Top 50 Most-Commonly Used Words

Your child must spell some words by automatic reflex, because she uses them time and time again. Here are the 50 most common words of all — the ones you need to help her get to know *really* well:

the	he	at	but	there
of	was	be	not	use
and	for	this	what	an
a	on	have	all	each
to	are	from	were	which
in	as	or	we	she
is	with	ine	when	do
you	his	had	your	how
that	they	by	can	their
it	I	word	said	if

The Handiest Mnemonics

Mnemonics, or memory joggers, are really handy and helpful things. The mnemonics that I give here can help your child figure out some of those tricky spellings that trip up just about everyone at one time or another:

- **Necessary:** One cap, two socks.
- **Ought words:** **O**nly **u**gly **g**irls **h**ate **t**oothpaste.
- ***ight* words:** **I**ndian **g**irls **h**ave **t**eeth (they *like* toothpaste and brush often!).
- **Friend:** A friend stays to the *end*.
- **Rhythm:** **R**hythm **h**elps **y**our **t**wo **h**ips **m**ove.
- **Business:** There's a *bus* in business.
- **They:** There's no *hay* in they.
- **Because:** **B**ig **e**lephants **c**an **a**lways **u**nderstand **s**mall **e**lephants.
- **Here, there, where:** All have *here* in them and are all about position.
- **Two:** Two twins.
- **Government:** The government *governs* the country.
- **Secretary:** A secretary keeps *secrets*.
- **Four, fourteen, forty:** If you're bidding, you stay in at *four* and *fourteen,* but "u drop out on *forty.*"

For Dummies: Bestselling Book Series for Beginners

Teaching Kids to Spell For Dummies®

Cheat Sheet

Thirty-two Words that Kids Often Misspell

Teachers see these words misspelled every day of the week. If you make sure (check) that *your* child can spell all of them, you give his teacher one less student draining her red ink.

about	friend	once	they	were
are	have	people	too	when
beautiful	house	play	until	with
because	I'm	pretty	very	would
Christmas	know	said	want	
could	like	should	was	
excited	my	there	went	

Common homonyms

Homonyms are words that sound the same. Dozens of homonyms can be found in the language, but the ones that I give you here are the most common of all. Your child is bound to grapple with some or all of them at some point, so if you help him in advance, you can make his efforts more productive and less frustrating.

- there, their, they're
- see, sea
- for, four
- by, buy
- passed, past
- which, witch
- son, sun
- who's, whose
- hole, whole
- write, right
- to, too, two
- threw, through (you may want to look at *thought* here too)
- cereal, serial
- principal, principle

Three hot spelling chunks

This book is jampacked with useful spelling chunks. You get families like *all, call,* and *wall;* endings like *ing, ly,* and *ent;* spelling rules for sounds like *ee* and *oa,* and heaps more besides. But if you want my three favorite spelling chunks — the ones I'd probably show your child straight off — here they are

- *ou,* like in loud, shout, and around
- *ight,* like in right, might, and tight
- *tion,* like in action, fraction, and direction

For Dummies: Bestselling Book Series for Beginners

About the Author

Tracey Wood was born in England. She went to teachers college in Leeds and graduated with an honors degree in Psychology and Education. She taught in a special school for four years and loved it. But sunnier climes called and she left England for a backpacking vacation in Australia. Twelve years later, she was still enjoying the warmth of Australia and had traded her backpack for a husband and two kids.

In Australia, Tracey earned a Diploma in Special Education and a Master's degree in Education. For several years she ran a high school special education unit and then started her own reading clinic. In the 90s, Tracey moved to the San Francisco Bay Area, where she set up a reading and writing clinic, helped in her kids' school, led two scouting troops, instructed for the Red Cross, created her Web site (www.readingpains.com) and wrote her first book, *See Johnny Read! — The 5 Most Effective Ways to End Your Son's Reading Problems.*

Still on the move (with her husband's job), Tracey relocated to Toronto and wrote her second book, *Teaching Kids to Read For Dummies* (Wiley). Tracey is now a literacy consultant, writer, and public speaker. She's the kids' reading and writing expert on www.LDonline.com and www.kidslinktoronto.com, she contributes articles to magazines like *Big Apple Parent* and *Teachers of Vision,* and she's committed to steering (albeit unsteadily) her two children through childhood with all their limbs and faculties in tact.

Dedication

When I asked my youngest child what she'd like me to say about her if I were to mention her in my book, she said I should say, "Her beauty is greater than the golden sun high above." When I asked my oldest child the same question, she said, "Say I'm more beautiful than her." So there you are, I said it. This book is for both of you, so utterly and equally amazing!

Publisher's Acknowledgments

We're proud of this book; please send us your comments through our Dummies online registration form located at www.dummies.com/register/.

Some of the people who helped bring this book to market include the following:

Acquisitions, Editorial, and Media Development

Project Editor: Natalie Faye Harris

Acquisitions Editors: Mikal Belicove, Natasha Graf

Copy Editor: E. Neil Johnson

Editorial Program Assistant: Courtney Allen

General Reviewers: Susan Byers, Andrea M. Richter

Senior Permissions Editor: Carmen Krikorian

Editorial Managers: Christine Beck, Michelle Hacker

Editorial Assistants: Hanna Scott, Melissa Bennett, Nadine Bell

Cover Photos: © Charles Thatcher/ Getty Images/Stone

Cartoons: Rich Tennant (www.the5thwave.com)

Composition Services

Project Coordinator: Adrienne Martinez

Layout and Graphics: Carl Byers, Andrea Dahl, Heather Ryan

Proofreaders: David Faust, Jessica Kramer, Carl William Pierce, TECHBOOKS Production Services

Indexer: TECHBOOKS Production Services

Publishing and Editorial for Consumer Dummies

> **Diane Graves Steele,** Vice President and Publisher, Consumer Dummies
>
> **Joyce Pepple,** Acquisitions Director, Consumer Dummies
>
> **Kristin A. Cocks,** Product Development Director, Consumer Dummies
>
> **Michael Spring,** Vice President and Publisher, Travel
>
> **Kelly Regan,** Editorial Director, Travel

Publishing for Technology Dummies

> **Andy Cummings,** Vice President and Publisher, Dummies Technology/General User

Composition Services

> **Gerry Fahey,** Vice President of Production Services
>
> **Debbie Stailey,** Director of Composition Services

Activities at a Glance

Chapter 1: Thinking Like a Spelling Teacher

What's in a word? 13

Chapter 2: Understanding the Reading, Writing, and Spelling Mix

Sharing a journal 39

Chapter 3: Getting to Know the Pieces and Parts of Spelling

Finding three little words 54
Marathon spelling contest 60

Chapter 4: Spelling with Short Vowels

Back-to-front syllables 75
Filling in missing letters..75
Cutting extra letters 76
Riddles of things you shouldn't do 78
Rhyming riddles 78
Changing a first letter 81
Changing a last letter 82
Changing a vowel...82
Ten words in a chain 83
Spelling circle...84
Finding the gap 86
Spelling by flashlight..88

Chapter 5: Blending Letters Together

Making great use of a pizza box...96
Seven super shapes...97
Sorting your double-*c*'s 100
Looking at ex words 101
Extending yourself with *ex* words 102
Always *ct* (never *kt*)...104
Making sense of *c*, *k*, and *ck*..106

Chapter 6: Choosing ch (and sh, th, ph, and wh, too)

Mastering *ch* with the Lay-3 card game 111

Sorting long-vowel words with *ch* endings 113

Rhyming time with *sh* 114

More challenging *sh* rhymes 114

Creating *th* word crosses 116

Cracking the *ph* cryptic code 117

Chapter 7: Putting a Firm Pen on Bossy e

Back to front and front to back 125

Finding 18 errors 126

Three Bossy *e* quizzes 127

Thinking in threes 129

Joking around with Bossy *e* 130

Forming Bossy *e* pictures 131

Chapter 8: Taking Charge of Words with Two Vowels Together

Listening up for long vowels 136

Four pairs of vowels 136

Changing between short and long vowels 137

Five up 138

Sounds right; looks wrong 139

Pairs of vowels 140

Two-vowel word quiz 141

Spelling buddies 143

Chapter 9: Writing y Instead of a, e, or i

y-at-the-end quiz 153

Half and half 154

Sorting sounds into groups 154

See it, say it, spell it 156

Toothpicks 156

Coffee for the jockey and me 157

License plates 159

Finishing words 160

Marking up words 161

y Quiz 162

Chapter 10: Getting Into Word Family Mode

Spelling folder 170

Spelling continents...180

Spelling back to front 181

Chapter 11: Guiding Her Pen to Bigger Word Families

Looking, marking, and writing (then doing it some more) 185

Finding an *our, oar,* or *oor* match 189

Finding an *ear* match 189

Eight itchy gnomes have ticks 191

Only ungrateful girls hate toys 192

Colors and chunks..194

oy-oi quiz 197

Extravagant excuses 200

Which word? 202

Changing the last letter 203

Chapter 12: Spelling Sight Words: A Different Family

Color-coding sight words 207

Ten neat word families..210

Building word families 210

Finding your spelling strategies 212

Chapter 13: Being Vocal about Silent Letters

Clever cards (two players)...223

Eight-square bingo 225

Writing a loony letter 228

To *b* or not to *b* 228

Which word does this describe? 229

Pictures and mnemonics 230

Chapter 14: Spelling Some Letters "Softly"

Spotting soft *c* spellings..235

Dictated spellings...236

Silly sentences 236

Tackling a tampered-with story 237

Spotting soft *g* spellings..239

3 by 3 by 3 240

Imagining sentences...240

Fixing a muddle...241

Chutes and ladders with chances 241

Chapter 15: Cheerfully Chunking Sounds

Clapping out syllables...246

Spelling compound words...249

Making sense...250

Twins (Spelling double-consonant words)................................250

High five...252

Right or wrong? 252

Choosing your spelling list...254

Easy, medium, and hard 256

Sorting prefixes...257

Prefix run..258

Demon dozen 263

Mancala Spellorama!..264

Chapter 16: Finishing Off with Suffixes

Adding s's quick and easy 268

Taking the word away! 270

Pointing and spelling 271

Sorting your tomatoes and heroes...273

Finding the word..274

Finding, running, and writing..275

Placing your bets...277

Doubling the letter to keep the vowel short..............................278

Making a word longer 279

Adding able or ible 281

Ending for thirty points 283

Finding ten ending mistakes 284

Adding a quick ending 285

Matching up words and endings 286

Remembering and spelling..289

Charades...291

Chapter 17: Spotting What's in a Contraction

Count and figure out 297

Listen up...298

Poem search..298

Apostrophes in contractions and possession 299

Who has what?...300

Getting it right with its...301

Who's or *whose* 303

You're and your 304

30 proverbs; 20 apostrophes 305

Look who's talking..306

Ha, ha 306

Chapter 20: Ten (or More) Group Activities That Rock

Battling with simple word ships..329

Battling with intense word ships..330

Whole-word bingo 331

Word-part bingo...331

Hands on the table 332

Finding your word family 333

Racing and writing...334

Racing and finger-writing 334

Racing and defining...335

Drawing boxes with words...337

Drawing pictures with words..338

Oh, no!..338

Wake up and spell the word! 339

Chutes and ladders (with spell-to-throw) 340

Chapter 21: Ten Spelling Games for Car Trips

Fortuneteller 347

Contents at a Glance

Introduction 1

Part I: Understanding the Basics of Good Spelling 7
Chapter 1: Thinking Like a Spelling Teacher 9
Chapter 2: Understanding the Reading, Writing, and Spelling Mix 31
Chapter 3: Getting to Know the Pieces and Parts of Spelling 49

Part II: Getting Easy Words onto Paper 65
Chapter 4: Spelling with Short Vowels 67
Chapter 5: Blending Letters Together 93
Chapter 6: Choosing ch (and sh, th, ph, and wh, too) 109

Part III: Coming to Grips with Long Vowel Sounds 119
Chapter 7: Putting a Firm Pen on Bossy e 121
Chapter 8: Taking Charge of Words with Two Vowels Together 133
Chapter 9: Writing y Instead of a, e, or i 151

Part IV: Using Word Families 165
Chapter 10: Getting Into Word Family Mode 167
Chapter 11: Guiding Her Pen to Bigger Word Families 183
Chapter 12: Spelling Sight Words: A Different Family 205
Chapter 13: Being Vocal about Silent Letters 221
Chapter 14: Spelling Some Letters "Softly" 233

Part V: Spelling Words in Chunks 243
Chapter 15: Cheerfully Chunking Sounds 245
Chapter 16: Finishing Off with Suffixes 267
Chapter 17: Spotting What's in a Contraction 295

Part VI: The Part of Tens 309
Chapter 18: Ten Word Families 311
Chapter 19: Ten Ways to Correct Your Child's Spelling 317
Chapter 20: Ten (or More) Group Activities That Rock 329
Chapter 21: Ten Spelling Games for Car Trips 343

Index 349

Table of Contents

Introduction *1*

About This Book 2

Foolish Assumptions 2

What You're Not to Read 2

Conventions Used in this Book 3

How This Book Is Organized 3

Part I: Understanding the Basics of Good Spelling 3

Part II: Getting Easy Words onto Paper 3

Part III: Getting to Grips with Long Vowel Sounds 4

Part IV: Using Word Families 4

Part V: Spelling Words in Chunks 4

Part VI: The Part of Tens 4

Icons Used in This Book 5

Where To Go from Here 5

Part 1: Understanding the Basics of Good Spelling *7*

Chapter 1: Thinking Like a Spelling Teacher 9

Understanding How Learning Works 9

Showing and practicing 10

Sharing 10

Knowing when to back off 11

Solving problems 11

Having a reason to spell well 12

Having your child say and then spell words 12

Keeping things short and sweet 14

Lightening up 14

Making a big deal about motivation 15

Charts 17

Gathering Your Tools 17

Kits 18

Flashcards 18

Dictionaries 19

The computer spell-checker 20

Watching for Readiness 20

Getting an early start 21

Paying attention to posture and pencil grip 22

Keeping an eye on your child's vision 24

Listening for hints about your child's hearing 26

Moving in the direction of reading and writing 26

Jargon Busting 26
    Brushing up on familiar terms 27
    Catching up on new terms 29

Chapter 2: Understanding the Reading, Writing, and Spelling Mix . . .31

Why the Janitor's Son Is a Genius 31
Reading to Your Child 32
An Unequal and Sometimes Lumpy Mix 32
Reading with Your Child 32
    Partners and practices 34
    Listening to your child read to you 35
    Correcting your child's reading mistakes 35
Writing to Your Child 37
Writing with Your Child 38
    Putting up posters 38
    Sharing a journal 39
    Putting sass into stories 40
    Giving a big hand to handwriting 41
    Having your child write to you 41
    Spelling with your child 41
Getting the Most from Drills and Drafts 42
    Looking, saying, covering, writing, and checking 42
    Doing dictation 43
    Persevering with proofreading 44
    Using memory joggers 45
Correcting Your Child's Mistakes 46
Keeping Stress at Bay 46

Chapter 3: Getting to Know the Pieces and Parts of Spelling 49

Listening First 49
Listening for Chunks Of Sound 51
Playing with Pronunciation 52
Looking at Letters 53
    Words within words 54
    Mistakes 55
Having a Few Tries 57
Dictation: Doing It and Doing It Again 59
Having a Few Spelling Rules under Her Belt 61
Being Secure with Sight Words 62
Skimming through Suffixes, Silent Letters, and Other Stuff 62
    Suffixes 63
    Prefixes 63
    Silent letters 63
    Soft c's and soft g's 64

Part II: Getting Easy Words onto Paper 65

Chapter 4: Spelling with Short Vowels 67

Checking on Single Sounds 68
Tackling Letters in the Right Order 68
Beginning Simply 68
Being Clear about "kuh" 69
Surfing the Several-Sounds Consonants 76
Dealing with the Doubles 76
Putting the Vowels into Perspective 79
Spelling Short Vowels 80
Spelling in Chunks 85
Spelling Long Words From Short Sounds 85
Writing Short Vowels Inside Sight Words 87
Taking One Vowel at a Time 88
    Attending to the a's 88
    Enter the e's 89
    Including the i's 89
    On the go with o 90
    Up and away with u 90
    A word about open syllables 90

Chapter 5: Blending Letters Together 93

Blending Two and Three Letters Together 93
Writing Words with Blends at the Front 94
    Choosing between sc and sk 97
    Strangled eggs 99
    Spelling with cc and x 99
Writing Words with Blends at the End 103
    Doing away with kt 104
    Sorting c, ck, and k 105
    Nosing through ng and nk 107

Chapter 6: Choosing ch (and sh, th, ph, and wh, too) 109

Delving into Digraphs 109
Chewing Your Pencil Over ch 110
Showing Your Child sh 113
Thinking About th 115
Passing through a Phase of ph 116
Asking wh Questions 118

Part III: Coming to Grips with Long Vowel Sounds 119

Chapter 7: Putting a Firm Pen on Bossy e 121

Bearing with Bossy e 121
Spotting Bossy e Words 122

Spelling Bossy e Words 126
"Joke" is a Bossy e word 130

Chapter 8: Taking Charge of Words with Two Vowels Together ...133

Explaining the When-Two-Vowels-Go-Walking . . . Rule 133
Hearing Long-Vowel Sounds 134
Sorting Through Long and Short Sounds 136
Spelling Long Sounds 138
ee and ea Words 139
A Mix of Long Sounds 141
Copy-Cat Vowels 142
i before e 142
Except after c 144
Eight neighbors 144
e before i 145
Dreadful bread 145
Chairs and stairs 147
Scared of bears 148

Chapter 9: Writing y Instead of a, e, or i 151

Getting Used to the Different Sounds of y 151
Hearing It; Spelling It 151
y Sounding Like Long a (day, say, and play) 152
y Sounding Like Long e (happy, funny, and silly) 152
y Sounding Like Long i (my, by, and cry) 158
y Sounding Like Short i (Mystery and System) 162

Part IV: Using Word Families 165

Chapter 10: Getting Into Word Family Mode 167

Looking at What's in a Word 167
Introducing Word Families 168
Getting Friendly with Simple Families 168
Introducing the Spelling Folder 170
Sailing Through One-Syllable Word Families 171
Taking the Stress Out of Schwas 177
Schwa at the beginning 178
Schwa at the end 179
Schwa in the middle 180

Chapter 11: Guiding Her Pen to Bigger Word Families 183

The Distinctive-Looking all and alk Families 183
Being Savvy with Vowel+r Words 184
Recognizing other ways of using or and ar 187
Moving ahead to two vowels+r 188
Igh and ight Words 190
Eight, ought, and aught 191

Enough and Some 193
Swooping In on the Two oo's 195
Choosing from Two Good Spellings 196
    Oy and oi 196
    Ow and ou 198
    Aw and au 200
Taking Care with are, ear, and air 202

Chapter 12: Spelling Sight Words: A Different Family **205**
Introducing Sight Words 205
Skipping through the Families 207
Taking Time with the Individuals 211
Looking for Spelling Rules 214
    Bossy e 214
    When two vowels go walking 215
    Y making long-e or long-i sounds 216
Getting Faster at Spelling Sight Words 216
Having Fun With Sight Words 217
    Seeing and writing 217
    Hiding and seeking 217
    Racing the clock 218
    Keeping track 218
    Making the most of mediums 218
    Games to go 219

Chapter 13: Being Vocal about Silent Letters **221**
Knocking with your Knuckles 221
Plunging into a Sea of Silent Letters 222
Delighting over your Daughter 222
Wriggling your Wrist 224
Squealing and Squirming 224
Disguising as a Guard 226
Being Vague about the League 226
Gnawing on a Sign 227
Combing the Lamb 228
Walking and Talking 229
Being Honest at the Exhibition 230
Listening to Whistles 231
Going Psycho! 231
Feeling Solemn about the Column 232

Chapter 14: Spelling Some Letters "Softly" **233**
Hearing Hard and Soft Sounds 233
Relaxing with Identical Sounds 233
Scanning the Soft-c Rule 234
Recognizing Soft-c Words 234
Writing Soft c Words 236
Deciding Whether to Write c or s 237

Scanning the Soft g Rule 238
Recognizing Soft g Words 238
Writing Soft g Words 240
Deciding Whether to Write g or j 240
Sorting your cs and juggling your gs 241

Part V: Spelling Words in Chunks 243

Chapter 15: Cheerfully Chunking Sounds 245

Syllables or Chunks of Sound 245
Hearing Syllables in Words 245
Keeping Letter Friends Together 246
One Syllable Is a Cinch 247
Two Syllables Are a Pic-nic 248
    Cruising through compound words 248
    Dealing with double letters 250
    Taking on two consonants 253
    Hearing open vowels 255
    Putting prefixes first 256
    Running a marathon for serious spellers 259
    Quickly peering at suffixes 261
Three or More Syllables Are Pre-dict-a-ble 261
Quickly Revising Key Spelling Patterns 263

Chapter 16: Finishing Off with Suffixes 267

An Ending by Any Other Name 267
Playing with Plurals 268
    Adding s 268
    Adding es 269
    Adding to f words 273
Staying Calm with Tenses 275
    The sounds of ed 275
    Adding ed to short-sounding words 276
    Adding vowel endings (like ing and ed) to words that already
        end with e 278
    Deciding between able and ible 280
Adding to Words That End in y 282
Mixing Suffixes and Endings 285
Adding tion, sion, or cian 286
Adding ent or ant 287
Adding le and al 288
Adding full and all 290
A Grand Finale of Suffixes 290

Chapter 17: Spotting What's in a Contraction **295**

Disappearing Letters 295
Understanding What's Going on with Contractions 295
Getting to Know the Words That Contract 296
Possessive Apostrophes 299
Avoiding Mistakes 301
    It's versus its 301
    Can't versus can,t 302
    Who's versus whose 303
    You're versus your 304

Part VI: The Part of Tens *309*

Chapter 18: Ten Word Families **311**

The Easy All and Or Families 311
The Straightforward ight Family 312
The oi and oy Families 312
The ou and ow Families 313
The er, ir, and ur Families 314
The au and aw Families 314
Soon, spoon, and moon 315

Chapter 19: Ten Ways to Correct Your Child's Spelling **317**

Seeing and Hearing; Slouching and Shifting .317
Lightening Up 318
Homing in on Handwriting 318
Telling Your Child a Word Versus Making Your Child Figure It Out 320
Looking for Families 321
Looking for Spelling Rules 321
    Rule One: Bossy e 322
    Rule Two: When two vowels go walking, the first one does
        the talking 322
    Rule Three: y behaves like a vowel 322
    Rule Four: i before e except after c (when you hear ee) 323
Deciding to Remember the Look of a Word .323
Using Spelling Lists 324
Having Sight Words Down Pat 325
Doing Dictation 326

Chapter 20: Ten (or More) Group Activities That Rock **329**

Simple Battleships 329
Intense Battleships 330
Word Bingo 331
Bits-of-Words Bingo 331
Putting Your Hands on the Table 332
Finding Your Family 333

Run and Write 333
Run and Finger-Write 334
Run, Figure Out, and Write 335
Boxes 336
Pictures 337
Oh No! 338
Wake Up! 339
One More! Just for Two 340

Chapter 21: Ten Spelling Games for Car Trips **343**
Cards in the Car 343
Hangman 344
Describing and Drawing the Letters 344
I Spy with My Little Eye 345
Going to Aunt Maud's 345
Names 345
Shopping at Macy's 346
Songs 346
Word Find 346
Fortunetellers (or Origami Cruets) 346

Index..*349*

Introduction

*W*ant to steer rather than drag your child through words like *beautiful* and *they're?* Mystified that she can read the entire works of Tolkien (if she really wanted to) but can't spell *throat?* Hoping to preempt spelling saboteurs like *meny* and *untill?* Have I got great news for you!

Ta-da! The cavalry has arrived! This book gives a resounding boot to the typical tedium of spelling lessons and champions the cause of concerned but busy people like you (who can easily doze off at the mere hint of blah, blah, blah). *Teaching Kids to Spell For Dummies* is exactly right for you. It gives you practical activities that really work. It's easy to follow, pick and choose from, and come back to. It doesn't ask you to buy extras, and all you really need for an immediate start is paper and pen. Oh, and there's an added bonus. Right here in these pages I put jokes that are, let's just say, acute.

But what about your child, what's in this book for him or her? I can almost hear that devilish groan, so just for your child, I've packed this book with memory joggers and appetizing, bite-sized pieces of information. If your child makes careless spelling errors, this book can sharpen his eye with the proofreading and dictation activities that I dole out in The Part of Tens. If she can't write long-vowel sounds, she'll make quick progress with the easy rules I provide in Part III. If he's been making basic mistakes for a while, he can rebuild his skills from the short-vowel sounds that I give you in Part II.

To help your child get a solid grasp of spelling, you need practical, good sense information. And that's exactly what you find here in these pages. Welcome!

About This Book

Regardless of whether you're a shaky speller or friends marvel at your adverbs, whether your child's a beginner or practically a veteran, or whether you're apprehensive about teaching or can't wait to begin, this book is for you. That's because you can surf through it or immerse yourself chapter by chapter, as you need. So much spelling information is here in this book that you're assured of getting the guidance you're looking for, whatever your needs. And you'll love "The Part of Tens" at the end of this book, where you get quick lists, each of ten items, of all the really handy stuff.

Foolish Assumptions

Because you're reading this book I'm assuming:

- ✔ You'd like to help a child become a better speller but need cheerful, plain-talking guidance.
- ✔ You have interest and enthusiasm but not unlimited time.
- ✔ You'd like pointers as you go so you know whether you're doing things right.

What You're Not to Read

Many books about spelling are full of forced rules. They have you making strange pronunciations and give you rules that hardly ever work even after you've stretched and rolled your tongue obligingly. This book isn't like that. It gives you a few rules that really work, and if I use jargon, I warn you in advance so you can skip it if you want to. In addition to a few bits of jargon, I spice up each chapter with sidebars. Sidebars offer bonus or additional information that may be anything from a cute story to illustrate a point to a quick detour into an extra activity you may think you'd like to try out. In other words, you can skip the sidebars if you're in a rush; but if you like quirky stuff and diversions, you'll definitely enjoy them.

Conventions Used in this Book

To "he" or not to "he?" In this book I clean up that sticky dilemma by using "he" and "she" interchangeably. You can be sure that this book is for and about all kids, and after you're used to switching between he's and she's, you'll probably think all other books should do the same.

How This Book Is Organized

This book has six parts:

Part 1: Understanding the Basics of Good Spelling

Some kids seem to have an amazing-speller gene. Most kids have to work at it. Your child probably thinks twice about how to spell *twice* and scrabbles for scrap paper to figure out *probably*. The good news is that the tips, rules, and activities in this book can help your child. This part of *Teaching Kids To Spell For Dummies* outlines them for you along with the best ways to teach them. You get a lightning tour of stuff like digraphs, letter orientation, and phonemic awareness, so you don't feel like you never got the memo when you read more about them later.

Part II: Getting Easy Words onto Paper

You're going to hear quite a bit about short vowels in this book. Short vowels are solid and predictable letters that your child writes in an awful lot of words, putting them into words like *put* and *can* and stringing them into big words like *introduction*. Part II shows you how to take your child carefully through the short-vowel words and spelling chunks to build a set of spelling skills on a strong foundation.

Part III: Getting to Grips with Long Vowel Sounds

This part of the book shows you how to make short work of spelling long-vowel sounds. Long-vowel sounds are a definite problem area for kids, but this section gives you three simple rules to make things easy. In addition, you find out the ins and outs of sight words or most common words. You're told why teachers fuss so much about sight words, and how to get one step ahead. I give you a list of 220 sight words that comprise a whopping 70 percent of all the words in regular text. When you explain how to spell these words, you iron out any frequent errors that your child makes.

Part IV: Using Word Families

Words are easier to remember when you classify or group them. *All,* for example, is a forgettable word until you show your child that it fits snuggly inside a whole army of words like *ball, call, tall,* and *small.* Words like *right* belong with *fight, might,* and *tight,* and there's no end to the words your child can make from a spelling chunk like *ou.* Part Four shows you these word families.

Part V: Spelling Words in Chunks

Part V shows you how to make sure that your child figures out words methodically, starting at the beginning, moving to the middle, and finishing up at the end. Here you show your child how to gain control of even the longest of words. I talk about contractions in this section, too. Not the stork-visiting-in-the-middle-of-the-night kind, but rather the ones that squeeze words like *has not* into *hasn't.* You see how syllables and contractions work and how to steer your child past the pitfalls that kids often fall into.

Part VI: The Part of Tens

The Part of Tens is where I boil down heaps of useful information into super easy lists. Here you get "Ten Word Families," "Ten (or More) Group Activities that Rock," and "Ten (Okay, Eleven) Spelling Games for Car Trips."

Icons Used in This Book

You see this icon whenever I give information that's really worth hanging onto.

Here's something you DON'T want to do. It's easy to make mistakes, so this icon warns you about land mines that cause them.

Here's your jargon alert. Skip ahead or brace yourself for the particulars!

This icon means I'm offering a golden nugget of handy advice that I've probably learned firsthand.

This handy icon helps you spot the fun activities that appear throughout the book.

Where to Go from Here

If you're ready to leap straight into action, go to Chapter 4. This chapter shows you how to muster a firm grip on short vowels not just so you can spell easy words, but so your child can spell the small chunks found inside big words later on. If you're working with a child who's already good with short-vowel sounds, go to Chapter 7. Long-vowel sounds also can trip up your child, so this chapter shows you exactly how to make the long-vowel thing clear. In Chapters 8 and 9, I continue talking about long vowels, because there's plenty to find out about them. From Chapter 10 onward, I explain stuff like word families and sight words, but don't worry, I inject fun into every task so you won't start off enthusiastically only to wake up with a stiff neck an hour later. If you're not in that much of a rush, you can enjoy the traditional journey through this book. Start at Chapter 1 and take a straight path all the way through the book. Although this book is arranged so you can pick and choose topics, it also follows a logical progression.

Part I
Understanding the Basics of Good Spelling

The 5th Wave   By Rich Tennant

"Oh, she's definitely ready to start spelling lessons.
She can already spell 'Guess', 'GAP', and 'Hilfiger'."

In this part . . .

You're going to help a child spell better. Do you need to focus on single letters? Do you need to know about phonics? Do you need a new dictionary? Part I answers all of these questions and much more. It tells you why chunks of sound are key, what a good eye is, and why you need to encourage your child to always "have a go" at spelling unfamiliar words.

Chapter 1

Thinking Like a Spelling Teacher

In This Chapter

▶ Introducing the cornerstones of good teaching

▶ Getting ready, getting set

▶ Making an early start

▶ Busting through the jargon

Great teachers take care of all kinds of kids. They climb aloft to reach the highly strung, fix their acts for the divas, and tread warily around kids who rule their parents with iron fists. They seem to have every kind of book and brainstorm at their fingertips and manage to serve it all up with a generous dollop of Zen. What's their thing? Can anyone else get some of it? Can others do effective work without piercing their tongues and going back to college to learn it? Of course! This book piles you up with easy, practical strategies and awfully shrewd insights. Although you may not get the whole Zen thing, and, of course, you miss out on tongue piercing, you nevertheless get a down-to-earth spelling plan. And to add to all that, you get quick yet constructive stuff to do while chugging the kids off to soccer or coercing a cart of chicken noodles and ice cream (you made the mistake of shopping with the kids) through that traitorous slowest-of-all checkout line.

For now, though, don't worry too much about the details, because this is your introductory overview.

In this chapter, I start you gently on your spelling journey by taking a look at learning principles, which are otherwise known as all that stuff that great teachers have on their minds before they even get your child to take his coat off.

Understanding How Learning Works

Great teachers are nice people. They know that your child learns best when he's happy and actively engaged, so they find cool kid things for him to do. They're flexible. They try to think from your child's perspective and inject fun into every activity. And they see your child and everyone else's pretty much as family — quirky, often difficult, and excitable for sure, but family nevertheless. So, you're asking, what, specifically, do great teachers advise? Read on.

Showing and practicing

You can't just pile information onto your child and expect it to stick. Instead, you need to help him become active and involved in learning — as soon as possible. To help you do that, here's a three-step guide for getting your child actively engaged:

1. Show your child what to do.

2. Give your child plenty of assistance as you practice whatever it is you're doing.

3. Watch and applaud whenever your child independently engages in a learning activity.

Sharing

Sharing also is an important part of learning. Your child thrives on your company, attention, and (deserved) praise. Whenever you can, join in your child's learning. When he's figuring out spellings (that is the entire idea, right?), hang with him and give him your support. A number of good ways to do your part in supporting your child include

- ✔ Showing that spelling in chunks (as in *ac-count*) makes more sense than spelling in single letters. I talk more about spelling in chunks in Part V.

- ✔ Showing that some sounds are spelled with single letters (like *t*) but others are spelled with two or more letters (like *ch, ou,* and *eigh*).

- ✔ Letting your child know that most words are spelled in logical chunks of sound (that match, or sort of match, the spelling chunks), but that odd words, like *who,* aren't worth sounding out. In those cases, your child just needs to get to know how they look.

- ✔ Writing common word families on a poster for your child to refer to (like the *ight* family: *light, sight,* and *might*) and telling your child about any new families whenever he comes across them. I deal with word families in Chapters 10 and 11.

- ✔ Taking time to check that your child writes all the sight words easily. If a few of them happen to get away, have him jot them down and focus on them for a few days. You can find all the ins and outs of sight words in Chapter 12.

✔ Explaining how some sounds are spelled in more than one way (like *bait* and *bay; sent* and *cent*).

✔ Explaining that vowels always represent a few sounds (like in *mat* and *mate*).

✔ Walking your child through common spelling chunks (like *ou* and *oi*).

✔ Explaining that developing a good eye for correct spellings is as much a part of being a good speller as knowing all the rules. (Which word looks right, *they* or *thay*?)

✔ Showing your child that sometimes a letter is written when there's no sound at all (like in *gnat* and silent *e* on the end of words like *cute*). In Chapter 13, I delve into silent letters, and you can find out about the silent-*e*-on-the-end rule in Chapter 7.

✔ Making sure that you tell your child that proofreading is really important.

Knowing when to back off

Have you ever had someone show you a photo album by holding onto it possessively while pointing out each shot? You know, someone who's so interested in the photos that she doesn't realize how irritating it is for you. Hanging onto stuff while showing it also switches off your child's interest. Just like you, your child wants to be the one doing the holding and showing. She wants to get that cool feeling of being in control. Whenever you can, let your child hold the book, the pens, or the worksheet. Having ownership and control means she can learn much more than if she thinks she's learning only *your* stuff. Make your child a willing and engaged learner by backing off and giving her a lead role. Your role needs to be that of facilitator, supporter, and guide — not hog-everything, bossy-britches.

Solving problems

You can help your child figure out spellings in different ways. If he's stuck on the word "library," for example, you can tell him, "Library's spelled *l-i-b-r-a-r-y,*" or you can say something like, "Library can be tricky, because it's spelled *li-bra-ry*. Jot all of that down, and see what you get." The first option works, but the second works better. It makes your child do the things that good spellers do. A good speller:

✔ Says the word to herself

✔ Breaks the word into chunks

✔ Jots down the chunks

✔ Looks to see whether the finished word looks right

When your terrific speller has done all of that, something occurs to her. She mentally notes that, yes, she *can* figure out spellings by going through logical steps. Even if her very last step is to ask you to correct her word, that's still fine. She's gone through the whole process by herself up to that point, so she's actively learning. In the process, she's remembering the spelling a zillion times better than when her very first step was to give no thought to the word other than to try to weasel the spelling out of you.

Have your child figure out as much of the word as possible before asking you for help finishing it off, but bear in mind that some words really try a child's patience. Take the word *patience*. If you insist that your child figure it out alone, you may just be driving him into a frenzy. Cut him some slack. Adopt a general policy of having your child take a try before demanding satisfaction, but give her help with words whose parts he isn't yet familiar with.

Having a reason to spell well

Your child likes to have a genuine reason to spell. Ask your child to write lists and notes as often as you can so he sees that spelling isn't just a classroom thing but rather is a necessity, or at least an asset, in the real world. If your child isn't convinced, you may want to run these reasons why kids need to learn to spell well past him:

- ✔ Teachers and classmates expect good spellers to be pretty clever all-round.
- ✔ Good spellers are more likely to be called upon by teachers to do responsible jobs that require some writing (like making posters to advertise school performances).
- ✔ Good spellers get better grades for written work.
- ✔ Computer spell-checkers don't catch all spelling errors.
- ✔ Job applications with spelling errors get rejected.
- ✔ People judge you by your spelling (and that includes friends, boyfriends and girlfriends, and people in workplaces).

Having your child say and then spell words

You're going to hear a lot about the importance of having your child say words in chunks and then jot down those chunks. Even when this habit sounds downright obvious to you, your child may not do it instinctively and instead may need you to make things clear. After you do, your child will be off and running. To quickly take your child through the saying-in-chunks part of spelling, lead her through the "What's in a word?" activity.

And the winner is . . .

This kind of conversation usually strikes a chord with parents:

You: It's not a competition.

Your child: I know, but if it was, I'd win.

You: Yes, but it isn't.

Your child: But I'd win.

You: It is *not* a competition!

Your child: I'd still win.

Your child likes to win. Build some healthy competition into spelling activities whenever you can. Lose competitions to your child if you want to (after all, you *are* the adult), but be convincing. Your child won't like being patronized.

Activity: What's in a word?

Preparation: Open your copy of *Teaching Kids to Spell For Dummies* to the list of words in this activity.

Follow these steps:

1. **Read these words out loud to your child.**

2. **Ask your child to tell you what chunks of sound she hears in them.**
   Demonstrate by saying, "*Inside* is made of *in-side*."

I talk about breaking words into chunks in Chapter 15. I tell you the rules for breaking words into chunks but let you know that it really doesn't matter where your child breaks words as long as she says all the bits. In this activity, don't worry about where those breaks go (your child may say *di-no-saur* or *din-o-saur*); just listen to make sure your child gets the basics of chunking.

1. football

2. pencil

3. puppy

4. distance

5. window

6. player

7. garden

8. friendship

9. neighbor

10. table

11. dinosaur

12. introduce

13. demonstrate

14. partner

15. sister

16. recorder

17. satellite

18. festival

19. parachute

20. prison

Keeping things short and sweet

Sometimes you see a fixed look in your child's eyes and know that he isn't listening to a word you're saying. You're telling him stuff that you already said a thousand times before ("Put your shoes in the closet"), but you're using 60 words rather than 6 ("Shoes get in the way and people trip over them. They bring dirt in and . . . "). That, or he has far more interesting things on his mind. To save yourself disappointment, get real. Your child has a short attention span and is easily distracted. It isn't his fault when he gets that fixed stare, and in any case, he's the kid, and you're the grown-up. Keeping things short and sweet is up to you.

Lightening up

When you teach your child how to spell you have to be organized and authoritative, but other factors are just as important. When kids are asked what they want in a new teacher, they say that they want the teacher to:

- Like them
- Care about them
- Be nice to them

- ✔ Smile at them
- ✔ Be happy
- ✔ Not yell
- ✔ Look nice
- ✔ Understand what a kid's life is like

So maintain a warm and happy tone. That way you keep your child equally as sweet-tempered.

A kitchen timer can come in handy for taking breaks. Have your child set the timer for a 10-minute break so she knows what's happening and when and that she has plenty of control.

Making a big deal about motivation

When the word "motivation" crops up, most people think of tangible rewards. Tangible rewards (like toys, candy, and extra TV) do, of course, motivate, but rewards that involve your child's feelings and perceptions are even better. If your child wants to please you or feel proud, she's naturally motivated, and

---

Mood lifters

To ward off that heinous "How much longer?" question, try these temper-sweetening tactics:

- ✔ **Change scenery.** Move onto the floor, into another room, or onto the porch.

- ✔ **Have a snack.** Give your child's spirits and blood sugar a lift with high-protein snacks like peanut butter on toast.

- ✔ **Take a break.** Your child's best attention span is pretty short, and yours probably isn't as long as you'd think.

- ✔ **Get moving.** A few shots at the hoop or a walk around the block can get all those feel-good chemicals whizzing around in your brains.

- ✔ **Put on your child's favorite CD.** Soft or familiar music is soothing and helps your child focus better.

- ✔ **Give your child a hug.** Touch is a natural calmer.

- ✔ **Offer your child incentives.** Avoid giving food and TV time if you can. Opt instead for games together, outings to the playground, and extra bedtime reading.

- ✔ **Have timeout for you.** If you get tense and frazzled, your child will. too, so don't let things go that far.

- ✔ **Give your child choices.** Let your child decide when he does his activities and takes breaks. ("You have a violin lesson at 4:30, do you want to do your 30 minutes of spelling before then or after dinner?")

you don't have to buy new toys and videos in the process. Natural (or internal) motivation is inexpensive, wholesome, and enduring. In practical terms, your child gets a natural boost when you're with her when she does her spelling. The same is true when you offer helpful suggestions (without steamrolling her) and when you comment on her perseverance, neatness, and cleverness. Praising her correct spellings and sympathizing with her when she struggles, having her take breaks and change activities frequently, and singing her praises to friends and family also are as beneficial as hanging with her after spelling sessions to shoot basketballs, throw a baseball, or simply chat.

The kinds of comments that count as downers or mood busters include ones like these:

- ✔ "I told you already to get your book!"
- ✔ "We looked at that word yesterday; you must know it!"
- ✔ "You're not trying."
- ✔ "Think!"
- ✔ "Look at the word!"
- ✔ "Concentrate!"

Charts — The vital measurements

I know, I know, I just wrote, "I won't bore you with the details," but a thought just occurred to me. What if you actually haven't heard much about making charts? Well, this sidebar is for readers who want or don't mind checking out a few pointers:

- ✔ Phrase your points in positive (rather than negative) terms. Instead of using phrases like, "Don't yell at your sister (or one day I swear I'll crack!)," make points like, "Talk in a polite way."

- ✔ Limit points to only three or four; otherwise, your child (an you for that matter) may find remembering everything she's supposed to be doing a hard thing to do.

- ✔ Get maximum input from your child. Discuss why you need a chart, what she'll gain from it, and what information needs to be listed. Have her make final decisions (after you artfully elicit what you want, of course). Have her write the chart, decorate it, and post it where she wants it to be (again after you've steered things in the right direction).

- ✔ Figure out a manageable rewards system. Start with things like play dates or sleepovers for 20 points rather than a holiday for two in Barbados.

- ✔ Never, ever take points away.

Points and profanity

My youngest child recently discovered the joys of expressing herself with profanities. It flummoxed me. If I ignored her, I ran the risk of the neighbors hearing. If I responded, well then she's gotten the attention she's after. It was a delicate situation, so I responded with a walloping heavy hand. I presented my daughter with a three-checks-and-you're-out system. An expletive earned her a check, and three checks meant no Girl Scout camp. The system was airtight. She soon got three checks and sobbed. . .and sobbed. I had a new dilemma on my hands. Was she truly remorseful? Does remorse excuse past indiscretions? How come I'd been fool enough to deprive myself of possibly the only peaceful weekend that I'll get this year? Well anyway, I don't want to use you readers as my personal psychotherapists, so

I'll cut to the chase. Out of this whole sorry business came a new chart. My daughter asked if she could write a positives chart (like we used to use in the days when I still had a heart). She scurried off with markers and poster paper and surfaced with a new system. She explained it to me, asked if she could start her good behavior immediately (like I'd say, "Uh no, maybe you should stick with the bad behavior for a few days") and went off to sweep and dust my basement, organize the new bookshelf, bring firewood in, and clean the windows. When my house looked like someone else's, I fetched her chart. Putting past differences behind me (pretty graciously I thought), I awarded her four whole points. (Oh, and at the time of this writing, camp's still on.)

Charts

Small kids like points charts (one point for nice manners, one point for a tidy room, and so on). If you get your child to make his own chart, he'll probably like it even better. I won't bore you with the details of allocating points for good behavior and limiting yourself to only three or four sought-after behaviors, because you've probably already heard that to death, but remember to include charts in your mental list of cool writing tasks.

Gathering Your Tools

A friend of mine once told me that his personal, all-to-himself space steadily diminished from the time his kids were born. Before kids, he said, his whole house was his personal space, give or take a few square feet for his wife. When his kids were toddlers his personal space was a room. When his kids were mobile, but still small, his space became a desk. At the time of our conversation, with school-age kids, he maintained that his personal space was one drawer that he, luckily, still had the key to. I know just what that friend feels like. My kids frequently lose their own scissors, tape, and erasers and have no compulsion about pilfering my desk. "But I have to hand this report in tomorrow," or "I'll put it back," they say. Yeah, right! Gather (and hide) your personal items, and organize and stow safely away the pens and paper that you need. Achieve this state of grace through iron resolve and a keep-your-thieving-hands-off policy (or by squirreling these items away under sofas and piles of socks just before spelling time).

Kits

Scour your toyshop, and you're sure to find some kind of word-building kit. Often it's a nifty case in which letter tiles and activity cards all fit snuggly. Kids love kits and do miles of spelling with them. They like fitting tiles into their right places, getting the better of whole stacks of work cards, and carrying the case around. Add a kit to your games stash, and you'll be glad you did. Don't forget to admire the case and it's owner; otherwise, with no one to notice it, the ensemble (and its benefits) won't be half as attractive to your child.

For educational games you can view and buy on the Internet, check out www.EducationalLearningGames.com. A particularly good spelling kit for beginning spellers is Spell Time by Cadaco, which has the Parenting Center seal of approval, and a favorite spelling game for the entire family is Quiddler. To view both games and many more, click on the "Spelling" option in the menu.

If you're in an Internet-surfing mood, check out home-schooling Web sites for good spelling resources and games. The reviewers do their reviewing conscientiously and with fervor.

Flashcards

Flashcards sometimes get a bad rap. People grab handfuls of cards from boxes they buy at the store, wave them at their child and wonder why she goes off to watch TV instead of getting caught up in the excitement. Flashcards aren't a substitute for absent adults, but they're great learning tools when you use them with your child in a systematic and interactive way. The trick is to take part but not take on too much in one go. If you're showing your child how to spell *ain* words, a bunch of *ain* flashcards are all that you need. Two hundred mixed spellings, all flashed at your child in one sitting, won't help him much. That said, here are some terrific, inexpensive sets of flashcards. They come in sturdy boxes that you can take with you everywhere, and you can pick them up at any good school supplies store.

✔ *Easy Vowels* by Frank Schaffer

✔ *Easy Blends and Digraphs* by Frank Schaffer

✔ *Beginning to Read Phonics: Fishing for Silent "e" Words* by Judy/Instructo

✔ *Beginning to Read Phonics: Word Family Fun, Long Vowels* by Judy/Instructo

✔ *Easy Sight Words* by Frank Schaffer

Dictionaries

Chances are that, unlike one friend of mine, you don't read a dictionary for relaxation. But do you own one? Do you keep it in a place that's accessible to your child? Does your child see you head to it when you're halfway through

---

Hands-on with flashcards

Not sure what to do with the flashcards you bought? First, select from your cards only the ones that you want your child to focus on for now. Then:

✔ Have your child look at one word at a time, cover it, and either spell it out verbally to you or write it down. (The verbal response is good for in the car.)

✔ Have your child spread the words face down on the floor, pick out one word at a time, peek at it, and then spell it verbally to you.

✔ Have your child write or verbally spell the words that you read out loud.

✔ Have your child look at ten words for one minute then spell them (in writing or verbally) as you call each one out.

✔ Have your child look at ten words and then spell them back to you as you read them out in clue form. ("This word starts with *st*.")

✔ Have your child spread ten words face up on the floor and study them for one minute. Take a word away, have him guess which word's missing, and then have him spell it out. To make this task more challenging, mix up the cards after he's had his first look.

✔ Have your child look at ten words from a word family (all, call, ball, and so on) and then spell out as many of the words as he can remember.

✔ Give your child rhyming clues for spellings. ("This word rhymes with pear.")

✔ Get your child to spell homonyms ("What's the other way to spell *s-o-n*?"). For this you can use *Homonyms Match* flashcards by Judy/Instructo.

✔ Have your child spell words from picture clues. A good set of cards for this is *Easy Action Picture Words* by Frank Schaffer.

Let's hear it for the boys

By now you've all heard that boys lag behind girls in picking up books and jotting down stories. Boys consistently score lower in reading tests than girls, and when they're asked about books and libraries, they say that they're really not all that interested. The good news is that much more is now known about making reading better for boys. Many of the things that we know about boys and reading also apply to boys and spelling, including that boys like:

- Information in short blasts
- Nonfiction
- Searching for information to solve real problems
- Comics, magazines, sports pages, and computer games

Ah ha. Computer games. You can make the most of that. A study of boys' spelling in the United Kingdom found that computers actually help boys with their spelling. When groups of boys spelled words and then fixed them either with pen and paper and a dictionary or a computer spell-checker, the spell-checker kids made spectacular gains. How so? Researchers believe that using the spell-checker doesn't imprint spellings on boys' minds, but rather it engages kids in active inquiry. The spell-checker kids had to put their words into the checker and then consider whether the answers they got applied. Whenever the answers didn't apply, they had to resort to paper and pen. All the problem solving and figuring out fired up the boys' interests so that their answers were best. The message for parents: Don't fight your son's computer worship, tap into it.

---

some smart newspaper article and hit a word like *ontologism*. You do? He does? That's great. Regular, routine habits like these influence your child the most.

For an online dictionary, check out `www.dictionary.com`.

The computer spell-checker

When my husband first plunked a computer down in our spare room, I was skeptical. Did we *really* need to fancy up our lives quite so dramatically. That was a long time ago, and now I'm practically tethered to my computer. And I get more and more dependent on the spell-checker. Your child will too (if it hasn't happened already), so now you see where all that proofreading that I talked about earlier comes into its own. Is your child's proofreading keeping pace with his lightning-fast reflex for clicking on the spell-checker?

Watching for Readiness

When it comes to spelling, what's normal comes in a wide range. Your child develops prespelling skills, such as hearing the parts inside of words and drawing circles and lines, at around age 2. Later, when your child starts kindergarten or school, she brings home never-ending strings of writing with no spaces between words. In the next few paragraphs, I take a look at the pieces that come together to set your child securely on the path to spelling well.

Getting an early start

Plenty of the things that you do with your preschooler set the stage for your child gaining spelling prowess. You probably don't even realize that you're already doing a great job of preparing your child to spell. In fact, take a look at this list and for every activity that you get your child to do, give yourself a pat on the back.

✔ **Bats, balls, and bicycles:** Toys like these, which make your child move, help develop gross motor coordination. You may not think these skills have much bearing on your child's future spelling, but studies show that when kids go through a course of motor skill development, their academic performance also improves. Some learning centers make the most of this benefit by having kids bounce on trampolines or jump rope for a while before settling down to write.

---

35 percent satisfaction guaranteed

You can find this poem on a zillion Web sites. It shows just how wrong your child's writing can be even after she's run it through a spell-checker. If she hasn't already come upon the poem in school, find out whether she can correct the mistakes now. Moral: Don't dispense with the noble practice of proofreading just yet.

Eye halve a spelling checker

It came with my pea sea

It plainly marcs four my revue

Miss steaks eye kin knot sea.

Eye strike a key and type a word

And weight four it two say

Weather eye am wrong oar write

It shows me strait a weigh.

As soon as a mist ache is maid

It nose bee fore two long

And eye can put the error rite

It's rare lea ever wrong.

Eye have run this poem threw it

And I am shore your pleased two no

Its letter perfect awl the weigh

My checker tolled me sew.

— Sauce unknown

✔ **Modeling compound (Play Doh), beads and thread, LEGOs, puzzles, and blocks:** When you provide all this nice stuff for your child to play with, you're not just giving him fun things to do, you're also helping his fine-motor coordination. Be especially conscious of your son's fine-motor coordination because it lags a little behind his sister's.

✔ **Pens, pencils, markers, crayons, paper, whiteboards, blackboards, and paint:** These media encourage creativity, something that your child can never have too much of.

✔ **Rhymes, songs and poems:** Nice-sounding rhymes, songs, and poems get your child listening to sound chunks. Later, your child starts to spell by repeating those sound chunks either out loud or to herself.

✔ **Listening and word games (like "I Spy" and "Going to Aunt Maud's," described in Chapter 21):** Again, the hearing part of spelling is important, and these kind of games home in on that.

✔ **Educational TV and CDs:** Fun, clever and easy avenues for your child to discover spelling techniques.

✔ **Books, comics, magazines and posters:** With short blasts of text that need to be watched especially closely, these works help your child develop an ever-so-helpful good eye for spelling. An extra bonus that accompanies comics and magazines is that they usually include word games.

✔ **Cards, letters, and notes:** Again, reading and writing these items makes your child looking closely at spellings, and that's always good.

Kids love to have their own space stocked with pencils, paper, glue, scissors, and markers. Regardless of whether it's a cardboard box or a real desk, a messy or tidy zone, or whether it's situated in the kitchen or in your child's own room, it can be a creative haven.

Paying attention to posture and pencil grip

Are you amazed by how your 9-year-old still starts a meal with his chair at a 45-degree angle about a foot away from the table? I am. It isn't just meals that can send your child into a daze; the same thing can happen when he writes. When your child gets ready to put his pen to paper, make sure that his chair is pulled comfortably to the table and he looks relaxed but not on the verge of snoozing. Teachers typically tell beginning writers these kinds of things:

✔ Hold your pencil between your thumb and pointer finger and then let it rest on the third finger.

✔ Hold the pencil on the paint, not on the exposed wood near the point.

Finger Olympics

If you think that your child's fine-motor skills can use a workout (so your child holds and guides a pencil better), try some of these finger Olympics. Have your child:

✔ Turn a pencil over again and again, eraser end up then lead end up, using only one hand.

✔ Pick up small objects, like LEGO blocks, using only one hand and keeping them in that hand until it's full. Then have your child put the blocks back down, one at a time, and still one-handed.

✔ Pick up small items, like dried beans or pasta shells, with tweezers. For an easy start use cotton balls.

✔ Draw around stencils and templates.

✔ Put some tape on the bottom line of the page to help remember not to write on it.

✔ Use a finger or Popsicle stick to help remember to leave spaces between words.

✔ Trace many shapes and objects. Make laminated sheets by covering regular sheets of letters and words with transparent adhesive book covering (which you can buy at stationary stores). Pick up some erasable whiteboard markers and a cloth to complete the kit.

✔ Draw between lines (draw parallel lines like roads).

✔ Use dot-to-dot activity sheets.

✔ Warm up her hands before writing by shaking them, clasping them together, and then stretching her arms up and overturning her hands, and by rubbing her palms together.

A few of the things you can do to help your child keep this hold are

• Put a rubber band on the pencil above the exposed wood near the point so your child's fingers touch it and she remembers where to hold on.

• Put a pencil grip on the pencil.

• Push the pencil through a practice golf ball (the kind with lots of holes).

• Put clay around the pencil.

• Have your child use long (not short) pencils (throw out the short pencils).

✔ Have your bottom (yes your rear end, caboose, or tushie) to the back of your chair.

✔ Put your feet flat on the floor.

Oh, my aching back

Does your child carry absurd amounts of who knows what in his school backpack? If he does, he can develop a lopsided posture or back and shoulder pain, and that can make sitting down and writing for long periods uncomfortable for him. Here are a few things that your child can do to keep his back and shoulders in good shape:

✔ Get a backpack with wide, padded, adjustable shoulder straps.

✔ Wear the straps tightened.

✔ Always carry the pack over both shoulders.

✔ Regularly sort through the contents, and *take out the extraneous stuff.*

✔ Place your forearms on the writing surface.

✔ Slant your paper (to the left for right-handers, to the right for left-handers). Tape the paper to the desk, if that helps.

✔ Use your helper (or opposite) hand to hold the paper down near to the top of the sheet.

✔ Take 2-minute stretch breaks from writing every 20 to 30 minutes.

Keeping an eye on your child's vision

If you're worried about your child's eyesight, have your child's vision tested, and don't hesitate to get second and third opinions. You can keep a watchful eye on your child's vision (especially when other family members have vision problems) by being aware of these indicators of possible vision problems:

✔ Your child tilts his head.

✔ Your child squints.

✔ Your child rubs his eyes, especially after looking at books.

✔ Your child complains of headaches.

✔ Your child feels dizzy pretty often.

✔ Your child seems to tire easily after reading.

✔ Your child holds books at an unusual angle or distance.

I'm neither a doctor nor an optometrist, so the information that I give you here is just what parents have told me. It's always good, though, to hear advice from people who have overcome problems, so here's what my sources say:

Making accommodations for your lefty

The world is pretty much made for right-handers. So if your child is a southpaw, she may sometimes need some extra help. This list offers a few pointers that can make your lefty's life more comfortable:

✔ Give your left-handed child room on her right, um I mean, left (or strong) side. She takes up more than the usual space because of the angle at which she writes. If an insensitive, brutish righty plunks down to your child's left, elbows bump, and the jostling begins.

✔ If your lefty develops an awkward writing posture, it's probably to avoid smudging her work or writing hand or so she can see what she's writing — or, more likely, both.

✔ Your lefty hates conference-style desks with a right-handed rest. They're nigh on impossible for her to use.

✔ Your lefty may find that leaning on pads and books makes writing easier than when she writes on single sheets of paper and that notebooks with the spiral on top make her life much easier. And guess what, you can get specialty notebooks with the spiral binding on the right but notebook holes on the left — how cool is that?

✔ Your left-handed child probably isn't too fond of whiteboards. Using erasable markers makes it awfully easy for her writing

hand to erase what she's just written. (Tilting the board can help.)

✔ Make life easier for your lefty by getting her left-handed writing tools. Ever seen a left-handed rule? It has a zero on the right and numbers running toward the left. Pens with fast-drying ink (you have to experiment) also are a good idea.

✔ Your lefty actually has an easy time with keyboarding, because, just like you, she does 50 percent of the typing with her left hand. The number keypad on the right can cause her problems, though, but you can buy a special keyboard.

✔ The biggest problem your lefty may have with computers is using a right-handed mouse. You can either move the mouse to her left (if no right-handers use the PC or it's set up for all household members to switch back and forth) or buy her a left-handed mouse. Your child may instead prefer to simply get used to using the mouse right-handed. Doing so is easier than making changes and has benefits. With the rise in popularity of video games, being able to use your weak hand is a distinct advantage.

✔ If your son seems to lag a little behind where your daughter was with reading and writing at the same age, don't jump to the conclusion that his vision is impaired. Statistically, boys develop language skills later than girls.

✔ Roughly gauge whether your child sees letters and symbols clearly by having him play with activity books that include activities like spotting the differences between shapes and letters and matching identical shapes and letters.

You can easily do your own regular minitests of your child's vision. When you're waiting for food at your favorite takeout restaurant, ask your child to read off a few items. If she's slow or unable to respond, take a trip to the optometrist.

Listening for hints about your child's hearing

Spotting whether your child has a hearing problem can be tricky, because all kids shout and ignore their parents when it seems like a good idea to them. But parents whose kids have hearing problems say to watch for these indicators:

- ✔ Your child has many ear infections.
- ✔ Your child shouts and talks excessively loud just about all the time.
- ✔ Your child doesn't answer you, even when you're saying good things.
- ✔ Your child quite often doesn't hear words the right way.

Statistically, boys are more prone to ear infections than girls.

Moving in the direction of reading and writing

One of the best things that you can show your child when he starts jotting down spellings is where to lead his pen. He needs to move from top to bottom with individual letters and from left to right with his words and sentences. Letter shapes go in all directions, but the starting point for printing always is somewhere at the top. Up-to-down and left-to- right printing doesn't directly give your child great spelling skills, but indirectly it makes all the difference. If your child writes in a smooth flow, he has brainpower to spare to figure out spellings. If he uses half of his brainpower trying to speed up and improve his writing, it's an unnecessary waste of good grey matter.

For downloadable writing sheets with options for tracing and dot-to-dot exercises, visit www.handwritingworksheets.com.

Jargon Busting

In this book, you come across a smattering of jargon. Most of it is stuff you've already heard, like *phonics* and *dictation*, but a bit of it, like *phonemic awareness* and *digraph*, is quite, well, classroomy. This section gives you a rundown of familiar and new jargon so that you won't run into any surprises farther down the track. If the new words seem a bit scary right now, fear not. When I use them in this book, I give real-life examples to show exactly what I'm jabbering about.

Brushing up on familiar terms

Relax. Table 1-1 is full of terms that you'll probably feel completely comfortable with. It's Table 1-2 that you want to watch out for!

Table 1-1	Familiar Terminology
Term	*What It Means*
apostrophe	This punctuation mark looks like a comma, but sits up high rather than down on the line. It's used to show possession like in "Sally's book." Your child can put it in contractions like "It's Tuesday," but she mustn't put it in phrases like "Yesterday was its birthday," because this kind of "its" is what technically is called a possessive personal pronoun and it doesn't require an apostrophe.
blends	*St* and *str* are blends. When two or three letters blend one into the next but each keep their own sound, that's a blend.
comprehension	A fancy word for understanding.
consonants	Letters that aren't vowels. The five vowels are *a, e, i, o,* and *u.* The rest of the letters in the alphabet are consonants. *Y* sometimes functions as a vowel.
contractions	Words (like *can't* and *I'm*) that are made by shortening other words (*cannot* and *I am*).
dictation	When you say or read text aloud for your child to write.
fine-motor skills	Small physical movements like writing and threading.
gross-motor skills	Big physical movements like kicking and jumping.
homonyms	Words (like *sun* and *son*) that sound the same.
learning styles	How each child learns things in a number of ways. A child has more than one kind of learning style, so teachers must tap into all of them — seeing (visual), hearing (auditory), and doing (kinesthetic).

(continued)

Table 1-1 *(continued)*

Term	*What It Means*
mnemonic	Memory joggers like "*i* before *e* except after *c*" and "there's a *bus* in *business*."
multisensory learning	Learning that uses as many of your senses as possible. Teachers often use it to describe the way they have kids look, say, and write.
nouns	Names of actual things (like man, pen, and book).
phonics	Showing your child how letters of the alphabet represent sounds.
plurals	More than one. Words like *man, pen,* and *book* are singular, while *men, pens* and *books* are plurals.
possessive apostrophe	When your child uses an apostrophe to show possession, like in "*Sharon's dog*" or "*The man's shoe*."
prefixes	A chunk of letters added to the beginning of a root word (a root word is a word all by itself). Chunks like *un, dis,* and *pre* are prefixes. Your child writes them in words like *uneven, disappoint,* and *preconception.*
proofreading	Looking over what you've written to check that it's right.
proper nouns	Names of specific, not general, things. Words like *man* and *book* are nouns, but *Mr. Brown* and *Huckleberry Finn* are proper nouns.
root word	A word that can either stand alone or have prefixes and suffixes added onto it. *Appoint* is a root word, because it can become *disappoint* and *appointed.*
silent letters	Letters that your child writes even though he can't hear them when he says the word. Silent letters are letters like *k* in *knee* and *gh* in *night.*
soft letters	*C* and *g* have soft sounds in words like *city* and *gem.* The soft sound of *c* is "*ss*", the soft sound of *g* is "*j.*"
suffixes	A chunk of letters added to the end of a root word (a root word is a word all by itself). *Ed* and *ing* are suffixes that your child uses often in words like *spelled* and *spelling.*
syllables	Sound/spelling chunks. The word *sound* has one syllable (you say it in one chunk) whereas *spelling* has two syllables.

Term	What It Means
vowels	The five letters a, e, i, o and u. *Y* sometimes functions as a vowel, as in *sky.*
word building	Spelling words in their respective parts. Your child may start with *an* and build it into *ant,* and then *pant,* and then *panted.*

Catching up on new terms

Now's the time to brace yourself, take deep breaths, or reach for the candies you've been saving for times of stress and high need. Table 1-2 is where I give you a bunch of terminology that any teacher would be proud of. Pace yourself, drink plenty of fluids, and don't even think about skipping the stretches. Otherwise, you'll pull some embarrassing or unsightly thing and have only yourself to blame.

Table 1-2	Upscaling Your Terminology
Term	**What It Means**
contextual cues	Clues that your child gets from the context or gist of the text. Let's say that your child's reading a book and gets stuck on the word *"gypsy."* She looks to the rest of the text, the illustrations, and the grammar to help her figure out the word. Those are contextual cues.
digraph	Two letters that together make a new sound that isn't the sound of them blending together. *Ch, th,* sh, and ph are consonant digraphs.
graphophonics/ phonographics	Looking at the sounds and shapes of letters in words.
phoneme, phonograph, phonogram	Chunks of sound/spelling like *st, sm, ee,* igh, and *ou.*
phonemic awareness	The awareness that letters and chunks of letters represent sounds and are used in many different words.

(continued)

Table 1-2 *(continued)*

Term	What It Means
schwa vowels	Vowels that make an indistinct *"uh"* sound. The end *a* in *camera* is a schwa vowel.
sight words	Words that are so common that your child needs to read and write them fluently (or risk being a stop-start sort of reader and writer).
visual discrimination (and auditory discrimination)	Being able to see the difference between letters and letter chunks in words. (*Auditory discrimination* means being able to hear the difference between letters and letter chunks in words.)
word families	Groups of words, like *about, shout,* and *out,* that share a spelling and sound pattern.

Chapter 2

Understanding the Reading, Writing, and Spelling Mix

In This Chapter

▶ Reading to your child

▶ Getting the hang of reading *with* your child

▶ Correcting your child's reading mistakes with grace

▶ Adding purpose and pep to your child's writing

▶ Joining in and helping your child with spelling

I wouldn't know a spark plug from a sprocket. That's okay, though, because I drive a new car, and the nice dealership people fix stuff that goes wrong with it — no questions asked. Last week, a red warning light lit up on my dashboard. Guessing that maybe my spark plugs needed dusting or my sprockets needed jiggling, I headed to the dealership. It turns out that that cute warning light signifies that any of about 80 million things can be wrong. As a result, my car had a sleepover at the dealership so the mechanics could unravel the problem. When your child learns to spell, he won't have to unravel 80 million different options, but he will have to pull apart the sounds inside of words and match letters to those sounds. To do it, he uses some skills he already has from reading and writing. This chapter strips down the parts that keep the whole spelling machine running and explains that, like you do with your car, you need to keep the whole shebang properly serviced.

Why the Janitor's Son Is a Genius

Comparing your family to other people's families is normal. You sometimes wonder, "Will the kid down the street do better in school than your child, because in his life, money's no object?" Will the little girl, new to the block and the country, and under opposite circumstances, be disadvantaged? Will your efforts with your child really make much difference? According to the National Education Association (NEA), whether you're a jillionaire or a janitor doesn't really matter. Whether you're new to the country or you left school early yourself doesn't matter all that much either. The more important question to answer is whether you encourage your child's learning to improve her chances of success in school.

Reading to Your Child

In this section, I extol the virtues of reading to your child. I tell you that reading to your child makes him comfortable with the look and workings of text. I tell you that when you read to your child you show him that you're a participant in this whole literacy thing and not a do-it-because-I-say-so onlooker. (And if you *are* reading, it must be fun, right?) I tell you that people who know a bunch about this sort of thing (like the NEA) say that reading out loud to your child is the single most important thing you can do to increase your child's chances of being a good reader. But reading isn't spelling, is it? Nope, but here's the thing: When you read to your child a heap of spelling things happen. Your child scans the words, makes mental images (without even knowing he's doing it), and ta-da, has a handy blueprint already in mind when he jots down words for himself. The system, of course, isn't foolproof, but you can be sure of one thing. If you share plenty of text with your child, he's much more likely to notice spellings than if you don't.

An Unequal and Sometimes Lumpy Mix

Your child learns to read, write, and spell in an unequal mix; moreover, she learns to read quickest of all before getting better at writing, and finally learning to spell. The mix of learning these three skills can get lumpy. Your child can be great at reading but weak at writing or spelling or both. You get no guarantees, either. You can submerge her in stories and bury her under books but still discover that spelling seems to throw her. The system can unfair, but regardless of whether your child picks up spelling incidentally or has to study practically every word she commits to paper, you can help. By making sure that your child does plenty of reading, writing, and practicing her spellings from this book, you can see her make marked progress.

Reading with Your Child

Just about everybody tells their children to read. Many people also read to their children. Not many people, however, read *with* their children. It's a pity, because reading with your child is a cool thing to do. Here's why:

✔ Sending your child off to read alone can make her think of reading as a chore — a bit like making her bed. Reading with your child gives her a distinct reading-is-so-good-that-I-do-it-too message that can mean the difference between your child remaining a reader, or not.

✔ Reading together bridges the gap between your child being a beginning or reluctant reader and her becoming a fluent, all-by-herself reader.

✔ Reading together fills in the gaps in your child's still-developing skills. When she isn't sure about a word, she can ask you for help right away, which, of course, boosts not only her confidence but also her fluency and comprehension. She keeps plot and meaning in her mind when she's fluent. Stop-start readers lose the sense of what they're reading, because keeping all that stuff in your head is hard when your concentration's all used up trying to figure out a bunch of hard words.

✔ Reading with a buddy is just plain fun. Snacks and a good range of books (or magazines and comics) make things even better.

Increase your chances of turning your child into a reader by making sure that he sees you (and other significant adults and peers) reading. The fancy term for letting your child see you read is *modeling,* and even if you're just skimming through a few work journals in front of him, you're being a model.

Being *Nuts About Nuts*

On my bookshelf, I have a children's book of verse. When I'm feeling wistful about the days when I could fit both my kids on my lap at the same time, or just want to take my mind off their campaign to share nothing, communicate in yells, and never take turns, I pick it up. Here's how some of it goes:

I'm nuts about nuts

nuts are great

crack seven

crack eight

or

pack a packet in your luggage

pack a packet in your pocket

pack a packet in your rucksack

pack a packet in your rocket.

Ah. At one time, my kids loved that rhyme. I still love it. Substitute "books" for the "nuts" part (except for the very first one) and there, in a nutshell, is sound advice for helping your child soak up spelling conventions without ever realizing he's doing it.

(*Nuts About Nuts* was written by Michael Rosen and published by HarperCollins.)

Partners and practices

Now that I've extolled its virtues, you're probably wondering exactly how you go about reading with your child. Luckily, this question has been answered by scores of teachers. The three kinds of reading with your child are

- ✔ **Choral:** You and your child read the same text out loud together at the same time.

- ✔ **Alternated:** You and your child take turns reading text, usually a story, out loud.

- ✔ **Interrupted:** You read text to your child, usually a story, and stop at an exciting point in the plot. The hope is that your child becomes so engrossed that he reads on.

Choral reading is a satisfying thing to do. Your child feels comfortable because she can listen to you whenever she's flummoxed by a word, and you get to discretely listen in to how she's doing. As you get better at staying in synch, you can read a hair's breadth behind your child so that she feels like she's taken the lead (which she actually has).

Taking turns reading with your child (alternated reading) is a great way to nudge her toward reading more for herself. Read to her, of course, but make deals. You read a page, and she reads a sentence. You read a chapter, and she reads a page. Start as small as you need to, which may be very small, if your child is reluctant. Read every night, and gently move your child from sentences to paragraphs to pages.

What's a good book for my child?

A good book to read with your child is one that doesn't overwhelm him (or you). The perfect book is just slightly taxing for him with well-spaced and appropriately sized text and nice pictures. Choose books that:

- ✔ Interest your child

- ✔ Have only a few words that are new and hard for your child

- ✔ Have text that's easy on the eye and nicely spaced

- ✔ Have an all-round appealing look

If you worry that your child reads stuff that's below his grade level, relax. It's better for him to read a few easy books confidently, and want to read more, than it is for him to labor over one hard book and want to run a mile whenever you suggest that he read another one.

You and your child can make selecting books easier by focusing on series. You can get the lowdown on popular book series by asking at your child's school library or at your local public library.

Make alternated reading easier for your child by reading text to him and then having him read the same text back to you.

Interrupted reading is ever so slightly sneaky — Oh my gosh, I'm right out of time and can't possibly read any more — but productive. You usually find that as long as the story's good, your child perseveres. When she reads on for herself, she gains confidence and the nice feeling of being in control.

Listening to your child read to you

Listening to your child read to you is so valuable that you've already heard all about it. You know that it's important to listen — maybe for the 18th time — to his rendition of the classroom text. You know that your child makes the best progress of all when he reads out loud to you every day. You know that you have to maintain a you're-doing-great tone and you're even cruising along with his reading log. However, the one thing that you'd like to get all sewn up are his reading mistakes. Should you correct all of them or just some of them? Should he sound out the words or can you tell him the answers? If he walks off after being stuck for half an hour on *ought,* should you track down his teacher's home phone number? Good questions. In the next section, I give you pointers that should keep you off the teacher's black-list of nuisance callers.

Correcting your child's reading mistakes

When your child starts to read, your life takes on a new dimension. You prepare breakfast while listening to her read. You drive to school while listening to her read. Afternoon snack time is punctuated by you listening to her read. Homework means listening to her read. She's at your side reading as you load the dishwasher, washing machine, and microwave. Supper is, of course, a good time for her to read to you (between mouthfuls) and everyone knows that bedtime reading is practically mandatory. With all that reading going on, there's a fair chance your child will make a few reading mistakes that cause tears to fall, sometimes hers and other times yours. How can you tread lightly on her ego? How will you make her feel like a winner when she makes a bunch of mistakes? Does it really matter that you let her read a bunch of gob-bledygook, because you're too nervous to correct her errors? In this section, I help you maintain a relatively normal household *and* make a few corrections to her mistakes (unlikely as that sounds). There's no yadda, yadda, yadda either, just this handy list of practical tips:

✔ You don't need to correct all of your child's reading mistakes. If she's reading a beginner's, one-sentence-per-page kind of book, you can correct all of her mistakes, because errors probably send the meaning of the text askew. However, with longer text, you can be flexible. If your child makes a mistake that doesn't interfere with meaning, and she's steaming ahead and enjoying herself, relax. Correct her only on words that are critical for keeping the meaning intact and let minor errors slide.

An error to let slide may be, "He let *her* dog run," instead of, "He let *the* dog run." Errors you'd want to correct are things like "He *lost* her dogs *rag*," instead of "He *let* the dog *run*."

If you're wondering why letting some errors slide is okay, you can end up interfering with the flow of your child's reading when you interrupt all the time. He needs to keep the meaning of the text in mind as he reads, because that's what gives him clues about what's coming next in the text. Another thing about being more discerning with your interruptions is that beginning readers need to keep a can-do attitude. The more you tell him that he's wrong, the less capable he feels, and the more you're pretty much caught in a Catch-22.

✔ Sometimes your child figures out words that she's stuck on if you draw her attention to the chunks of sound in the word. Sometimes she can't. Say, for example, that she comes across the word *enough* and has never seen it before. Furthermore say that she hasn't been through that particular incarnation of the *"ou"* spelling with you. She doesn't have much hope of figuring out "enough." In that case, the sensible thing to do is to flat out tell your child about the word "enough," make a note of it, and then let her move on with the story. You can always show her the background for words like *enough, rough,* and *country* later on. (To read more about the sounds represented by *ou*, you can check out Chapter 11).

✔ You can help your child figure out some words by drawing his attention to the gist of the text. If he reads ahead and looks at illustrations, he has a better chance of figuring out unfamiliar words. That's why teachers often tell your child to read to the end of the paragraph or chapter, and then, armed with this extra information, backtrack to the unknown word.

When your child reads around a word by looking at pictures and reading ahead, she's using contextual cues. She's looking at the word in context and searching for clues (or cues in teacher-talk) from that context.

✔ When you correct your child's errors, be kind. Say things like, "That's not quite right," or simply point to the offending words. If your child can't fathom the word after a few seconds, tell him what it is and continue on. You can always go back and focus on a few of the words your child misread later on in what is known as *word study*. You can get the most from word study by putting misread words into word families whenever possible. A *word family* is a bunch of words that share a spelling and sound pattern (like *all, call, ball,* and *tall*). I talk more about word families in Chapter 10.

There's no "hay" in "they"

When your child picks up a spelling list, he doesn't have to park his imagination.

Word study actually is fun. Have your child be bold with highlighter pens, brazen with circles, and brash with underlines. Have him draw stuff in and around words or think up rhymes and acronyms so he remembers them. I've seen kids draw a worm (wearing a cap) from the *eau* part of beautiful and tell me cool stuff like, "There's no hay in they." I guess that imagination was around long before spelling.

 A useful technique for helping your child correct errors is to say, "Can you read that again? I missed something." That way your child goes back with no worries of having made a mistake already and can get it right second time around.

Writing to Your Child

Much as I adore my kids, I sometimes avoid them. Maybe they rolled into my office, clenched in a half nelson just as I was on the phone explaining to an editor how I have my parenting skills all sewn up. Maybe they drank the last of the milk, so that I have to delay my caffeine buzz until I've manically raced to the store. Or maybe I just heard them exchange one too many "Well, duh's." Anyway, at times like that, I write them notes. I write things like, "I will check your room in 15 minutes, please have all your clothes in the right places." I calm down. My kids read my note (in case anything good is in it, which some-times there is) and best of all, clothes often find their way into laundry baskets. I'm sure that I don't have to persuade you that writing notes to your child is an excellent thing to do, but you may find it handy to have a few getting-started and keeping-going ideas up your sleeve. So here they are:

- ✔ Write thank-you notes.

- ✔ Write your schedule for today for your child.

- ✔ Write a note to let your child know what's on today's menu.

- ✔ Write to-do notes, which are especially handy when you're heated up and don't trust yourself to ask for things in reasonable tones.

- ✔ Write reminders about things like feeding the cat or dog or putting extra mittens in schoolbags.

- ✔ Write "I'm proud of you" notes.

- ✔ Write jokes and put them in lunchboxes.

- Write "I love you" notes (of course!).

- Tell your child who called for her. (This suggestion works well with older girls who can corner you for hours with questions about what tone was used and whether you're sure that that was all that was said.)

- Ask your child what he wants you to add to your shopping list.

- Write posters of rules or daily chores.

- Write checklists to keep daily routines running smoothly.

And, of course, after you get all of those notes written, feel free to go to work.

Writing with Your Child

No matter how many bags of stuff I take to donation bins, my house never seems to stay tidy for more than an hour or two. I mount regular lets-get-serious campaigns with my kids and have plenty of good ideas, but in real terms, nothing much changes. One thing that comes out of my sporadic frenzies, though, is the occasional poster. The posters are well-intentioned lists that I write with my kids. Only today my 9-year-old asked what she should do with our last poster. It read

Rules

1. No TV talk.

2. Keep your hands on your own body.

3. No answering back.

4. Clean up after yourself.

5. Have fun.

And although I follow the advice in parenting books and encourage my child to phrase things in positive terms, my child had added a dire postscript:

> Whoever breaks these rules WILL be PUNISHED (with a 10- to 30-minute timeout).

Putting up posters

Kids love making posters of things like rules, friends' telephone numbers and to-do lists. You may want to get involved, though, because eager poster-makers often use up several posters in about two minutes, haphazardly scribbling on each one. Show him how to use a ruler and pencil to first sketch a rough draft on paper. When he's created one great poster idea, consider helping him with a poster of word families that he'd like to get to know (*there where; were, her,* or *would, could, should,* for example). He can also make a "Tricky spellings" poster and put words like *who* and *because* on it. When you've got a stack of finished posters, have your child grab a clump of poster puttyand choose prominent spots to display them.

Your school supplies store is a good source of inspiration for word-family posters. Visiting one, you can get really groovy posters listing all kinds of word types for less than five dollars each — a great investment.

Don't go broke! Dollar stores have the best prices on poster board and often drugstores put it on sale. Sides of boxes work well, too

Sharing a journal

Years ago one of my kids had to keep a shared journal with a parent as a school project. She told me all sorts of things in the journal, and I could hardly wait to read her entries. I was even able to point out a few spelling errors to her without having to back nervously toward the door as I did it. I kept that journal. It moves from one place to another every time I have that tidy-house fantasy. The "Sharing a journal" activity up next explains the ins and outs of sharing a journal with your child so you can start making your own treasured memento.

Activity: Sharing a journal

Preparation: Buy your child a hardback notebook of his choosing and pick up some nice pens.

Follow these steps:

1. **Decide on a journal-writing schedule.** Your child can write entries at the end of a school week, on the weekend, or even daily.

2. **Encourage your child to write whatever comes to mind, especially things he may not have had time to tell you in person.**

3. **Encourage your child to include requests, such as what he'd like as a reward for good grades, and to explain things he's doing, such as what he's saving his money for.**

4. **When your child's done writing an entry, write your response.** Say things that you may have been too busy to say sooner and fill your entries with praise and encouragement.

Your child probably will start your shared journal with a burst of enthusiasm and write entries every day only to find that daily writing becomes a burden. Advise your child to write only one entry each week, and then if she wants, decide upon a time for finishing up completely.

Putting sass into stories

Your child may immediately take to writing stories. He may write reams of disjointed, waffling text and present it to you proudly. Your job is to be interested. Take heart. He gets better and better with his stories, because the more you encourage him, the more he does and the quicker he learns to trim excess baggage. Letting spelling mistakes slide is the best course of action in the early days. As your child's stories grow more sophisticated (and hopefully, shorter), you can make the odd but tactful spelling suggestion. When your child's about ready to begin his autobiography, you can point out more errors — maybe even all of them, but again, be sensitive. You can say things like: "That word doesn't look quite right," or "You may want to read this sentence again." Or you can ask whether he'd like you to put a discreet pencil mark under the words he may want to revise.

Little kids like to do close activities with favorite stories. A *close activity* is a piece of writing in which words have been deleted for your child to fill in. Making a close activity means getting one of your child's favorite stories, making a copy of it and blacking out key words. Key words that you black out for him to fill in can be simple, frequent ones like *they* and *was* or harder ones like *followed* or *proud*. An alternative to blacking out words is covering them with sticky notes so your child can write the missing words on the sticky notes before peeling them off to see if he was right.

If your child needs inspiration for story writing, go through a few typical story lines with her (bullied girl finds a hidden talent that attracts friends; boy perseveres with soccer skills and scores winning goal). Jot down promising words too so she can use them if she wants to. Boys usually like active, task-based stories (with words like *throw, hurl, compete, champion,* and *proud*) and girls like to talk about friendships and personal experiences (with words like *secret, lie, loyal, kind,* and *alone*). Animal stories — heroic dogs, talking horses, alien cats — are popular with most kids.

Internet message boards and chat rooms

Your child may know more about the Internet than you do, and it's a pretty safe bet that she knows more than I do. So I don't to go into much detail about the whole message board and chat room thing, except to remind you about it. Climb aboard the message board/chat room juggernaut with your child, because even if she isn't yet on it, it's going to happen. Peek at what she's writing but keep a nonjudgmental tone. Oh, and be ever vigilant about online safety. Tell your child never to give out her real name, address, or phone number to strangers (even if they become online friends) and to exit scary or yuk stuff ASAP.

Giving a big hand to handwriting

Handwriting drills can feel like one big drag. Your child spends night after night stretching the lines on *t*'s to the proper height and shaping *o*'s into perfect spheres. He often lets you know just how resentful he is, and you wonder whether it's at all worthwhile. Well, I don't think that any child needs to labor over the same ground when he's already proficient, but smooth handwriting helps your child spell. When your child writes fluidly, he doesn't spend so much time and effort forming his letters properly, and that leaves him with more brainpower to commit to spelling. That's why getting your child's handwriting up to scratch is a commendable — if at times a tad dull — pursuit.

Having your child write to you

Oh my gosh. Who doesn't love getting notes from their children? Some notes make you cringe ("I'm sorry I was bad."), some make your knees go wobbly ("I love you and I always will."), and some tell you things you might never have found out otherwise ("I know my manners are bad, but I'm upset about school."). Encourage your child to write notes to you and for that matter to anybody else. Here are some of the many good reasons for having your child write notes:

- ✔ Your child can write notes to say things she can't say in person like "sorry" and "I love you."

- ✔ Your child can leave you reminder notes like: "I get cookies in my lunch on Fridays."

- ✔ Your child can write notes when angry, explaining things that you may not be aware of, such as "You only told me off, but Shaun laughed at me and poked his tongue out while you were telling me off."

- ✔ Your child can ask you for special things, giving reasons why she deserves them or can be trusted. For example, "Ashley's mom lets her stay home alone as long as their neighbor is home and she calls her every half hour. "

- ✔ Your child can write you weekly schedules of what she has to do and what she'd like to do. For example: "Monday: Math homework. Can I play with Ashley from 6 to 7 p.m.?"

Spelling with your child

Nothing is like having company to make a task go by quicker and easier. As long as you aren't stuck with your archenemy, and as long as you aren't hung up on being boss, company is great. When you buddy up with your child to figure out spellings, you can achieve a great deal. You get stuff done in a warm, friendly way, and helping your child out is easier when he sees you as a buddy and not an interference (heaven forbid). Here's a sketch of how to get cozy and cooperative with your speller:

Use an inquisitive manner when you spell with your child. You want to convey the feeling that you're two supersleuths figuring out how to spell in a partnership. Your child knows that you're not too bad of a speller, but he won't care, because he's having fun with you. Here are some six steps for accomplishing these goals:

1. **Each of you grabs pen and paper or pen and whiteboard.**

2. **Try spelling out a word at the same time together, with each of you writing the word on your own paper.**

3. **Compare each other's results as you go.**

   Talk about what comes next.

4. **Sound out chunks of spelling as you go.**

   Scribble possible spellings at the side of your paper for your child to see and contribute to.

5. **Soup things up by not showing each other your papers until you're both done and then comparing answers.**

6. **Make your child laugh or shift into extraobservant gear by jotting down a few deliberate mistakes.**

Getting the Most from Drills and Drafts

I'm the kind of person who likes routine. I'm agitated when I don't get my morning coffee at the same time every day, and buying a new brand of toothpaste can throw me into panic. Routines are good things, especially for neurotics like me. Spelling has some routines that you definitely want your child to get into. I'm not talking about elaborate stuff, like pointing your boots northwesterly with the laces hanging to the left, but rather easy-to-remember, quick practices. The practice that you hear most about in classrooms is "Look, Say, and Write," which gets stretched into the more descriptive "Looking, Saying, Writing, and Checking" method.

Looking, saying, covering, writing, and checking

When handing out spelling lists, the teacher tells your child to: Look, Say, Cover, Write, and Check his spellings. This formula means that good spellers look carefully at a word and then say it to themselves. Then, without peeking

at the word again, they write it down in the chunks they're saying to themselves. The cover part of the formula reminds your child not to peek so
that he develops the look-say-write habit. Good spellers develop this form
of self-sufficiency without peeking at the word at the drop of a hat. The check
part of the formula reminds your child to check his spelling. When checking
the spelling, your child corrects it against the original word whenever necessary, and remembers better than when you point out any errors. The whole
look-say-cover-write-check formula gets your child actively doing the spelling
for himself and is one of those great multisensory strategies that people rave
about. Your child uses his eyes, ears, mouth, and hands with this strategy,
and what's more, if he doesn't, it can set him back. If your child doesn't
look carefully at words, doesn't say words in chunks, doesn't jot down the
words, and doesn't check what he's actually written, he may not gain the
confidence and skill that he needs to move forward with spelling.

If instead of using the look-say-cover-write-and-check formula your child tries
to learn things by rote, he learns them without any real understanding. Your
child thinks of the information as an isolated chunk of stuff that must be
drummed into his memory. The whole business is inefficient. Your child
learns things much better when he fits them into his own frame of reference,
like when he mentally files a word like *fight* with *might, tight,* and *sight,* to
create a word family. (I talk about word families in Chapters 10 and 11)

Doing dictation

Oh my gosh, here's my favorite thing. I love dictation. If you regularly dictate
words for your child to write and spell, good things happen. She grows more
confident at spelling, makes fewer silly mistakes (like *thay, I'me,* and *meny*),
breaks words into chunks better (because she's slowing down and really
thinking about each word), and starts habitually checking (or proofreading)
her own writing. These advantages are all great for a budding speller, so who
in their right mind wouldn't try dictation every night for a few weeks?

What exactly is dictation? What are its pitfalls? What's the no-fuss way to do
it? *Dictation* is reading text aloud and having your child write it down. The
factors that you need to consider when giving your child dictation are

- ✔ **Choosing text that's at your child's level (which doesn't necessarily
  mean grade level).** The right level is the level at which your child reads
  comfortably. You want to give him words that make him really think but
  not so many that he gives up. Having your child do several easy dictations is better than doing only one that's too hard and switches him
  right off spelling altogether.

- ✔ **Giving your child just one or two sentences to start, especially when
  he's a slow writer.** Build up to more dictation over a few days. Gauge
  the level of your child's cooperation and make your dictations suit his

mood, energy, and competence. Again, a few easier but successful dictations are better than one lengthy but coerced dictation.

If your child struggles with writing and does better on a keyboard you may want him to type the dictation — with the spell-checker turned off!

✔ **Reading the entire text first and then breaking it into bits.**

✔ **Speaking clearly and, if you think it's helpful, exaggerating some pronunciations and offering tips to remind your child of letter sequences.** Words like *chocolate* warrant this sort of help. Instead of the normal "choclut" pronunciation, say, "Choclut is spelled choc-oh-late."

✔ **Helping your child with spelling patterns like *tion* and *ought*.** You can have your child jot them on a poster or whiteboard so he can refer back to them whenever he needs to.

When your child does dictation and wants a perfect score, you need to lead him through proofreading and correcting.

You can do dictation in the car. It works especially well when your child has a lap desk.

Persevering with proofreading

Some of the things that you do with your child may raise big, fat question marks in your mind. You pick up her clothes and wonder whether you're choosing your battles or raising a messy child, you remind her to do her homework and wonder whether you're prioritizing homework or raising a lazy child, and you let her question you and wonder whether you're raising an analytical child or just a rude one. Thank heavens for proofreading. Regardless of whether you nurture or nag your child to always proofread her writing, you can be certain that you're doing the right thing.

When your child reads her own writing and spots mistakes, she probably can correct the mistakes on her own (after all, she knows that the offending words aren't right). Encourage your child to have a go at jotting down spelling options on scrap paper. With a word like *option,* she may try *opsion, opcian* and *option.* If she spots the right word, that's great, but if she doesn't, well the more she gets into the habit of jotting down options and scanning them for the one that looks right, the better her accuracy becomes. If she can't fathom the spelling at all, write it down for her, point out the unique features (*op-tion*), and have her write it out for herself a few times. Another way to proofread is to do it together. Your child spots mistakes but you contribute. You say things like, "Hmm, this word doesn't look quite right," and then give her time to correct it if she can. One last option that older kids like is correcting the dictation and then underlining any words with which they're really having difficulties. Your child then brings the underlined culprits to you, so you can dole out liberal servings of your wisdom. Alternatively, you can reach for the dictionary or computer spell-checker.

Poorfreading for Pros

I don't go into much detail about style and grammar in this book, but now and then I offer some style suggestions that I think you'd like to know about. If your child enjoys proofreading jokes, and you want to run a few points about style past her, check out this silly but sophisticated list of do's and don'ts. You may have to explain things like double negatives and metaphors — told you it was sophisticated.

✔ Check to see if you any words out.

✔ Don't use no double negatives.

✔ The passive voice is to be avoided.

✔ Even if a mixed metaphor sings, it should be derailed.

✔ Don't use commas, that aren't necessary.

✔ Its important to use apostrophe's right.

✔ a sentence should begin with a capital and end with a period

✔ In letters compositions reports and things like that use commas to keep a string of items apart.

For more trivia and jokes, go to `www.niehs.nih.gov/kids/jokes.htm#index`. This site is for the National Institutes of Health (NIH), Department of Health and Human Services (DHHS), and its kids' pages are fun. Most of the material on the site is in the public domain, so your child can use or copy it.

Take detours away from proofreading to show your child word families. A word family for *option* includes words like *action, fiction,* and *inspection.* I talk about word families in Chapters 10 and 11.

Using memory joggers

Whenever I give talks about kids' reading, a parent of a little child usually asks, "Is it okay for my child to parrot a story without *really* reading it, even though he thinks that he *is* really reading? Should I be making him sound out the words?" The answer is that beginning readers use a few prereading skills. Parrot reading is one of them, and it's perfectly okay. In fact, it's really useful as long as it's used as a steppingstone to real reading. When your child spells, he uses many other steppingstones. Memory joggers, such as "There's a *bus* in *bus*iness," and "Fri*end*s never *end*," are helpful steppingstones. You can also encourage your child to use rhymes or any other kind of mnemonic that helps him spell. After a few hundred uses, your child probably will drop them, but even if he doesn't, using them isn't a problem. I still say "*i* before *e* except after *c*" whenever I write *receive,* and I'd bet good money that plenty of other closet mnemonic-users just like me are out there. If you're bursting with mnemonics of your own and want to check out my repertoire, skip over to Chapter 11 and flit through the Cheat Sheet at the front of this book.

Correcting Your Child's Mistakes

Uh, oh! Here's the part about eggshells. You know, those glaring mistakes that you try to pirouette around whenever you see them in your child's writing — because you're wary of pointing them out to her. Correcting her spelling mistakes can be a thankless business. She doesn't want your input, hates you to see even a missing comma in her compositions, and if you point out a missing letter, shrieks with the kind of outrage you'd expect if you'd just sold her into forced child labor. Are there things you can do to ease the pain? You bet. You can find heaps of help all through this book, and for starters, here are a few tips to serve as an immediate analgesic:

- Use an "I think" or "maybe try this" kind of an attitude, and use those phrases when helping your child, too.

- Ask your child whether she wants your help instead of just barging in on her show.

- Tell your child that you're nearby, if she needs or wants a quick hand now and then.

- Don't be shy about saying things like, "Yeah, that word really used to outfox me, too," or, "Watch out for the *"ough"* spelling, it catches everybody by surprise."

- Ask your child to pencil in any words about which she'd like your advice.

- Let your child know that you think spelling can be a hard nut to crack but that it's worth getting right. Tell her the story of the rejected job application. . . you know, the one where the kid, very much like her, writes everything beautifully in her job application but (aargh) makes spelling mistakes.

- Help your child find spelling chunks that match the sounds in her words. Tell your child that in some words doing so is easy — like in *dramatic*, but in others, like *ought*, she must rely more on her visual memory.

- Help your child cruise through word families (like *all, call, ball,* and *fall*) any time she spells a word that belongs to a family. (Words in a family all share a common spelling and sound pattern. I tell you more about word families in Chapter 10.)

- Remind your child, again and again, to proofread.

Keeping Stress at Bay

I wish that I were calmer. I'd like to be one of those composed kind of parents — you know, the kind whose kids do what they're asked and gladly accept their advice. In the real world, I'm not blessed with vast reserves of patience and my kids eye me warily much of the time. Neither of my kids is the tai chi or meditative type either. They haven't picked up serenity, or even forbearance, from any of their teachers, even though I've sent them to school for years. So, in our shut-the-door-so-the-neighbors-don't-hear-us-yelling household, I frequently refer to books and lists that reintroduce me to that concept of being calm. I'm sure that *you* don't need more calm, but maybe you know someone who does. Tell her to read this list:

- ✔ **Make sure you and your child are fed and watered when you tackle spellings.** This idea sounds obvious right up until you hear your stomach rumbling louder than your bad temper.

- ✔ **Provide your child with needed solutions, not blame.** If you tell him that he should've listened better or practiced more in class, you create bad feelings and won't make headway.

  The big thing to remember about having your child spell for you is that he wants to succeed. If you ask him to spell from a cold start, you may be setting him up for failure. Before asking him to spell single words or a list of spellings from school, make sure you run though the words first and help him break them into chunks and highlight tricky ones.

- ✔ **Take breaks.** Your child's best attention comes in bursts of about 20 minutes. Of course, he won't become fatigued after 20 minutes of absorbing Nintendo play, but you can pretty much count on it happening in the middle of spelling homework. It happens to you, too. Attention spans are short things, so taking a cookie-and-milk break every now and then is okay. In fact, it's best to. When you get 20 minutes of willing effort from your child, instead of a grueling hour of complaints, you'll be glad you listened to me — except that unlike me, you won't, of course, have the experience of wading through that bad hour for comparison, so actually you'll have no idea what I'm fussing about!

- ✔ **Delegate.** The things that I lead you through in this book are simple. If you can pin down your partner, mother, or an older child, and whiz through the basics with them, do it. Anyone can make a difference to a child's spelling and now that you have this book to incite you, maybe you can harangue a few people into helping you out.

- ✔ **Help your child to spell words, one chunk at a time.** Tell him that some chunks like *atch* are easy, some like *ight* and *ow* are fairly easy, and some like *eigh* take a little ingenuity. Not to worry, though, when he gets a few spelling chunks under his hat, he can use them to spell masses of words.

- ✔ **Look for words that are spelled similarly to other words (like *should, would,* and *could*).**

Some people swear that their short-term memories (STM) don't handle any more than two or three thoughts at a time, but in truth, your short-term memory typically hangs onto five to ten bits of information. So if your child tries to memorize random words by sight alone, she can't store any more than ten at most. It's hard for her to remember random, unrelated words that don't follow any pattern. Her brain isn't fond of that kind of information. It plunks it in her short-term memory and keeps it there only briefly. If, however, your child finds tricks for remembering those words, like spelling them out in chunks and using mnemonics (memory joggers) like *i before e except after c*, she remembers more and for longer periods of time. Words that are drenched in meaning or patterns move into your child's long-term memory (LTM). So what I'm really saying is: Show your child how to spell in chunks and use memory-jogging techniques, and have her focus on getting to know ten words at a time really well before adding any more. Whenever you help your child tackle new words, think LTM. (It's official; STM is *so* yesterday.)

Make sure that your child knows what a word means before you ask him to spell it. Doing so is key to establishing it in his LTM.

Chapter 3

Getting to Know the Pieces and Parts of Spelling

In This Chapter

▶ Beginning with your child's ears

▶ Being practical about pronunciation

▶ Looking for patterns and peculiarities

▶ Having a few tries

▶ Dictating the rules

*W*hen I was a kid, I was impressed by a rhyme about a kingdom that fell into ruin because of a nail. The rhyme starts out with a horseshoe. The horseshoe is missing a nail, but no one goes to get one and therein begins the demise of the entire kingdom. For the want of a nail, the shoe was lost; for the want of a shoe, the horse was lost; for the want of a horse, the rider was lost: and, well, I'm sure you get the picture. A battle ensues, the kingdom falls, and the original lazy culprit no doubt feels pretty stupid. When you teach your child the skills needed to be a good speller, don't get caught in the lurch like the person who wouldn't go get a nail. Don't skip the "looking hard" part — that's what this chapter is all about.

Listening First

What do you think the most important thing for you to teach your beginning speller happens to be? The alphabet? The looks of key words? Phonics, maybe? No. Well, actually, yes and no. All of these things are really handy for beginning spellers, but the first thing that your child needs is phonemic awareness. I'm beginning to sound technical, right? Phonemic awareness does have a scary sort of a ring to it, I confess, but I'm not going to give it a technical-stuff icon, because honestly the term phonemic awareness has *so* much more bark than bite.

No room for seven

A friend of mine has a son who used to recite the numbers from one to ten like this: "One, two, three, four, five, six, eight, nine, ten." Puzzled, my friend told him that he'd forgotten seven. "No," the son replied, "I don't like seven." My friend still doesn't know why seven fell from grace with her son, but she thinks that it has something to do with the fact that all the other numbers up to ten are pronounced with only one syllable. Her son may have decided that the word "seven," with its two syllables, just didn't sound the same as or even fit in with the other numbers. With such an attentive ear for word patterns, chances are that when this little guy starts school, he'll breeze happily through his spelling lists.

Phonemic awareness is probably *the* hottest phrase among teachers of reading, writing, and spelling these days. It gives plain old phonics quite a hefty boot — meaning you no longer hear many teachers talking about phonics. They say "phonemic awareness" and leave ordinary, unsuspecting parents baffled the way you are at this point.

So what on earth are they going on about and how come they think regular people have heard of it? Don't worry, teachers often get caught up in their own jargon simply because it's so familiar to them. They forget to clue the rest of us in. After all, parent/teacher conferences are already jam-packed with other information, but that's okay, because I give you the lowdown right here: *Phonemic awareness* is what your child has when he hears that words are made of chunks of sound and realizes that those same chunks also pop up inside of other words. If your child has phonemic awareness, he can hear the "*at*" in *cat, mat, hat,* and *fat,* or the "*buh*" at the beginning of *boat, brick brother,* and *ball.* He's able to finish off the rhyme, "Roses are red, violets are blue, sugar is sweet, and so are —." Phonemic awareness is all about hearing patterns in words. It's a hot-button topic in school, and you want your child to latch onto it!

The key to remember about phonemic awareness is that it follows a horse-and-cart sort of principle. You want your child to get the hang of sounds *before* he starts trying to jot them down on paper, just like you'd put your horse before your cart or risk an unorthodox, not to mention slow and difficult journey.

What's the difference between the old phonics and the newer phonemic awareness? Not much. But never say that to any ferociously adamant devotee of phonemic awareness, or you're in for a long-winded explanation. Phonemic awareness reminds teachers that kids need to understand all about sound chunks *before* they begin matching letters to them. Phonics, some say, didn't stress sounding out chunks like that. Instead, the theory goes, phonics left the door open for teachers to just teach kids that "*a* is for apple" and "*b* is for belligerent," oops I mean "ball." Phonemic awareness is a really useful term, but I seriously doubt that teachers didn't already know the phonemic awareness stuff before the actual term was invented. Good teachers always have taught kids all about chunks of sound and moving them around to make new words, but now everyone has phonemic awareness as a reminder. Whatever you do, don't get caught saying "phonics" to the phonemic-awareness watchdogs.

Listening for Chunks of Sound

The kinds of chunks of sound that you want your child to be able to distinguish in words are single-letter sounds, blends, digraphs, and rhymes. Table 3-1 gives you an at-a-glance account of what these terms mean and where to start rustling up a few sounds for your child to tune in to.

Table 3-1	Getting Your Child Used to Sound/Spellings
Sound/Spelling Pattern	*Practicing It*
single letters	Start your child in spelling by having her write down the first letter she hears in the words that you say to her. When she writes *t* in response to you saying *top*, *b* when you say *big*, and so on, she's getting the hang of beginning single-letter sounds. From there, move her onto ending sounds, and then finish single-letter spelling by having her jot down short-vowel middle sounds like the *a* in *cat* and the *e* in *hen*.
blends	When your child can jot down single letters (first, last, and middle short vowels), introduce her to blends. Start with blends at the beginnings of words, like *st* in *step* and *br* in *brown*. Read words to her until she's comfortable with jotting down blends that she hears at the beginning, and then move her to blends at the end. Read words like *ring* and *held* until she's jotting down blends like *ng* and *ld* almost as fast as you read them out loud to her.
long vowels	Long vowels are where your child really has to tune in. The next spellings to show your child are long-vowel spellings. The first step in mastering long vowels is hearing them. To spell words like *pain* and *tale,* your child must first hear that *ay* is different than the *a* in *apple*. After that, she can put her energies into figuring out exactly how to spell long-vowel sounds because a few different options can be used. At this point, your job is to give your child plenty of practice spelling word families like *pain, rain,* and *mail, pale, whale,* and *stale,* so that she navigates her way through all the spellings of all the long vowels.

Table 3-1 (continued)

Sound/Spelling Pattern	Practicing It
digraphs	Sooner than you think, your child will come across words like *loud* and *boil* and will see a brand-new kind of spelling that sits in the middle of words like these — a two-letter cluster called a digraph. Digraphs result in unexpected kinds of spellings (why *loud* and not *lawd*?), but luckily digraphs are all around the spelling world, so your child will encounter plenty of words (like *proud, cloud, out,* and *shout)* to practice. Your job, as usual, is to show her heaps of *ous, ois,* and other digraphs.
rhymes	You probably never thought of rhyming as being much more than a fun thing to do with your child, but rhyming is one of the more valuable spelling strategies that you teach her. Rhyming helps your child group words together like *lean, clean,* and *mean.* Groups of similar-sounding (and looking) words are known as word families (in this case, the *ea* family). Word families help your child spell whole bunches of words. When spelling a word like *misdeed,* for example, she can refer to the word families she already has filed away in her brain (*miss* and *mistake/need, feed,* and *greed).* Even tricky words like *subconscious* and *numb* usually fit into word families (*conscious, delicious,* and *suspicious/thumb, comb,* and *bomb*), so you can see how rhyming and making word families can help your child more than any other spelling strategy.

Playing with Pronunciation

Any spelling teachers who are worth their salt understand that your child needs to have a few spelling strategies up his sleeve. Your child has to be able to hear the chunks in words, jot them down (not be afraid to make guesses), and check what he's written. When your child is learning a spelling list, he must group words into families whenever he can, look for familiar spelling chunks (like *ai* or *ay*), and highlight tricky new spelling patterns (like the *eigh* in *neighbor*). He must jot down his spellings a few times and proofread them to see whether they look right. Sometimes he can even overpronounce his spelling, because some words seem to be crying out for a little phonetic pronunciation.

Subtle sounds

If you're not totally convinced that tweaking or exaggerating the pronunciation of some words helps your child to spell them, take a look at the pairs of words in the list that follows. Your child needs to say each word clearly to himself to get exactly the right spelling. Even after trying that, the spelling still can be difficult.

accept and except

affect and effect

advise and advice

belief and believe

choose and chose

diary and dairy

desert and dessert

loose and lose

purpose and porpoise

sense and since

through and thorough

thought and though

quiet and quite

once and ounce

trail and trial

And while I'm on the whole business of your child overpronouncing or phonetically pronouncing words, consider the words *different* and *separate*. When exaggerating the pronunciations of words like these ("dif-fer-ent" and "se-par-ate"), your child avoids the spelling pitfall of leaving out bits and pieces of words. By contrast, when your child pronounces the words the way people normally say them, she can be forgiven for writing *diffrunt* and *seprut.*)

A word like *Wednesday* is ideally suited to phonetic pronunciation. Your child says, "Wed-nes-day," and can spell it. Is overpronunciation a wise thing to do though? Yes, of course. If overpronunciation helps your child spell certain words then it's a useful strategy for her. Researchers say that attention to detail is a handy trait for your child to have when it comes to spelling, and they add, phonetic pronunciation of tricky letters is a great way for your child to fix them in her mind. Relax. Your finicky, strange-talking child may be a finely tuned spelling machine in the making.

Looking at Letters

Looking at letters is pretty much the theme for this entire book. Your child needs to look at letters so that he develops a good eye for telling whether he's reproducing the spellings accurately. What kinds of factors help your child develop a good eye for looking at letters?

Knowing what's frist and lsat

Spelling every single letter in a word in the right order is important for your child, and yet interestingly enough, if he doesn't, you may still be able to read his writing. Check out the paragraph that follows.

Aoccdrnig to a rscheearch at Cmabrigde Uinervtisy, it deosn't mttaer in waht oredr the ltteers in a wrod are, the olny iprmoetnt tihng is taht the frist and lsat ltteers be in the rghit pclae. The rset can be a toatl mses, and you sitll can raed it wouthit porbelm, bcuseae the huamn mnid deos not raed ervey lteter by istlef, but the wrod as a wlohe.

This text has found its way into hundreds of web pages. No one's really sure of its origins or even whether a study actually exists, but everyone can read it! To catch a big discussion about it and versions in dozens of other languages, visit `www.mrc-cbu.cam.ac.uk/personal/matt.davis/Cmabrigde/`.

Words within words

In this book, you hear plenty about spelling chunks, but here's another factor on which you need to have your child focus. Many words contain other smaller words inside, so when your child spots them, it becomes another feature that helps him recall the sequence of letters in the word. Sometimes words within words practically jump out at your child, like in *sometimes,* but in others, finding the words within isn't as easy. In the word *other,* for example, your child can find *the* and *her,* and in *feature,* he finds *eat* and *at.* Those little words may not always be pronounced as distinct words when they're inside of a bigger word, but your child can have fun spotting them all the same.

Activity: Finding three little words

Preparation: Make a copy of the word list that follows.

Follow these steps:

1. **Read each word in the list out loud to your child.**

2. **Have your child find three smaller words inside each word on the list.** The words must already be in the word and may not be rearrangements of the letters.

   1. believe (*answers: be, lie,* and *eve — belie* counts, too)

   2. carefully (*answers: car, care,* and *full — careful* counts, too)

   3. consonant (*answers: on, son,* and *ant — con* counts, too)

   4. fantastic (*answers: fan, ant,* and *as — tic* counts, too)

   5. father (*answers: fat, at,* and *her*)

   6. football (*answers: foot, ball,* and *all*)

7. forget (*answers: for, or,* and *get — forge* counts, too)

8. hotdog (*answers: hot, do,* and *dog*)

9. important (*answers: port, or,* and *ant — import* counts, too)

10. splendid (*answers: lend, end,* and *did — id* counts, too)

When you and your child are done with the list, finish up on a high note by finding out how many words you can find inside the word *information.* (Aim for ten words as a good goal.)

For more words within words and more information about anagrams (PTO), similes (A man like an ox), and oxymorons (uh? I have to be cruel to be kind), check out "The Wacky World of Words" at www3.bc.sympatico.ca/teach well/wwwpage.htm.

Mistakes

Many people say that you learn best when you make mistakes along the way. When your child learns to spell, he inevitably makes mistakes. Mistakes are a big part of learning to spell, so encouraging your child always to have a try is important. If you don't, these nasty things happen:

✔ Your child won't have confidence in himself.

✔ Your child will limit his writing to only those words he can spell and thereby gets limited practice on harder spellings and vocabulary.

✔ You child won't get to try out and polish up the spelling strategies you're showing him.

So now you can see that mistakes are an important part of your child's natural development and nothing is wrong with making plenty of them in the early days. You don't need to correct your child's early mistakes at all, and when you *do* start pointing out errant capital letters and spellings like *thay* rather than *they*, do it selectively and with sensitivity. Point out only the errors that you think your child understands and can benefit from seeing. As your child grows more capable, you can point out more mistakes.

By judiciously correcting your child's spelling mistakes in the early days, you help her gain the confidence to write a lot. When your child reaches the stage where she's writing plenty of sentences, correct just enough of her spelling errors for her to remember them but not feel overloaded. (And after you've achieved this fine balance, award yourself top marks for impeccable judgment.)

Was it a rat I saw?

If you and your child have five minutes to fill, try asking him to solve this puzzle. It takes some careful observation.

Question: What do these words have in common? *Level, radar, madam,* and *kayak.* (And while we're

on the subject, what's special about the title of this sidebar?)

Answer: They're all *palindromes,* words or phrases that are spelled the same forward and backward.

Your child didn't learn to walk without ever falling down and the same goes when he's learning to spell. If you try to make his early writing perfect, he may end up thinking of writing as drudgery that's doomed to fail. Focus on and praise his efforts and ideas. Restrict yourself to one or two spelling suggestions. You need to see steady progress in the amount of words that your child spells correctly so that by about grade two he can write pretty tidy text. If it seems that your child's progress has come to a halt or he's lagging far behind his classmates, see his teacher right away. Draw up a plan of exactly what you'll do in practical terms that can be measured.

When beginning spellers write sentences like "I lik gwing tow the mwll," teachers call it emergent writing with invented spellings inside. Emergent writing and invented spellings are good things, and you need to encourage your child to do as much of them as she reasonably can. In time, she improves by getting better at remembering letter sequences, and she makes fewer mistakes. This abundant warming up at a tender age stands her in great stead for her later epics.

Confessions in the night

When I went into my child's bedroom to tuck her in a few nights ago, she had a furrowed brow and a guilty conscience. "Mom," she said, "I did something pretty bad in school today. I wrote this really good story in my very neatest joined-up writing, but the teacher put her red pen on it in three places. She found these three really, really small mistakes, and put her red pen on them. If she'd used a pencil, I could've erased

the marks and kept the story. I just couldn't bear to look at my spoiled sheet. Mom, I wanted it to be perfect, and I was so mad at the teacher that I threw the whole story in the garbage."

I talked the whole diabolical thing through with my daughter and then headed to my desk to move my two red pens out of temptation's way and sharpen a few pencils.

Having a Few Tries

When I grew up in England, a very common expression was, "Have a go." If ever spectators were urging you to "wallop" a soccer ball or belt out a song on stage they'd say, "Go on love, have a go!" I still use that expression — even though my kids give me odd looks — and I want to encourage you to give your child the same message in whatever terms you like. Encourage your child to always "have a go," because when she jots down loose approximations of real spellings, it gives her a frame of reference to look at and tweak several times until she arrives at her best shot. Then she can ask you for advice or consult a dictionary, and that's okay. Having tried a few times before, she asks for your help, establishes good habits, and refines that good eye for spelling.

If you read other books about spelling, you may come across the terms homophone and homograph. *Homo* means same, and *phone* means sound, so *homophone* means sounds the same. Words like *sun* and *son* are homophones. *Graph* means picture or visual representation, so *homograph* means looks the same. Words like *grave* in a cemetery and the *grave* as in very serious are homographs. Check out Table 3-2 for more about these and more word-related terms.

Table 3-2	Defining Word-Related Terms
Term	*What It Means*
homonym	A general term for words that are the same in sound but not spelling (like *son* and *sun*), or the same in spelling but not sound (like *bow* in your hair and *bow* of a ship), or the same in both spelling *and* sound (like *grave* in a cemetery and *grave* as in serious).
homograph	Words that are spelled the same, like *bow* in your hair and *bow* to the king. Homographs are a subset of the bigger, general group called homonyms.
homophone	Words that sound the same, like *you* are nice and the farmer has a *ewe* (sheep). Homophones are a subset of the bigger, general group called homonyms.
antonym	Opposite words in meaning, like *big* and *little*.
synonyms	Same words in meaning, like *little* and *small*.

Tables 3-3 and 3-4 up next have some tricky words in them. Don't be scared. This book doesn't keep getting harder and harder. In fact, you come to some easier bunches of words in Chapters 4, 5, and 6, but it just so happens that many homonyms and homographs are fairly sophisticated words. Remember that you can skip from one part of this book to another whenever you want. You can file these words under "things to do" and come back to them after your child practices spelling words that don't look quite so serious.

The words in Table 3-3 are not for the fainthearted, but if you want to crank up the gears and show your child a few words to test both his spelling and vocabulary, this is the table to use. All the words in it are homographs — words that have two distinctly different meanings but nevertheless are spelled the same.

Table 3-3	A Gross of Homographs (Give or Take a Few Dozen)	
bass	bow	buffet
close	compound	converse
desert	does	dove
entrance	frequent	grave
gross	intimate	invalid
lame	lead	live
minute	nail	object
patient	polish	present
project	putting	record
refuse	resume	row
shower	sow	tear
tower	wind	wound

In case you're wondering about the dual meaning of some of these words, here are a few definitions:

- **Desert:** Either those dry arid places you wouldn't want to be lost in or how you can leave or *desert* a place.

- **Grave:** Either the kind in a cemetery or the very serious or *grave* situation.

- **Gross:** Either large or yuk or the old-fashioned measure.

- **Nail:** Either you have one on your finger or you *nail* down a job.

- **Patient:** You can be this either when you're teaching your child to spell or when you're confined in a hospital.

Homophones are words that sound the same but usually are spelled differently and mean different things. Table 3-4 provides quite a few to keep you going.

Anytime I say "homograph" or "homophone," I can equally well say "homonym" instead, because homonym is the general term that incorporates both.

Table 3-4	A Hat Full of Homophones	
aloud/allowed	ate/eight	blue/blew
board/bored	break/brake	buy/by
cereal/serial	deer/dear	for/four
groan/grown	hair/hare	hear/here
hole/whole	knot/not	lead/led
meet/meat	naval/navel	no/know
pain/pane	pair/pear	passed/past
patience/patients	peace/piece	plain/plane
principal/principle	rain/reign/rein	real/reel
rode/road/rowed	sale/sail	scene/seen
scent/sent/cent	seam/seem	see/sea
sew/so/sow	sight/site	some/sum
son/sun	steal/steel	straight/strait
symbol/cymbal	tail/tale	there/they're/their
threw/through	thrown/throne	tide/tied
to/too/two	wear/where	week/weak
whether/weather	who's/whose	witch/which
write/right		

Dictation: Doing It and Doing It Again

Giving your child dictation is a great thing to do, especially when you want to iron out those little mistakes like *untill, thay,* and *I'me.* Get into the routine of giving your child weekly dictation, and you give her a time when she can check her writing for those kinds of mistakes. Keep a cheerful, positive tone, though, so that your great idea doesn't turn into a great big drag. Using a points system can cheer up proceedings, and you don't have to think up a bunch of whiz-bang rewards. Instead, try awarding your child three free points that allow her to make three errors in a paragraph, but if she makes more than three errors, she must work on another sentence or paragraph.

Activity: Marathon spelling contest

If your child brings spelling lists home every week, you probably find that by about week four, the novelty wears pretty thin. Try making a spelling chart that gets harder as your child gets better at spelling and includes all your kids' scores (if you have more than one child), so you can extend a spelling routine's natural life span.

Preparation: Gather together award certificates, stickers, a bulletin board, individual photos of your children, and a trophy. You'll also need several lists of spelling word equal to the number of weeks you want the contest to continue, paper, and pens. This activity can last a few weeks to an entire school year.

Follow these steps:

1. **Draw a "Spelling Champion" board.**

2. **Plan a routine by which the name of the weekly champion gets posted on the same day every week.**

   Whoever scores 100 percent has his or her photo posted in the champion's spot and receives formal applause from significant family members and other participants. For this activity to work, you need to act duly ceremonious and enlist Dad to shake hands or hug the champion and siblings to high five her.

3. **Read the spelling words for the week out loud to the participants.**

4. **Determine the scores for the week and who the weekly champion is.**

5. **Award stickers and prepare to award a grand prize during the next school break to the child with the most stickers.**

6. **After winter break, make the contest harder.**

   Now the spelling champion must score a 100 percent on spelling tests for two weeks in a row. Every two weeks, the Spelling Champion is honored for her achievement.

   After spring break, increase the difficulty again by determining the champion via a 100 percent rating for three-week intervals!

7. **When the school year ends, you may want to award your grand champion a trophy or mark his or her effort in some other extraspecial way.**

For classroom ideas that you can adapt to your child, visit www.busy teacherscafe.com.

Remembering to read

If you regularly sit down with your child and look at spellings, give yourself a great big pat on the back, and then take a break and put a few books in front of your child. When you read often and extensively to your child, or have your child read on her own, you do as much for her spelling as you do with your advice and guidance. Every time that your child looks at written text, she sees not only individual spellings but also spelling patterns — typical arrangements and strings of letters, abundant vowels, and things like apostrophes and hyphens. Keep your child reading by taking her to the library, surrounding her with cool-looking books, and showing her that you're a reader, too.

Spelling is a family issue. Your child needs to see you doing all the things that you tell him to do. If you really plan to help your child, you have to walk the talk.

Having a Few Spelling Rules under Her Belt

Some people dislike spelling rules. I can't say that I blame them, because they probably have bad memories of tedious spelling lessons in which they were drilled in dozens of complex and often convoluted spelling rules. Well, I'm not about to burden you with a whole heap of rules that have you yearning for a nap or a call from the telemarketers. However, I *am* about to tell you about a handful of the more effective spelling rules.

When your child spells *make,* he can use the Bossy-*e* rule to help him do it. When he spells *main,* he can think about the when-two-vowels-go-walking-the-first-one-does-the-talking rule. When he gets on top of those two simple rules, he adds hundreds of words to his spelling repertoire (like *make, take, came, same, like, life,* and *pain, rail, nail, trail, sail, and main*) and sees that he's really moving into superleague spelling. In this book, I walk you and your child through these two simple, nonthreatening rules and throw in just a couple more equally nice ones so that your child puts together a simple but reliable arsenal.

Throw together a five-minute spelling contest by setting up a white board or poster and having players run to it to write down spellings. Only one player is the runner, while the others have to figure out the spelling and jot it onto a slip of paper for the runner. Give teams lists of misspelled words (or ask them to write homonyms from Table 3-3) and a time limit.

Putting the social into spelling

Because your child is a social creature, just like everyone else, she likes to do things in company. Any time you can recruit friends or family into spelling activities with your child, do it. In case you're thinking to yourself right now, "Oh yeah, right, just like that, huh?" here are a few practical pointers to set you on your way:

✔ Ask other people (or older kids, grandparents, aunts, and uncles) to give your child a quick dictation. Spice it up by having your child try to beat the clock. He can get help but only with yes/no answers to his questions.

✔ Get interested others to brainstorm with your child. They can think of Bossy-*e* words, or *er* words, or any other spelling pattern.

✔ Ask computer-savvy relatives to download dual copies of word searches for your child and encourage them to do them together.

✔ Suggest that long-distance relatives become your child's pen pals.

✔ Suggest that grandparents give your child the occasional quick lists of ten misspelled words.

✔ Have friends ask your child to correct *their* misspellings.

✔ Play team games. Team leaders have question sheets to read to their teams. Teams must answer the questions but can get only yes/no answers to their questions from their leader. Write ten questions and see whether teams can answer them in less than ten minutes. (To see more about group activities, flip to Chapter 20.)

✔ Remind friends and relatives about favorite old games like Hangman and Scrabble (Junior version).

Being Secure with Sight Words

Sight words comprise most of what your child spells. They're words like *they* and *were,* and your child writes them all the time. Naturally, you want your child to spell these words with ease. Have your child read and write all the time (within humane limits), show her spelling patterns, and take her through the sight-word list in Chapter 12 so you can isolate the words that she hasn't yet mastered.

Skimming through Suffixes, Silent Letters, and Other Stuff

If spelling were a fancy meal, you'd start your child off with sight words. Sight words would be the perfect appetizer, because your child needs only a small serving. She probably knows how to spell most sight words already, so you serve her only the words that she needs more practice with. For her main course, you'd dish up some listening-for-chunks-in-words, some jotting-down-of-those-chunks, and some proofreading so she can see whether those written chunks look right. You'd also drizzle some word families onto the chunks so your child comes to grips with common letter patterns and clusters. For dessert you'd serve up three or four spelling rules and then finish up with the equivalent of those small chocolaty or minty things that come with your coffee. Your child's chocolaty and minty things in spelling are suffixes, prefixes, silent letters, and soft *c*'s and soft *g*'s. She needs to be comfortable with them, but they're not on the main menu. You get a calorie and fiber count on all this nibbly stuff in Chapters 13 (silent letters), 14 (soft-sounding letters), 15 (prefixes), and 16 (suffixes), but for now, the sections that follow provide a quick preview.

Suffixes

When your child can spell *run,* you want him to spell *running*. That's where suffixes come in. *Suffixes* are the endings that your child tags onto words to make them more impressive. Common suffixes are *ed, ing, er,* and *est,* but your child needs to follow some putting-together instructions before affixing some of them. Do you remember the drop-the-*e*-when-you-add-*ing* (pronounced "eye-en-gee") rule? No? Well, you can find out more about it in Chapter 16.

Prefixes

If your child ever tells you about his prespelling tests at school, he's already learning about prefixes. *Prefixes* are little bits of words like *pre* (meaning at the front of). Your child puts them at the beginnings of words to make new words with new meanings. Common prefixes are *bi, hyper, mono,* and *dis,* and I tell you much more about them in Chapter 15.

Silent letters

Know anything about *plumbing*? Well, if you don't (and I'm taking the liberty of assuming that you don't), you won't know any more by the time you finish this book. But you *will* know more about silent letters (like the silent *b* in *plumbing*) and so will your child. More silent letters exist than you probably thought, so in Chapter 13 I *bustle* you through a whole *plague* of them.

Soft c's and soft g's

The scent that you sent wasn't worth a cent. Now there's a few soft *c*'s, silent *c*'s and absent *c*'s for you! Your child needs to write soft *c*'s and soft *g*'s every once in a while, but probably not as often as she thinks. The softies are fun for your child to get to know, but you have to be around to make sure that things don't get out of hand. Interpretation: Your child will be tempted to slap soft letters in all sorts of unlikely words, so you have to help her exercise a measure of restraint. Sure, she can try words like *cent* and *gem*, but steer her clear of bad mixes like *cet* and *gello*. In Chapter 14, I help you turn your child into a responsible and occasional soft-letter user.

Part II

Getting Easy
Words onto Paper

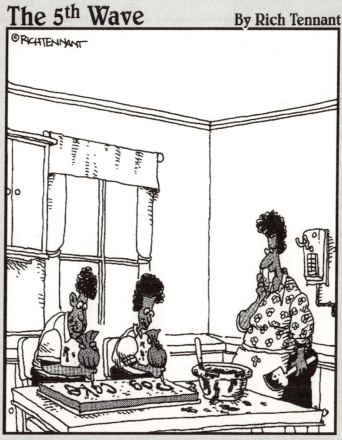

The 5th Wave

By Rich Tennant

"I'll say this - a piping bag full of frosting and a sheet cake go a long way toward getting your kids to practice spelling."

In this part . . .

Almost every word contains a vowel, so helping your child get to know them well makes pretty good sense. This part of the book introduces you and your child to short vowels. It shows you blended letters, like *st* and *ng*, too, so that your child can tag them onto short-vowel words like *and* and end up with words like *standing*. It gives you a tour of consonant digraphs *ch, sh, th, ph,* and *wh,* so that words like *chatting, dashing,* and *whisking* come easily to your child.

Chapter 4

Spelling with Short Vowels

. . . .

In This Chapter

▶ Casting an eye on colorful consonants

▶ Discovering what a short vowel is

▶ Getting to know common chunks of short-vowel spellings

▶ Moving from saying to spelling

▶ Having fun with long words spelled from short chunks

. . . .

"*R*umplestiltskin" is a fairy story about a princess who guesses the name of her captor (Rumplestiltskin) to win her freedom. The story culminates with the princess declaring emphatically, "Your name's Rumplestiltskin." Now had that princess smugly declared, "Your name's Rumplestinkskin," she'd have been in big trouble. Hearing, pronouncing, and ordering sounds were important for the princess, and they're important for your child. Your child can spell the short vowels that I tell you about in this chapter only if he hears, says, and orders them accurately. In this chapter, I explain how to verify that your child does all those things. I have you move him from saying to writing, because that's the path that good spellers follow. I show you a few common or sight words made from short vowels. Lastly, I give you long words made from short vowels strung together so that your child gets a kick from power spelling.

When I say that your child must pronounce short vowels accurately, you don't have to worry about whether he rolls his *r*'s or says the occasional *"th"* rather than *"s."* You don't have to worry about accents, either. As long as your child says a consistent form of each short-vowel sound to himself, he's doing fine. Whether he pronounces words in his own unique way or speaks in the queen's English won't matter. Speech therapists can help you whenever your child mispronounces words in a big way or over a long time, but slight deviations from the typical way most people speak don't cause problems. If they did, the many accents that people have would cause mayhem, and second-language kids would have a hard time learning to use English in school. In fact, kids who use English as their second language right from an early age use it as competently (or as poorly) as they use their first language.

Checking on Single Sounds

Because only 26 letters are in the alphabet but hundreds of sounds are in the English language, it stands to reason that you need to let your child know how those 26 letters work and combine together to make loads of sounds. Here are a few hints:

- ✔ Most single letters make (or represent) one sound (*m, b,* and *d,* for example).
- ✔ Each of the five vowels makes (at least) a short sound and a long sound.
- ✔ A few consonants make more than one sound (*c* and *g,* for example).
- ✔ Certain clusters of letters (like *ight, ou,* and *ar*) make unique new sounds.
- ✔ Sometimes you write letters in a word and they make no sound at all (*k*nee and *cam*e, included).

These five points give you a rough sketch of how spelling works, and I discuss them in much greater detail throughout this book. For now, however, I home in on regular, single-letter sounds and the short-vowel sounds.

Tackling Letters in the Right Order

The order in which you and your child tackle letters is important. When your child's an absolute beginner, you need to show her the easiest letters first, the ones like *m* that never change sound. As she starts to string letters together to spell words, you need to make sure that she jots down the letters in the right order. When she writes longer words you have to keep her moving from one sound chunk (or syllable) to the next. I talk about chunks of sounds in the section about "Spelling in Chunks" later in this chapter (and all through this book), but to start with, I talk about single letters. I tell you which letters are the best ones for absolute beginners to start off with, which consonants do a few things that your child needs to know about, and why vowels are the most important letters of all.

Beginning Simply

When starting out with spelling, you first need to introduce your child to single letters with hard sounds and vowels with short sounds. A *hard sound* is the regular, most typical sound that letters make. *Short-vowel* sounds are what your child hears in words like *mat, pet, ink, hop,* and *cut.* When your child says short-vowel sounds, they actually sound short when compared with the long sounds that vowels make in words like *mate, Pete, idea, open,* and u*nicorn.* The other single-letter thing to tell your child about is how a few consonants do some pretty quirky stuff.

With a letter like *c,* which makes more than one sound, the *"cuh"* sound, or hard-*c* sound, is the one to start with as opposed to the soft, or *"ss,"* sound that *c* makes when you pop an *e, i,* or *y* after it (like in *ceiling, city,* and *cycle.*

Being Clear about "kuh"

C does quirky stuff. It makes the *"kuh"* sound even though *k* does too. Both letters are used in plenty of words. How will your child know when to use one rather than the other? Well, I have some suggestions. In fact, they're more like set-in-stone rules, which is nice, because you don't find too many of those in spelling. Here are ten absolute, always, not open for discussion, never any different, solid rules to tell your child, about using *c* or *k*:

- ✔ **Rule 1: Always *ct*, never *kt*.** Many words end with *ct,* and many words have *ct* in the middle. Dictate some words from Table 4-1 for your child to spell and ask him what letters appear in each one. Ask him whether he can ever write *kt*. If you feel inspired, jot down some *ct* words from the table but put *kt,* rather than *ct,* in them. Have your child sort the words into right and wrong spelling groups.

Table 4-1	*ct* Words	
act	collect	compact
direct	duct	fact
factory	fracture	inspect
lactate	pact	picture
puncture	react	tact

- ✔ **Rule 2: *ic* (not *ik*) at the end of big words of more than one syllable.** *Horrific,* now there's a nice word. Show your child the rich, generous words in Table 4-2 and explain that alternatives to good and dumb do exist. Then you may want to try the misspelling routine that I just mentioned for Rule 1.

Table 4-2	*ic* Words	
alcoholic	ballistic	chronic
colic	comic	dramatic
economic	elastic	epic
fantastic	frantic	frolic
garlic	gothic	graphic
holistic	horrific	magnetic
mimic	panic	pathetic
pedantic	picnic	septic
specific	static	sympathetic
terrific	traffic	tragic

✔ **Rule 3: Write *ke* and *ki* to keep the *"kuh"* sound (not *ce* or *ci*).** You can read the details about soft sounds in Chapter 14. For a quick start, here's the scoop: When your child writes *ce* or *ci,* she makes the soft-c, or *"ss,"* sound like in *ceiling* or *city.* So if she wants to spell a word like *kettle* or *kite,* she must use *k,* not *c.* Have your child check out Table 4-3 so she sees just what I mean. Dictate a few words for her to spell and then flit through the other rules, picking and choosing words to suit your child's level and schedule. The tables contain easy and hard words to dip into and so many of them that you may want to pace yourself over a few days.

Table 4-3		*ke* and *ki* Words	
ke		***ki***	
kebab	kernel	kick	kindle
keel	kerosene	kid	king
keen	kestrel	kidnap	kip
keep	ketchup	kidney	kipper
keeper	kettle	kill	kiss
keepsake	key	kiln	kit
keg	monkey	kilt	kitchen
kennel		kin	kite
kept		kind	kitten

✔ **Rule 4: When you write** *ca,* *co,* **and** *cu,* **you keep that** *"kuh"* **sound.** If you think this is too much for your child to remember, don't worry so much about detailed explanations. Instead have your child write a few *ca, co,* and *cu* words (see Table 4-4) so she learns by practicing them. The distinctive thing about using *c* is that you get the *"ss"* sound from *ce (ceiling), ci (excite),* and *cy (cycle).*

Table 4-4	*ca, co,* and *cu* Words	
ca	*co*	*cu*
cabbage	coast	cub
cable	cobweb	cube
cake	cod	cud
calf	code	cup
call	coffee	cupboard
camp	coffin	curb
can	cog	curd
candle	coke	curl
capable	comb	curt
captain	comet	curse
capture	comic	custard
cast	cone	custom
castle	convenient	cut
catch	copper	cute
catalogue	cost	cutter

✔ **Rule 5: Write** *ske* **and** *ski* **to keep the** *"kuh"* **sound (not** *sce* **or** *sci*). This rule is just an extension of the *ce, ci,* and *cy* thing. Your child can write *sketch* and *skip* but not *scetch* and *scip,* because *ce* and *ci* make a *"ss"* sound (not the *"kuh"* sound you want). Again, you don't need to bog your child down with long explanations. Just walk him through a bunch of words from Table 4-5.

Table 4-5	ske and ski Words	
skeleton	skeptic	skeptical
sketch	skid	skill
skillet	skillful	skim
skimpy	skin	Skip
skirmish	skirt	skittles

✔ **Rule 6: Always *scr*, never *skr*.** How easy is this? Here's a sit-back-and-relax rule, because there's nothing to figure out. Always *scr*, never *skr*! Table 4-6 gives you 15 good examples.

Table 4-6	scr Words	
scrabble	scram	scramble
scrap	scrape	scratch
scream	screech	screw
scribble	scribe	scrimp
scroll	scrub	scrumptious

✔ **Rule 7: Write *ck* immediately after a short-vowel sound.** Whenever your child hears a short-vowel sound in the word she's spelling, she uses *ck* or *k* after it. To decide which one to use, have your child asks whether the *"kuh"* immediately follows the vowel. If the answer is yes, she jots down *"ck."* A whole bunch of words use this rule, and Table 4-7 gives you a sampling of them. You can see that *ck* words often are short and very easy to spell.

Table 4-7	ck Words	
back	black	check
clock	deck	dock
duck	fleck	flick
flock	kick	lick
lock	neck	pack

peck	pick	rock
sack	sick	slick
smack	smock	snuck
sock	speck	struck
stuck	thick	truck

> ✔ **Rule 8: *k* after a short-vowel sound + a consonant.** Whenever your child hears a short-vowel sound in the word he's spelling, he uses *ck* or *k* after it. To decide which one fits, have your child ask whether the *"kuh"* immediately follows the vowel or follows the vowel + a consonant (like *il* or *in*). When your child hears a vowel+ a consonant he jots down *"ck."*

Table 4-8	*k* Words	
brisk	bunk	chunk
desk	dunk	dusk
ink	junk	link
mink	milk	monk
pink	plunk	prank
punk	risk	silk
sink	skunk	stink
sulk	sunk	talk
tank	task	thank
think	tusk	walk

Here's a tough question for your child to ponder. Only three consonants can come before *k* (not ck) when *k* follows a short-vowel sound. What are they? Refer to Table 4-8 for some examples. (Answer: *n, s,* and *l.*)

Digraphs like *ar* and *aw* appear in front of *k* in words like *park* and *hawk.* I talk about digraphs in Chapter 10.

> ✔ **Rule 9: Write *ake, ike,* and *oke* to keep the *"kuh"* sound (not *ace, ice,* or *oce*).** Here's the *ce* spelling again (only the opposite). *Anytime* your child writes *ce,* she makes the *"ss"* sound. That's why she simply can't make the *"kuh"* sound by writing things like *mace, lice,* and *joce,* but can when she writes words like the ones that appear in Table 4-9.

Table 4-9	*ake, ike,* and *oke* Words	
ake	*ike*	*oke*
bake	bike	broke
cake	hike	coke
fake	like	joke
flake	pike	poke
lake	spike	smoke
make	strike	woke
mistake		yoke
rake		
sake		
shake		
take		
wake		

✔ **Rule 10: You can write *cc* in the middle of words but not *kk*.** The *cc*-in-the-middle bunch of words will really have you and your child thinking. Plenty of words have *cc* right in the middle, and most of them are long. Table 4-10 gives you a good selection with which to practice, so get settled in and comfortable and jot some of them down.

Because Table 4-10 is full of lengthy words, you may want to come back to it later on when your child has practiced with spelling chunks like *ai* and *er*.

Table 4-10		*cc* Words	
k Sound		*ks Sound*	
acclaim	accurate	accelerate	succinct
accolade	accuse	accent	vaccine
accommodate	accumulate	accept	vaccinate
accomplish	occasion	access	

k Sound		ks Sound
accord	occupy	accident
accost	occur	succeed
account	succulent	success
accredit	succumb	successive

✔ **Rule 11: Don't push French fries into the video player.**

✔ **Rule 12: Don't eat lint from the clothes dryer.**

What a lot of rules. Did you spot the fake ones? I thought that I'd add them to the end so that nothing went wrong while you were reading all the other real rules. The main thing is to take your time with these rules. Have your child write just a few words in each group. Skip or use the really tricky words, like *succumb*, as you like. Words like *accolade* can lead you into a bit of vocabulary practice. Others, like *accent*, sound tricky but aren't so hard after your child gets the hang of different ways to spell the *"ks"* sound. To give your child some *word study* (or looking hard at words and moving bits of them around), try out the next three activities.

Activity: Back-to-front syllables

Preparation: You'll need pen and paper and your copy of *Teaching Kids to Spell For Dummies* turned to this activity.

Follow these steps:

1. **Have your child write down ten two-syllable words.**

2. **Take the words and turn them back to front by transposing the last and first syllables.** You end up with words like *cesssuc* (success) and *takemis* (mistake).

3. **Have your child fix the jumbled words.**

Activity: Filling in missing letters

Preparation: Have pen, paper, and this book ready.

Follow these steps:

1. **Have your child write ten words that she thinks are pretty tricky.**

2. **Delete one or two letters from each of the words your child provides.**

3. **Have your child fill in the blanks, or missing letters.**

Activity: Cutting extra letters

Preparation: Have this book, a pen, and paper ready for your child to use.

Follow these steps:

1. **Have your child write ten words that he thinks are pretty tricky.**

2. **Add one or two extra letters to each of the words your child provides.**

3. **Have your child cross out the letters that don't belong.**

Surfing the Several-Sounds Consonants

What I tell you in this section isn't something that you have to study or memorize. It is, however, interesting information for you to refer to as the need arises. It gives you sort of well-rounded picture of how some of the consonants behave, so you can tell your child that: "Most consonants represent just one sound and are as easy as pie. You hear them and jot them down. Some, however, behave in different ways. You jot down those ways and choose the one that looks right." Table 4-11 gives you an at-a-glance picture of the spelling variants that your child will come upon. Remember, it isn't a test or something that you have to tattoo on the inside of your arm so that you never forget; it's just a handy bit of information.

Table 4-11		Different Spellings for the Same Consonant Sound				
ch	*f*	*j*	*k*	*s*	*sh*	*z*
chin	fin	joke	key	sun	shed	zero
catch	photo	bridge	come	cent	sure	is
picture	laugh	gentle	duck	scene	attention	please
righteous	coffee	giant	chorus	grass	initiate	busy
		soldier	bouquet		tissue	eggs
					Asia	ladies
					machine	

Dealing with the Doubles

In this section, you get two "nearly always" rules for helping your child deal with double letters that are easy to remember. Here's the first:

If a short, one-syllable word ends with the sound *s, l, f,* or *z,* your child (nearly always) writes a double letter.

If you're thinking something like "But *bus* only has one *s,*" you're spot-on. Remember that these rules are really handy, but they're "nearly always" rules. And if the *bus* thing drives you crazy, you may want to tell your child about words like *bus, yes,* and *us.* (Other rogue words are *quiz* and *whiz* and *nil* and *pal.*) Table 4-12 provides some examples of words with double letters.

Table 4-12		*ss, ll, ff,* and *zz* Words	
ss	**ll**	**ff**	**zz**
boss	drill	cliff	buzz
chess	dull	cuff	fizz
dress	fell	fluff	fuzz
floss	fill	gruff	jazz
fuss	grill	huff	
guess	hill	muff	
hiss	hull	off	(sizzle
kiss	ill	puff	drizzle
lass	kill	sniff	fizzle
less	mill	snuff	muzzle
loss	sell	stiff	nuzzle
mass	sill	stuff	puzzle)
mess	smell	tiff	
miss	spill		
moss	still		
press	tell		
toss	till		
	will		

A different way to have your child write spellings is to present him with riddles. See how he likes these:

In the "Riddles of things you shouldn't do" activity up next, I give you riddles in which your child moves spelling chunks around, an activity that often is called phonographics or graphophonics.

Activity: Riddles of things you shouldn't do

Preparation: Open this book to the activity that follows and have paper and pen ready for your child to work on.

Follow these steps:

1. **Cover the answers to the three riddles.**

2. **Have your child solve the riddles.**

    Riddle 1:

    1. Take *sm* off *smell* and put *t* there instead.

    2. Take *mo* and *r* off *mother*.

    3. Take the *l* off *loss* and put *b* there instead.

    4. Take *day* off *today*.

    5. Take *ard* off *buzzard*.

    6. Add *f* onto *of*.

    Answer: Tell the boss to buzz off.

    Riddle 2:

    1. Rhymes with *drill* but starts with *g*.

    2. Take the *corn* off *acorn*.

    3. Take the *p* off *press* and put *d* there instead.

    Answer: Grill a dress.

    Riddle 3:

    1. Rhymes with *pill* but starts with *f.*

    2. Take the *e* off *the* and put *is* there instead.

    3. Take the *n* off *nuzzle* and put *p* there instead.

    Answer: Fill this puzzle.

Activity: Rhyming riddles

Preparation: You'll need this book, some paper, and a pen your child to write his answers.

Follow these steps:

1. **Cover the answers to the three riddles.**
2. **Have your child solve the riddles.**

   Riddle 1: I rhyme with loss

   1. The dentist says that you should use me. I'm long and very thin. You pull me off a reel.
   2. I am green. I grow on rocks in shady damp places.
   3. I am in charge.

   Answers: Floss, moss, and boss.

   Riddle 2: I rhyme with till.

   1. I am big or small but never flat.
   2. I am a tool. I make holes. I fit screws into holes.
   3. Turn me on or light me up. I am hot. Cook on me.

   Answer: Hill, drill, and grill.

   Riddle 3: I rhyme with tiff.

   1. I'm in Table 4-12. You can climb up me (you may need climbing rope) or throw things off me.
   2. I'm what you do when you test a perfume.
   3. I'm the opposite of flexible.

   Answer: Cliff, sniff, and stiff.

Putting the Vowels into Perspective

When you lead your child through written words, you tell her many things. The one factor that probably has a wider application than anything else that you tell her is this:

You need to put a vowel in almost every word there is. In words like *why* and *cry, y* plays the role of a vowel. That's why teachers sometimes call *y* the other vowel. I talk about the *y-acting-like-a-vowel rule* in Chapter 9. You often put a few vowels into words, because they make at least two different sounds. The two sounds that each of the five vowels always make are short and long sounds. The short sound is in words like *mat, pet, ink, hop,* and *cut.* The long sound is in words like *mate, Pete, like, hope,* and *cute.*

So the perspective that you need to have on vowels is that vowels sure are important!

Spelling Short Vowels

Nearly any time that your child hears a short-vowel sound, like in *apple* (not *ape*), *egg* (not *eagle*), *ink* (not *idol*), *olive* (not *open*) and *up* (not *universe*), he uses just one vowel to spell it. How easy is that? In Table 4-13, I give you a glimpse of the trillions of words that your child spells with a short vowel. (He may think that they're beneath him now that he's already trotted through a whole heap of bigger words.)

Table 4-13		Words with Short-Vowels		
a	*e*	*i*	*o*	*u*
act	bed	blimp	block	blunt
ant	bell	click	clock	bump
black	bend	drink	cod	bun
blank	bet	flick	cross	bus
brag	deck	flip	drop	crust
camp	den	grill	flock	cup
clap	desk	grip	fog	cut
cramp	end	hint	fond	drum
damp	get	lift	frog	dull
drag	help	limp	frost	fun
fact	hem	link	hot	gulp
ham	jet	list	job	gut
hand	less	mint	jog	jump
lamp	mend	pink	log	lump
pack	nest	skin	lost	mud
plant	next	slim	lot	must
sack	press	snip	mop	nut
sank	rest	sprint	pop	pump

a	e	i	o	u
scrap	sell	still	rob	rug
slack	send	strip	rock	run
slam	smell	swim	snob	rust
smack	spend	trip	sob	stuff
snack	went	twin	sock	sunk
track	west	wind	spot	tub
trap	yet	wink	stop	tug

If you look closely at Table 4-13, you can see that short vowels follow a pattern. When your child writes a short word (with only one chunk of sound or one syllable) and puts a single vowel between consonants (or consonant blends like *st* and *mp)*, he makes a short-vowel word.

Some of the words that don't follow this pattern are words like *her* and *stork*. That's because these words have a vowel+r in them, and that's a whole different ball game. I talk about vowel+r words in Chapter 11. Words like *bread* and *said* defy the rule too, but you can show them to your child later, after he's practiced this easier spelling pattern.

Your child uses the same (consonant-vowel-consonant) pattern to write most short-vowel bits of words like in *mid*-night, home-*less* and car-*pet*.

What's the best way to get your child spelling smoothly with short vowels? Have her doodle with word patterns like *an, pan,* and *man; can, cat,* and *cap;* and *hat, hit,* and *hot*. These three kinds of doodling are in the "Changing a first letter," "Changing a last letter," and "Changing a vowel" activities that I give you next.

Activity: Changing a first letter

Preparation: Cut out small pieces of card or paper (about the size of sticky notes) and grab your pen and paper — a whiteboard and marker is even better.

Follow these steps:

1. **Have your child write each of the letters that follow on separate pieces of the paper you just cut out.**

   b, d, f, g, h, l, m, n, p, r, s, t, and *v*

2. **Have your child write** *"an"* **on his paper, and then move the lettered cutouts, one at a time, in front of** *an* **to help him make and then write words like** *tan, pan,* **and** *man.*

3. **Follow the directions in Steps 1 and 2, using** *ap, at, et,* **and** *ip* **in place of** *an* **and pointing out that not all the words your child makes will be real words.** Some will be nonsense words like *han,* so he can discount (and not write) them.

All teachers show children word families like the ones in the change-a-letter activities. A *word family* is a bunch of words that share a last sound. The words your child just wrote in the "Changing a first letter" activity were word families, and I tell you the ins and outs of them in Chapter 10. By the way, a teacher may talk of other kinds of word families — words that describe feelings is one — but the last-sound kind of word family is a favorite in spelling programs.

Chunks of sound, like *at* and *ap,* go by the names of *phonemes, phonograms,* or *phonographs* among people who like to use technical words. I can give you the fine details, but really it's still plain old chunks of sound that I'm talking about here. (Syllable is the same, a nice word, but again, chunk of sound pretty much says the same thing.)

Activity: Changing a last letter

Preparation: Cut out small pieces of card or paper (about the size of sticky notes) and have pen and paper or whiteboard and marker so your child is ready to write.

Follow these steps:

1. **Have your child write each of the letters that follow on separate pieces of the paper you just cut out.**

   d, g, n, p, and *t*

2. **Have your child write** *"bu"* **on her's and then move the lettered cutouts, one at a time, after** *bu* **to help her make and then write words like** *bug, bus,* **and** *but.*

3. **Follow the directions in Steps 1 and 2, using** *ba, ta,* **and** *pi* **in place of** *bu* **and pointing out that not all the words your child makes will be real words.**

Activity: Changing a vowel
Preparation: You need this book and pen and paper.

Follow these steps:

1. **Have your child change the vowel in each word in the list that follows into another vowel.** Changing the vowels turns the listed words into new ones.

2. **If your child's feeling smug, I suggest that you time his efforts.** Can he find the answers in three minutes?

1. bell	14. stuff
2. rest	15. swim
3. sank	16. slam
4. lamp	17. den
5. bed	18. sock
6. hint	19. cup
7. must	20. trap
8. tug	21. hut
9. gut	22. bog
10. bet	23. not
11. bun	24. fat
12. lot	25. slash
13. click	

After your child breezes happily through the changing-a-letter activities, she may feel that a change of direction would be nice. The "Ten words in a chain" activity stays with short-vowel spellings, but requires a bit more figuring out. The object is for your child to spell ten different words that follow a formula. But anyway, read on, you'll see what I'm getting at.

Activity: Ten words in a chain

Preparation: You need this book (turned to this exercise) and pen and paper.

Follow these steps:

1. **Cover the answers on the right of the list of words that follows.**

2. **Have your child change each word in the list one letter at a time, trying to make ten different words in all.** You're not allowed to repeat the same word twice. The starting words are *sank, lash,* and *chap.*

3. **Have your child write down each listed word.**

4. **After each word in the list, have your child make the word chains.**

   Look at the examples that I give to see how it works.

   1. Sank *(Answer: sink, silk, sulk, hulk, husk, dusk, dust, duct, duck)*

   2. Lash *(Answer: cash, cast, cost, lost, list, mist, most, mast, mask)*

   3. Chap *(Answer: chip, chop, shop, ship, slip, slap, slop, stop, step)*

After you finish the chains, let your child use many different colors to highlight the different short-vowel sounds — pink for *u,* green for *a,* and so on.

For a real challenge, you can give your child the first and the last words so that she has to figure out how to make the changes to get from one word to the other.

Doing puzzles is so much fun that I have to give you one more. The "Spelling circle" activity is a word-building puzzle in which you write a common spelling chunk, like *ap* or *an,* in the middle of a circle and then pepper a dozen other letters or blends, like *m* and *st,* all around it. You then ask your child to jot down words by mixing and matching the outside letters with the middle letters.

Activity: Spelling circle

Preparation: All you need is a piece of paper and a pen, and of course, your copy of this book.

Follow these steps:

1. **Have your child draw a large circle.**

2. **Tell your child to write a nice big "ap" in the center of the circle.**

3. **Have your child write each of the letters that follow inside the circle around the *ap* in the center.**

   m, t, l, s, c, f, g, n q, sl, and *sp*

4. **Have your child draw lines from the *ap* to the letters that make words (this is a nice visual exercise and a break from writing words).** How many words can your child make?

In Chapter 8, you hear about spelling chunks like *ea* and *oa.* You can make great spelling circles with them, too, because your child gets to add letters and blends to both ends (*mean, moat, speak,* and so on).

Spelling in Chunks

The best way for your child to spell is in chunks. Single-letter spelling is a long and inefficient way of learning to spell, and studies of good spellers show that they know all about short-vowel chunks like *ap, ack,* and *ell.* They're also on top of other chunks like *ight* and *eam,* but in this chapter, I try to stay with short vowels. Getting your child really comfortable with short-vowel chunks is a good idea. Instead of having him spell like this, *s-p-e-ll,* have him try this, *sp-ell.* Have your child practice spelling word families like *spell, bell, smell, shell,* and *fell* to help get him into the habit of spelling in chunks. When you show him plenty of short-vowel chunks, you find that doing so comes in handy not only for small words but also for big words. A chunk like *ant,* for example, shows up in impressive words like *distant, anterior,* and *cantaloupe.* In the next section, I give you some words that may at first look hefty to your child, but won't seem scary at all when she's breaking them into short-vowel chunks.

Spelling Long Words From Short Sounds

My 9-year-old firmly believes that she's old enough to wear makeup, shop alone at the mall, and ride her bike on the road without having me in slow pursuit. She wants to do everything *now,* regardless of whether it's preparing for the new century or knitting a sofa. Every now and then I relent. She gets to smear hot-pink makeup on her eyelids and cheeks and shop in the small nearby mall with me patrolling nervously a shop away. When you give your child a taste of grown-up things, she feels proud (not the least because she's browbeaten you into it). The words in Table 4-14 give your child that same satisfaction with her spellings. She can spell every mature word there, because they're all made from short-vowel chunks. Show her the lofty words. Dictate some for her to spell. Let her wallow in torrents of satisfaction. Let her flit cleverly through the "Finding the gap" activity to bring her gently back to earth.

Pronounce a few of these words slightly weirdly so that your budding speller can get her pen around them. Pronounce *children,* for example, as a clear "child-ren" instead of saying "childrun" the way you normally would.

Table 4-14	Long Words Made of Short-Vowel Spelling Chunks	
across	caravan	channel
chicken	children	collected
cricket	crossing	dashing

(continued)

Table 4-14 *(continued)*

dentist	distant	drifted
drilling	dusted	gasping
getting	gifted	grabbing
gritted	infected	insect
inspected	invested	kitchen
kitten	level	lifted
mattress	nodding	nesting
napping	picnic	printed
sitting	toboggan	twisted
umbrella	undress	upon

Activity: Finding the gap

Preparation: Make a copy of the ten questions that follow.

Follow these steps:

1. **Have your child find the three words in each of the strings of letters that follow.**

2. **Tell your child to look carefully, because each word overlaps into the next by one letter.**

3. **After your child has solved all 30 words, dictate some for him to spell.**

   1. cricketwistedistant *(Answer: cricket, twisted,* and *distant)*

   2. picnicollectedentist *(Answer: picnic, collected,* and *dentist)*

   3. umbrellacrossitting *(Answer: umbrella, across,* and *sitting)*

   4. kitchenappingifted *(Answer: kitchen, napping,* and *gifted)*

   5. investedriftedistant *(Answer: invested, drifted,* and *distant)*

   6. undressittingritted *(Answer: undress, sitting,* and *gritted)*

   7. collectedippingifted *(Answer: collected, dipping,* and *gifted)*

   8. infectedrillingetting *(answer: infected, drilling,* and *getting)*

   9. dustedashingritted *(Answer: dusted, dashing,* and *gritted)*

   10. nappingrabbingasping *(Answer: napping, grabbing, and gasping)*

Writing Short Vowels Inside Sight Words

My mom uses the expression, "You may as well be hung for a sheep as a lamb," and it seems to apply here, because I'm about to give you yet another big picture (sheep not lamb sized) of sight words (which I explain in nice easy steps in Chapter 12), because, well, I may as well be hung for a sheep as a lamb.

Sight words are really common words, so I spend a considerable amount of time on them in this book. They crop up again and again in text (any ordinary text that you care to read or write, for that matter), so naturally your child must be able to spell them again and again. I have to tell you right now that some sight words are pretty tricky, but guess what, I just pored through the 220 sight words that I offer up in Chapter 12, and I have some good news. Sixty of those words are straightforward, made from short-vowel chunks. You can show them to your child right now in Table 4-15, and he can spell them right now, unless of course, you've been kneeling down to read this lengthy chapter and you've lost all feeling in your legs or you've been waiting to go to the bathroom. In that case, loosen up a little or take that potty break, I'll still be here, and when you get back, I'll show you a novel way to make your child feel illuminated by flashing forward to the "Words by flashlight" activity.

Table 4-15	Sight Words Made from Short-Vowel Spelling Chunks			
a	am	an	and	ask
at	best	big	black	but
can	cut	did	drink	fast
from	get	got	had	help
him	hot	if	in	it
jump	just	let	long	much
must	not	off	on	pick
ran	red	run	shall	sing
sit	six	stop	tell	ten
thank	that	them	then	think
this	up	upon	us	well
went	will	wish	with	yes

Activity: Spelling by flashlight

Preparation: Have your child lie in bed in a darkened room with a flashlight in hand.

Follow these steps:

1. **When your child's lying in bed, and you're saying goodnight, grab a flashlight and hop onto the bed with him.**

2. **Dim the lights, and with the flashlight, print a word on the ceiling or wall for him to read.**

3. **Take a couple of turns each (and then act surprised when other family members complain that you hyped him up and he won't sleep).**

Taking One Vowel at a Time

As you flip through this book, you can find plenty of information about vowels. Vowels are up to all sorts of mischief. They each make a few sounds, partner up with some letters (like r) to make new sounds (*ar, er, ir, or,* and *ur*), make vague *"uh"* sounds in some words (like *idea* — *i-dee-uh*) and sometimes are silent like the *e* on the end of a whole battalion of words *(like, note,* and *cute)*. In this section, I give you a quick overview of the kind of things each vowel can do. Don't worry about getting an inside-out and back-to-front understanding because I discuss vowels in detail in Chapters 7 and 8. The information I give you here is for quick, optional reference, not prolonged, keep-the-caffeine-coming study.

Attending to the a's

Your child spells the regular or short sound of *a* with all-on-its-own *a*.

He spells the *"uh"* sound in words like *again* ("uh-gain") and *banana* ("buh-nan-uh") with *a*.

He makes the long-*a* ("ay") sound in a bunch of ways:

- ✔ *ay* like in *bay*
- ✔ *ai* like in *pain*
- ✔ *_a_e* like in *cane*
- ✔ *ei* like in *eight*
- ✔ *ei* like in *vein*

✔ *ea* like in *break*

✔ *a* like in *baby*

✔ *_e_e* like in *crepe*

Enter the e's

Your child spells the regular or short sound of *e* with all-on-its-own *e*.

She writes a silent *e* on the end of long-vowel words like *cane, pine,* and *cope.*

She writes *e* after *c* or *g* to make the soft-*s* and *j* sounds like in *cent* and *gent.*

She spells the long-i ("ey") sound with:

✔ *ee* like in *been*

✔ *ea* like in *bean*

✔ *_e_e* like in *here*

✔ *ei* like in *either*

✔ *ie* like in *niece*

✔ *y* like in *happy*

✔ *ey* like in *monkey*

Including the i's

Your child spells the regular or short sound of *i* with all-on-its-own *i.*

He spells the long-*i* ("eye") sound with:

✔ *_i_e* like in *like*

✔ *y* like in *my*

✔ *i* like in *find*

✔ *ie* like in *pie*

✔ *ei* like in *height*

✔ *uy* like in *buy*

✔ *ye* like in *dye*

On the go with o

She makes the regular or short sound of *o* with all-on-its-own *o*.

She spells the long-*o* ("oh") sound with:

✔ _o_e like in *cone*

✔ o like in *no* and *yolk*

✔ oa like in *road*

✔ ow like in *low*

✔ oe like in *hoe*

✔ ough like in *dough*

✔ ew like in *sew*

✔ oo like in *brooch (the jewelry)*

✔ ou like in *soul*

Up and away with u

Your child spells the regular or short sound of *u* ("uh") with all-on-its-own *u*.

He spells the long-*u* ("ewe") sound with:

✔ _u_e like in *cute*

✔ oo like in *moon*

✔ ew like in *new*

✔ eu like in *feud*

✔ ue like in *cue*

✔ ugh like in *Hugh*

✔ ie like in *view*

A word about open syllables

Sometimes your child writes a single vowel at the start of a word, and it makes a long vowel sound. Although it looks just like a short vowel, because it's a vowel all alone and often sits between two consonants, it's a long vowel nevertheless. It ends, or makes all by itself, the first syllable (or chunk) in words like *even (e-ven)* and *reply (re-ply)* and because it completes the syllable and isn't closed in, so to speak, by the next consonant, the syllable is called an open syllable. Table 4-16 gives you a bunch of open-syllable words so that your child can become comfortable with spelling them.

Always familiarize your child with the spelling chunks that he needs before asking him to go right ahead and spell a word.

Don't be afraid to skip words in Table 4-16 or any other table in this book. Even if you skip the whole thing, you can always come back to it later.

Table 4-16	Words that Begin with an Open Syllable	
acorn	apron	deliver
depart	detect	detest
digest	direction	divert
eclipse	economy	erase
erode	equal	equator
equipment	even	idea
ideal	item	recover
regret	relent	repeat
repent	reply	respect
respond	retire	unite

Chapter 5

Blending Letters Together

· ·

In This Chapter

▶ Introducing blends

▶ Getting to know good blends from outlawed blends

▶ Putting blends in their right places

· ·

Your child may write words like *pekt* and *klap*. When she does (and even if she doesn't), showing her that certain letter combinations simply aren't allowed is up to you — the spelling police say so. This chapter helps you lead your child away from bad blends, like *kt* and *kl,* and toward nicer blends like *cr, dr,* and *str.*

Blending Two and Three Letters Together

Look around, and you'll see blends everywhere. Right at this moment, for example, I'm sitting at a table with a box of laundry detergent at my elbow. (It's reminding me to go get my laundry before I delay anyone else's use of the washing machine. Don't let me forget.) On the detergent box, I see these words (along with a few hundred others that my morning eyesight isn't up to viewing): *detergent, product,* and *plastic.* All three words contain a *blend* — two (or three) side-by-side consonants that, well, blend together. Each letter in the blend keeps its own sound, but the first letter blends into the second, and the second letter blends into the third (if you have one). Your child writes blends all over the place, at the beginning of words like *product*(pr) and *plastic*(pl), on the end of words like *detergent*(nt), and in the middle of words that have endings added on, like *milked*(lk).

Blends pepper nearly all the spellings that your child uses, so he needs to spell them smoothly. The great thing about blends is that they're obliging. Your child hears them clearly and spells them just as they sound. Don't let him become disconcerted by their abundance. Although their numbers may seem like too much to come to grips with, your child soon will move through them with ease. In this chapter, I tidy up how blends work and organize them into manageable groups.

The blends in this chapter are made of consonants. Most teachers mean consonant blends whenever they talk about blends, but sometimes they talk about vowel blends, too. I discuss pairs of vowels, like *ea* and *ai* in Chapter 8. There's so much to find out about pairs of vowels (like which letters typically buddy-up) that they deserve their own chapter.

In Chapter 6, I talk about pairs of consonants called digraphs. The difference between a blend and a digraph (in case you're just itching to know) is this:

✔ A *blend* is two or three letters that merge into each other but keep their own individual sounds, like in *pr* or *str*.

✔ A *digraph* is two letters buddying-up to make a whole new sound that's different from the letters' two individual sounds, like in *ch* or *sh*.

Writing Words with Blends at the Front

Right here in the heading to this section, you see two words whose first letters are blends. The words "blends" and "front" start with the common blends, *bl* and *fr*. Your child needs to be able to write blends like *bl* and *fr* effortlessly so she can give more thought to the other letters in her words. Why, for example, is it *front* and not *frunt?* Hmm, that's a good question. Your child *can* either get all long-winded about "*uh*" spellings *or* jot down "front" a few times to fix it in her mind. (I know which one I'd choose.)

If you're right in the middle of showing your child blends and come across a tricky word like "front," have him jot "front" down a few times. Jotting down a word is a good way to help your child remember the spelling, and because it's quick to do, you stay on track with blends. Later, when you're done with blends (for the time being), show him how word families can help fix spellings in his mind. Show him, for example, that in words like *some, come, brother, mother,* and *front*, he spells the *"uh"* sound with an *o*.

Table 5-1 shows you common front blends. The only blend in the whole bunch that you may need to clarify for your child is *squ* (and even that's pretty easy). Your child writes "squ" even though she hears only a *sq* sound in the word she's spelling, because, get this, *q* always brings *u* along. Whenever your child hears a *q* sound, she jots down *qu*. The *u* is silent but you'll always find one after a *q,* just the same.

If you're on the ball, you'll notice that I'm talking about a consonant and vowel here, *q* and *u*, when I distinctly said I'd talk only about consonants. Well that's why the *q-u* marriage takes a little thought — *q* is an exceptional consonant. Because it never goes anywhere without u (except perhaps to Iraq!), your child treats *squ* as a consonant blend. The *s* blends into the *qu*, which makes just the *"q"* sound.

Look over the blends in Table 5-1 with your child, and then rummage through your recycling. Did you keep that pizza box from the weekend? If you did, grab it for the game that I tell you about next. If your box went out with the recycling, or you're not a pizza-loving family, don't fret. You can play the pizza box game by drawing a large, pizza-size circle on paper rather than using a pizza box.

Table 5-1	Blends at the Front
Front Blend	*Example Words*
bl	black, blink, blister, blot, blocks, blender, blimp, and blast
br	brown, brag, brick, bring, brooch, bread, broom, brilliant, break, and brain
cl	cliff, clown, clock, clasp, cloak, clap, clip, clamp, and clatter
cr	crust, creep, craft, crest, cream, crimson, Creole, crab, cry, and cringe
dr	drive, drink, draft, drool, drum, drop, and dry
dw	dwindle, dwell, and dwarf
fl	flood, flick, flash, flame, fleet, flan, flag, flip, and fly
fr	frost, fringe, freak, Fred, Friday, fry, fray, fruit, frog, and fresh
gl	glow, glide, glad, glove, glimpse, glee, glisten, and glade
gr	grip, grow, ground, grand, grouch, growl, green, Graham, Gran, grind, grin, grapes, and grub
pl	plan, please, plod, plaster, plow, plant, plug, play, and plate
pr	prick, prod, proud, pram, prim, pretty, pry, private, primitive, print, pride, prickle, and present
sc	scout, scamper, scale, scope, scab, scar, scarf, and scum
scr	scrape, scratch, scream, screech, screw, scribble, and scrub
sk	skip, sketch, skeleton, skittles, skunk, skin, and sky
sl	slip, slide, slant, sleep, slope, sloppy, slim, slipper, and slate
sm	small, smell, smack, smudge, smile, and smart

(continued)

Table 5-1	Blends at the Front
Front Blend	*Example Words*
sn	snail, snap, sneak, snoop, snip, and snatch
sp	spill, spin, spank, spade, spoon, spanner, spider, and spell
spl	splash, split, splinter, splendid, spleen, and splatter
spr	spread, spray, spring, and sprint
squ	squeal, squeak, squid, and square
st	stand, stack, stop, stammer, stupid, stamp, stampede, start, stolen, stink, stairs, stay, steel, and stem
str	strip, stride, stranded, stroke, strawberry, string, and stream
sw	swing, swim, switch, swindle, swell, swagger, swill, swat, sweet, sweat, and swollen
tr	tread, trip, tree, treat, trap, tribe, trend, trade, true, and train
tw	twang, twist, twin, twiddle, twenty, and twig

The pizza game is fun. Anytime your family has pizza, you can use the box for this game before sending it off for reincarnation. (You may want to get rid of any lingering bits of pepperoni or bacon first.)

Activity: Making great use of a pizza box

Preparation: Gather together a large pizza box, different colored pens, and some sheets of regular paper to jot scores onto.

Follow these steps:

1. **Have your child draw a 12-slice pizza on the box with a 1-inch circle in the very center (sort of like a dart board).** Use the side of the box that doesn't have so much printing.

2. **Have your child write a different blend on each slice.**

3. **Have your child hold a pen in one hand and cover his eyes with his other hand.**

4. **As you turn the box in a circle in front of your child, have him point (with the pen) to a place on the turning box (a bit like the television spelling game, *Wheel of Fortune*).** If the pen points to the center circle, your child scores ten points, but if it lands on a line, try again.

5. **Whenever your child lands on a slice, have him write a word, using the blend written on that slice.** Award one point for every letter in the word.

6. **Have your child cross off (or otherwise indicate) the slice that already has been played.** Pretend that slice has been eaten so that it can't be used for the rest of the game.

7. **Keep playing and keeping score.** Whenever a player lands on a slice that's already been eaten that player loses a turn and play proceeds to the next player. The first player to score 30 point wins.

Your child will get a kick out of spelling big words in the pizza game. Help her make words longer by adding suffixes (like *ing*), and try the same game again with other kinds of words or blends. A good variant is to mark slices with pairs of vowels (like *ee, ea, oa,* and *ai*), repeating them until all the slices are marked.

Another simple and fun word-making game, "Seven super shapes," starts off with your child drawing seven little shapes.

Activity: Seven super shapes

Preparation: Gather together paper and pen.

Follow these steps:

1. **Have your child to draw seven shapes (flowers, hearts, pizzas, cars, you name it).** You can draw them for you child, if you'd prefer.

2. **In each shape, have your child write a letter.** Make sure that you have two vowels and five common consonants (so you get a mix like *a, e, s, r, t, n,* and *d*).

3. **Ask your child to use the available letters to make more than seven words from the letters (like *rent, sent, send, stand, strand, rest, nest, tend,* and *trend*).** Each word must have a blend, but using a letter twice is okay.

Make this activity easier by allowing your child to spell out any kind of word, not just words with blends.

Choosing between sc and sk

Wouldn't it be fun if you could *whisk* me from my *desk* right now to jet off to your private island? You could teach me *scuba diving, skiing,* and *skydiving;* rustle me up some *scaloppini;* leave me in the care of your personal maids while you *scoot* off to attend to my kids. Sounds good, right? Alas, I'm *scheduled* for more prosaic things. I have a *sc* versus *sk* issue to deal with here.

Coping with words like kinder and cinder

Just in case you'd like to know a bit more about *k* and *c* stuff right now, I'll tell you a little about words like *kinder* and *cinder*. Spellings like *ki* and *si* aren't blends; blends are consonants like *cr* and *cl*. You can find more about the soft-*c* sound in Chapter 14. Anyway, *kind, king, kill,* and *kiss* all start with *ki. Ki* is a cool letter combination. *Ci* won't give you the same *"k"* sound, because it yields a soft-*c* sound, like in *circus*.

Kept, keen, kelp, and *kettle* all start with *ke. Ke* is good, too. Like *ki, ke* gives the *"k"* sound, but if you write *ce,* you make a soft-*c* sound again, like in *cent.*

Something's happening here, right? Yep. In a roundabout sort of way, I'm telling you to give your child this advice: You make the hard *"k"* sound, in phrases like "keep kissing," with *k. K* goes in front of *e* and *i.* And, on the other hand, in front of *a, o,* and *u,* you nearly always put *c,* like in *cat, cot* and *cut.*

Your child needs to know when to use *sc* and when to use *sk*. Here's the scoop: Your child writes *"sk"* (not *sc*) before e and *i*, like in *sketch* and *skin*. If she writes *scetch* and *scin,* she makes soft *c* sounds, like in *scene* and *science*. To keep the hard-*c* sound in words like *sketch, skim, skin, skill* and *skid* your child must jot down a decisive *k*. If you want to go get a quick lead on hard and soft sounds, you can flip over to Chapter 14 (I'll hang here for a while).

Ske and *ski* make hard-*c* sounds but *sce* and *sci*, make a soft-*c* sounds.

Okay, so now you're asking, "What about words like *scab* and *skate?*" Is there anything I need to bear in mind about which one my child should look for? The short answer is, "No." No hard-and-fast rule exists for choosing between *sca* and *ska,* but I have a sound piece of advice: When you don't know; have a go. In fact, I'd say that this piece of wisdom is so darned acute that it needs to be repeated with a "Remember" icon right after this paragraph. My advice isn't in the least bit like rocket science. It may even sound clichéd and worn, but it works. If you give your child too much "if this, then that" type of advice, she'll zone out. If, on the other hand, you encourage her to jot down all her options *(scab/skab, scate/skate)*, she gets better at spotting the spelling that simply looks right. So in a nutshell, tell her:

"When you don't know; have a go."

Tell your child to jot down the spelling possibilities he thinks of and then opt for the one that irks him the least. Even if he chooses the wrong spelling, he'll probably remember the right one next time, because of the nuisance it caused.

Okay, time for less talk and more action. Table 5-2 lays out *sc* and *sk* words for you to walk your child through. Explain that *ke* and *ki* make the hard-*c* sound (unlike *ce* and *ci*). When he spells words that have *sc* or *sk* followed by *a, o,* or *u*, like *scan, score,* and *skittle,* he uses the noble strategy of trial and error, or "When you don't know; have a go."

Table 5-2		Words Starting with *sc* and *sk*	
sc Words		**sk Words**	
scan	scar	skip	skeleton
scat	scratch	skin	sketch
scamp	scramble	skill	skewer
scab	scrub	skulk	sky
scalp	scrape	skull	skate
scant		skunk	

If your head is reeling with all these *c* and *k* quirks, here's some important advice: Watch out for *c.* That's it. Because *c* can make a soft sound *(ss),* just tell your child to watch out whenever it is paired with *e* or *i.* Words like *scene* and *science* show what happens with *sce* and *sci* words. Oh, and if another letter separates the *c* from the *e* or *i,* like in *schedule* and *school,* things get back to normal, and you don't need to worry about *c* making it's *"ss"* sound. The same thing applies to *scr,* which I talk about next (no need to worry about *c* making a *"ss"* sound, because it isn't right in front of *e* or *i*).

Strangled eggs

Oops, I mean "scrambled." I couldn't resist using cheap ploys to pique your interest. Are you piqued? Good. Here are a few words to consider: *screw, scream,* and *screech* (a motley assortment, aren't they?). Your child can write *scr* in front of *e* and *i* without a care in the world. In fact, he must use *scr,* because the *skr* blend is an outlawed combination. You don't see it, write it, or get caught up with it in any way. Spelling police don't miss much.

Your child spells many words that start with *scr,* but he won't ever spell a word that starts with *skr.*

Spelling with cc and x

By now you may be suspicious of *c* and *k.* They're slippery letters that combine in different ways and make different sounds. Don't worry. In this chapter, I give you all the permutations of *c* and *k* and a bit more besides. This section is part of that little bit extra. I want to give you a helpful snippet about popping *cc* into words like *accident* and *soccer,* so here it is:

Your child spells some words with *cc* more or less in the middle. The sound she'll spell with *cc* is hard-c, like in *soccer,* or hard-cs, like in *access.* Lead her through these spellings because that *"cs"* sound is just like the sound in *exit* or *exclude.* Your child needs to get to know the look of *cc* or *x* words so she isn't caught jotting down the wrong one. In Table 5-3, I show you *cc* and *x* words so you can help your child practice spelling them. If you're steadily leading your child through this book, you may want to tackle this table slowly, during the course of a few days. If your child's setting a fast past and wants to push ahead, have her take the whole table by storm. The activities that I give with this table help your child look for similarities in the words so that they're easier for her to remember later on.

Table 5-3		Distinguishing *Accept* from *Except*		
cc Sounds Like "c"	*cc Sounds Like "cs"*	*x Sounds Like "cs"*		
occur	accept	explain	exclaim	excited
account	access	explode	exhale	excellent
occupy	accent	expect	expert	example
accurate	success	expand	excerpt	examine
acclaim	accident	exclude	except	extinguish
soccer	vaccinate	excrete	exit	exhibit
		exhale	exert	executive
		excuse	exist	exorbitant
		extra	exhaust	exuberant
		excess	exact	exhilarating
		excel	exempt	

Activity: Sorting your double-c's

Preparation: Make a copy of this table and find some color highlighters.

Follow these steps (with dialogue in quotations):

1. **Say to your child, "In column one, there are words with two or three chunks of sound (or syllables). Color the two-chunk words in one color, and then color the three-chunk words in a new color."**

Help your child break the words into parts by drawing a pen line (or slash) between the chunks. Break the first chunk after the first *c*. Point out spelling features to watch out for, like the *ou* part of account and the *ai* part of acclaim.

2. **Tell your child to, "Read the words to yourself," and after she's done that say, "I'll read them for you to write, now."**

   Dictate the six words in the first column of Table 5-3 to your child. These are tricky words, so when your child has spelled them correctly, be generous with your praise.

3. **Repeat steps 1 and 2, using the words in the second column of Table 5-3.**

If your child has trouble spelling these words, make the task smaller. Focus only on the two-syllable words at first (there are four of them). Have your child say the words in chunks. Have him circle or underline tricky letters. Have him jot the words down a couple of times. Then dictate the words for him to spell (and cheer him on). When he's happy with the two-syllable words, add *accurate* and *occupy*. Break accurate into *ac-cu-rate* and occupy into *oc-cu-py*. Have your child jot down the new words a couple of times. Dictate all six words and then take a well-earned break. Later, when you've finished your cookies and milk or your two-hour, fully equipped, hike into town and back (if you enjoy moderate exercise), have one last quick test of the six words.

Activity: Looking at *ex* words

Preparation: Make a copy of Table 5-3 and a copy of the list of 23 exercises in Step 4.

Follow these steps (suggested dialogue is in quotations).

1. **Have your child: "Find *excited* in Table 5-3 and color all the two-syllable words before *"excited"* in one color.**

2. **Have your child: "Draw a line through each word that you colored, after the *ex*."**

3. **Ask your child: "What's the same about all these words?"** Wait for your child to answer that they're all made of two chunks or help her figure this out.

4. **Hand a copy of the list that follows to your child and tell her to: "Circle the correct words in this list."**

   1. explain — explane

   2. explode — expload

   3. expect — expect

   4. ecspand — expand

   5. exclude — exclood

   6. ecscrete — excrete

   7. exhale — ecshale

   8. excuse — excoose

   9. extra — ecstra

  10. excess — ecsess

  11. exsell — excel

  12. exclaim — exclame

  13. exhale — exhayl

  14. exclude — exclude

  15. expurt — expert

  16. exerpt — excerpt

  17. except — except

  18. exit — exitt

  19. exert — exurt

  20. exyst — exist

  21. exorst — exhaust

  22. egsact — exact

  23. exempt — exsempt

Activity: Extending yourself with *ex* words

Preparation: Make a copy of Table 5-3.

Follow these steps:

1. Find *excited* in Table 5-3 and color it and all the three-syllable words after it in one color.

2. Read each of the ten questions that follow to your child and write down, for him to see, the three-syllable *ex* word he has to find.

3. Have your child write each answer on his own paper and then move to the next question.

1. Can you find and write down a word with "bit" in it?

2. Can you find and write down a word with "cell" in it?

3. Can you find and write down a word with "cut" in it?

4. Can you find and write down a word with "rat" in it?

5. Can you find and write down a word with "rant" in it?

6. Can you find and write down a word with "mine" in it?

7. Can you find and write down a word with "tin" in it?

8. Can you find and write down a word with "ted" in it?

9. Can you find and write down a word with "ample" in it?

10. Can you find and write down a word with "orb" in it?

If your child's cruising along with ease, have her give you her paper and dictate the words for her to write from scratch.

Your child probably likes figuring out things side by side with you. By writing with and being alongside your child, you convey good things. Conversely, if your child's the keep-away-I-have-to-do-this-myself kind, you can give her all the words and make yourself scarce.

Writing Words with Blends at the End

Okay, just to show you how frequently your child needs to spell blends, let me refer you once again to the title bar (the heading above). I typed the title of this section without thinking about including blends, but guess what, they turned up anyway. Blends at the end are featured in the words, *writing, blends, words,* and *end.* That's four words out of seven. That's how common blends are (at least in this heading). You can be sure that your child needs to run his pen smoothly through *ngs* and *nds* and other companionable consonants. Table 5-4 shows you the blends your child needs to know and a bunch of straightforward words for him to practice with. Dictate the words for him to write and then lead him through the "Always *ct* (never *kt*)" activity, which focuses on the *ct* blend so he's not fooled into writing *kt.*

If you're wondering why I don't include *th* as a blend in this chapter, I deal with it (along with *ch, sh, wh,* and *ph*) as a consonant digraph in Chapter 6. Remember that a consonant digraph is a special spelling unit made of two consonants that together make one new sound that isn't like their individual sounds blending together.

Table 5-4	Blends on the Ends
End Blends	*Example Words*
ct	fact, pact, insect, direct, correct, inspect, reject, duct, detect, and defect
lk	milk, sulk, silk, and bulk
mp	lump, jump, bump, hump, stump, stamp, limp, lamp, and cramp
nd	end, bend, lend, fend, trend, spend, hind, mind, find, kind, hand, band, land, stand, and pond
ng	song, long, ring, sing, bring, fling, sting, wing, hang, bang, lung, tang, and clang
nk	sink, mink, blink, chunk, skunk, monk, wink, think, trunk, and bunk
nt	spent, sent, meant, tent, blunt, and bent
sk	tusk, mask, ask, risk, and task
st	mast, past, last, nest, cost, dust, frost, test, mist, list, best, pest, and trust

Doing away with kt

A simple spelling rule for the *ct* sound is that it's always *ct* and never *kt*. Just like that bad habit you're wanting to break, you simply do away with *kt*, never to be heard from again.

Activity: Always *ct* (never *kt*)

This activity (bidding *kt* bon voyage — poor girl) is quick and easy and it helps your child see that the *ct* blend is the one he needs to write on the end of words, while the *kt* blend is just plain weird looking. After your child circles the answers, you can dictate them back to him so he gets even more chance to fix ct in his mind.

Preparation: Make a copy of the ten questions in the list that follows.

Follow this step: Have your child to circle each correct spelling.

1. insect — insekt — insect
2. reject — reject — rejekt
3. currect — correct — correkt

4. dierect — direct — direkt

5. fact — fackt — fakt

6. inspect — inspeckt — inspecte

7. pakt — pact — packt

8. duct — duckt — dukt

9. detect — detect — deatect

10. defect — defect — defect

Here's how you can tell the difference between *pact* and *packed, duct* and *ducked,* and so on. The *ed* endings are tagged onto verbs, or doing-type words like pack and duck — as in watch your head. Pact and duct aren't verbs; they're nouns (things).

Sorting c, ck, and k

Do you have an *"ic"* sound on the end of a two- or three-syllable word? Spell it *"ic,"* like in *picnic, panic,* and *terrific.*

Hear *"c"* straight after a short vowel? Spell it *"ck,"* like in *lick, clock,* and *neck.*

Whenever you hear *"nk," "sk,"* or *"lk"* at the end of a word, spell it with a *"k."*

K, which always is accompanied by another consonant, is more common on the end of a word than *c* is.

By the same token, whenever you hear *"c"* after a long vowel sound, spell it *"k"* like in *cloak* and *peek* or *"ke"* like in *cake, joke,* and *spike.*

A *long vowel* is a vowel written in the middle of words like *mate, Pete, hike, slope,* and *cute.* It has a distinctly long pronunciation (like the names of the vowels *a, e, i, o,* and *u*) when compared with the pronunciation of the short vowel in words like *mat, met, mit, cot,* and *cut.*

Phew. Did I make that sound hard? If I did, I'm sorry, because after you and your child get into the swing of things, you find out that it gets easier and easier for your child to jot down the right spellings. He will see that some letter combinations just look all wrong from the start. The more words you have him try out, the better he gets at telling right from wrong. In Table 5-5, I lay out plenty of words for your child to peruse. When he's all perused-out, point him to the "Making sense of *c, k,* and *ck*" activity.

Table 5-5			Sorting through *c*, *k*, and *ck*
ic on the End	*ck on the End*	*nk, sk and lk*	*k after a Long Vowel*
panic	back	tank	like
electric	lick	sunk	smoke
specific	clock	think	cloak
terrific	stuck	task	peek
economic	neck	risk	tweak
frolic	truck	desk	flake
picnic	speck	dusk	joke
frantic	black	milk	strike
mimic	thick	sulk	spike
comic	sick	silk	mistake

Activity: Making sense of *c*, *k*, and *ck*

Preparation: Grab your copy of *Teaching Kids to Spell For Dummies*, and make copies of the ten questions in the list that follows.

Follow these steps:

1. **Explain to your child that, "The first letter of each nonsense word in the list of questions is correct and each answer has the same number of letters as the nonsense word."**

2. **Have your child write the real answers in place of the nonsense words that I've provided.**

   1. I made a funny jumd. *(answer: joke)*

   2. I ate so much cake that I got sgol. *(answer: sick)*

   3. I saw the sfasg from the fire. *(answer: smoke)*

   4. The cjidd showed it was one thirty. *(answer: clock)*

   5. My dpoy is covered with books and papers. *(answer: desk)*

   6. The night sky is jet bnazk. *(answer: black)*

   7. I thought that the play was tufklsmn. *(answer: terrific)*

   8. We packed sandwiches and cake for the pythfs. *(answer: picnic)*

   9. She swung her axe into the tree tjibd. *(answer: trunk)*

   10. I went to the wrong place by muwgule. *(answer: mistake)*

Hard? Not at all!

After sorting through the many computations of *c* and *k* you may be feeling like you need a rest. Maybe two weeks at some retreat? Maybe your own personal masseuse? Or maybe I can cheer you up by giving you a peek at a kid who tackles bigger and scarier spellings just for the thrill of it.

Fourteen-year-old David Tidmarsh from Indiana recently won the 2004 National Spelling Bee. David outdid 264 rivals (including one who fainted on stage but recovered to take second place). David's winning word was "autochthonous," which, by the way, means indigenous. His other spellings included "arete," "sophrosyne," "sumpsimus," and "serpiginous." Spellers were given a set time limit of 2 minutes to spell each word, followed by a final 30-second period with a countdown clock. And here you are, miffed because I threw a few measly *c*'s and *k*'s at you.

Nosing through ng and nk

Paying extra attention to the *ng* and *nk* endings is worth the effort, because they're not as clearly pronounced as other blends. They're called *nasal blends*. Apparently everyone makes the sound of these blends in their noses. I'm not great at telling nose-noises from other kinds of noise (with a few exceptions), but I know that your child may one day wonder whether to write *somethink* or *something*. He may get tied up with a bunch of *ings* and *inks*, so this section gives you a few to think about. Your child will whiz through Table 5-6, because every word has a dead-easy short vowel in it. Dictate them to him. For fun, set the timer and find out whether he can write all the words in less than three minutes.

Table 5-6		*ng* and *nk* Words
sing	sang	long
lung	sink	bank
bunk	honk	wing
bang	song	hung
wink	tank	hunk
sank	clang	trunk
drink	blink	blank
clank	fling	plank

(continued)

Table 5-6 *(continued)*

spring	gland	prank
grunt	bring	drank
frank	cling	string
clung	think	thing

Chapter 6

Choosing *ch* (and *sh*, *th*, *ph*, and *wh*, too)

In This Chapter

▶ Discovering consonant digraphs

▶ Getting to know the key pairs

▶ Guiding your child through *who*, *where*, and *were*

A few days ago, I was idly flicking through the pages of my daughter's magazines when a headline caught my eye. It read: "Get a beach-ready body in just two weeks." Knowing that I was being duped, but helpless to resist, I turned to the article. I was reading about the buttock clenching and belly crunching that I'd be required to do, when I saw an extra paragraph. It told me not to race off for my new bikini quite yet. To achieve sculpted perfection I'd have to do a few hundred hours of intense aerobic activity in between all that clenching and squeezing.

Don't you hate hidden extras! You won't find any of that in this chapter. The consonant digraphs that I tell you about here are exactly as they seem. You can give your child a good start with spelling them by helping him through the activities in this chapter. No extra laps are required.

Delving into Digraphs

Digraph is a scary name for something quite simple. *Di* means two, and *graph* means something drawn or written. Together, they cast no disparaging light at all on what's going on here! (A more helpful word would be "di-letters/new-sound" but I guess that's never going to happen.) A *digraph* is two letters that make their own new sound when put together.

Blends are two letters that keep their individual sounds when put together, such as *st* and *cl.* Find out more about blends in Chapter 5. Digraphs, by contrast, make a whole new sound, like *ch.* The main consonant digraphs are *ch, sh, th, ph,* and *wh,* although to my ear *wh* sounds just like *w.*

In this book, I don't dwell too much on the term "vowel digraphs," because when you talk about vowel digraphs you mean reams of spellings. Vowel digraphs are pairs like *ee, ea, ai, oa, oi,* and *ou* and spellings like *aw, ay,* and *oy,* that are made from a vowel and a consonant — because they make a sound that also can be made by vowels (*au, a, oi*). You can see just how elaborate the vowel digraph group can get, so in this book, I take a few vowel digraphs at a time and focus on other aspects of them. You see *ee, ea, ai,* and *oa* in Chapter 8, where I talk about the *when-two-vowels-go-walking-the-first-one-does-the-talking rule,* and in Chapter 11, where I talk about many different word families, like *aw* and *au, ou* and *ow,* and *oi,* and *oy.* Oh, another term that you see in some spelling books is *diphthong.* It's yet another fancy term to describe spelling chunks like *oi* and *ou* that are technically "gliding transitions from one vowel sound to another." With digraphs and diphthongs overlapping and covering so many spellings, it's easiest to talk about good old spelling chunks.

Chewing Your Pencil Over ch

The *ch* digraph is especially nice. It makes a sound unlike any other and after a bit of practice your child can easily use it. The words in Table 6-1 give the easiest *ch* words of all, the ones that start with *ch* and have a short vowel in them. Have your child read the words to you and write out a few that you dictate to her. Do the same with the words in Table 6-2, which are the next easiest words of all, the ones that end with *ch* and have a short vowel. Then play the Lay-3 card game I describe in "Mastering *ch* with the Lay-3 card game" activity.

A short vowel is the vowel your child writes in words like *mat, met, mit, cot,* and *cut.* It has the short pronunciation of *a* like in *ant, e* like in *egg, i* like in *igloo, o* like in *octopus,* or *u* like in *up.*

Table 6-1	Words Beginning with *ch*	
champ	chap	chat
check	chess	chest
chick	chill	chimp
chin	chip	chomp
chop	chum	chunk

Table 6-2	Words Ending with *ch*	
batch	bench	blotch
branch	bunch	catch
clench	clutch	crutch
ditch	drench	fetch
flinch	hatch	hitch
hunch	hutch	inch
itch	latch	lunch
match	much	munch
notch	patch	pinch
punch	ranch	rich
sketch	stench	stitch
stretch	such	switch
trench	twitch	witch

If you're wondering why I give you more *ch* endings than *ch* beginnings, it's because I'm using only short-vowel words and there are more of them in the endings group. I start talking about long-vowel words in Chapter 7.

Activity: Mastering *ch* with the Lay-3 card game

I adapted this card game from another one called Strip Jack Naked. Don't tell Jill. Actually, I played Strip Jack Naked with my grandma when I was a kid, so it isn't that bad. I never saw her remove so much as a hair curler, and I know I was always fully clothed, so the name still intrigues me.

Preparation: With 32 index cards, write the number *3* on 8 of them and write *"ch"* on 8 more cards, leaving the remaining 16 cards blank.

Follow these steps:

1. **Deal all the cards facedown, splitting them equally between the two of you.**

2. **Have your child lay down one card face up from the cards he's been dealt.**

3. **Take turns laying cards on the pile until one players lays either a 3 or a *ch* card.**

   When a player lays a 3, the other player gets to lay three of cards down. However, if that player happens to lay down a 3 in the middle of his or her turn, play shifts to the other player (who then tries to lay three cards down).

   If a player manages to lay down three cards in a row, finishing with a blank card, that player picks up the entire stack and adds those cards to his or her hand.

4. **Whenever a player lays down a *ch* card, the other player must write down a *ch* word and then lay one card down as usual.**

The first player to win all the cards wins the game, if that player also has written down an equal number of or more *ch* words than his or her opponent. If not, the players must play another round (and start the word list over).

Okay, here's the thing. Something is different about Table 6-3. Have a look at the words with your child and check out the *ch* and *tch* endings. "Ah", you'll say, "but there aren't any *tch* endings." And there you have it. Words with long-vowel sounds nearly always end with *ch,* but short-vowel words nearly always end with *tch* or *nch*. Glance back to Table 6-2 and note that these traits are true. Of all the words in Table 6-2, only a handful of words end with just *ch*. Ask your child to find them. After that task is accomplished, head to the "Sorting long-vowel words with *ch* endings" word-sort activity.

A long vowel is the vowel your child writes in the middle of words like *mate, Pete, hike, slope,* and *cute.* It has a distinctly long pronunciation compared to the pronunciation of the short-vowel in words like *mat, met, mit, cot,* and *cut.*

Table 6-3	Long-Vowel Words with the *ch* Ending	
arch	beach	birch
bleach	breach	each
church	coach	march
leech	lurch	perch
mooch	peach	porch
poach	pooch	roach
preach	reach	speech
scorch	screech	starch
teach	torch	

Activity: Sorting long-vowel words with *ch* endings

Preparation: Make a copy of Table 6-3, and grab some highlighters.

Follow these steps:

1. **Have your child group the words according to vowel or vowel+*r* combinations (like *ee* or *or* words).**

2. **Have your child color the *ee* words in one color, the *oa* words in another color, the *or* words in another color, and so on.**

3. **Dictate the words, according to their respective color groupings, or word families, for your child to write.**

Showing Your Child sh

Sh is another great spelling chunk with its own distinctive sound. Tables 6-4 and 6-5 give you some easy, short-vowel words that start or end with *sh*. Skim through them with your child and then dictate a few words for him to write. After that, try your hand at rhyming in the "Rhyming time with *sh*" activity that follows.

Table 6-4	Words Beginning with *sh*	
shock	shelf	shift
shack	shall	shell
shin	ship	shot
shed	shop	shock
shut	shrink	

Table 6-5	Words Ending with *sh*	
ash	brush	cash
crash	dash	dish
fish	flash	flesh
flush	fresh	gash

(continued)

Table 6-5 *(continued)*

gosh	hush	mash
mush	slosh	slush
smash	swish	wish
splash	trash	stash
bash	mesh	

Activity: Rhyming time with *sh*

Preparation: Make a copy of the list that follows and have it in front of you and have pen and paper for your child to use.

Follow these steps:

1. **Say the 12 words that I give you in the list that follows out loud to your child.**

2. **Have your child write words that rhyme with them that begin with *sh*.**

    1. Elf *(Answer: shelf)*

    2. Pack *(Answer: shack)*

    3. Pin *(Answer: shin)*

    4. Lift *(Answer: shift)*

    5. Bed *(Answer: shed)*

    6. Spell *(Answer: shell)*

    7. Lock *(Answer: shock)*

    8. Pot *(Answer: shot)*

    9. Pink *(Answer: shrink)*

    10. Cut *(Answer: shut)*

    11. Hip *(Answer: ship)*

    12. Hop *(Answer: shop)*

Activity: More challenging *sh* rhymes

Preparation: Make a copy of the next list and have it in front of you. Have pen and paper ready for your child to use.

Follow these steps:

1. **Say the 12 words that I give you in the list that follows out loud to your child.**

2. **Have your child write words that rhyme with them that begin with *sh*.**

   1. meet *(Answer: sheet)*

   2. foal *(Answer: shoal)*

   3. boot *(Answer: shoot)*

   4. peep *(Answer: sheep)*

   5. ape *(Answer: shape)*

   6. bark *(Answer: shark)*

   7. skirt *(Answer: shirt)*

   8. made *(Answer: shade)*

   9. line *(Answer: shine)*

   10. cry *(Answer: shy)*

   11. hopping *(Answer: shopping)*

   12. making *(Answer: shaking)*

Thinking About th

The digraph *th* has a distinctive but changeable sound. Some people describe the sounds of *th* as voiced or unvoiced. That explanation's a bit surreal for me, so I give you the two sounds to run through with your child (no theory needed) so that he gets a practical handle on them. The sounds are "*th*" like in *then, the,* and *this* and "*th*" as in *think, through,* and *three*. The difference in sound is subtle (at least it is to my boorish ears), but with a little practice you can have your child penning both sounds with ease. Tables 6-6 and 6-7 have enough words to give your child more than a little practice. Look over the words with him and then zoom forward to the "Creating *th* crosses" activity.

Table 6-6		Words Beginning with *th*
than	thank	that
theft	them	then
thick	thin	thing

(continued)

Table 6-6 *(continued)*

think	this	thong
thrash	thrill	throb
throng	thrush	thumb
thug	thump	

Table 6-7	Words Ending with *th*	
bath	cloth	fifth
math	moth	path
sixth	tenth	width
with		

Activity: Creating *th* word crosses

Preparation: You'll need a pen and paper for you and your child (white-boards work, too).

Follow this step: Write three word crosses each.

  ✔ A *word cross* is four words that make a cross shape when combined a certain way. The center of the cross is *th* (draw a circle around it) and the words branch to and away from the center.

  ✔ Two of the words start with *th* (the words going from center to bottom and center to right) and the other two end with *th* (the words going from top to center and far left to center).

Passing through a Phase of ph

Not all that many words have *ph* in them, but the ones that do can look pretty imposing. Check out Table 6-8 with your child and be prepared to get all deep and affected with *philosophy!* Highlight any spelling chunks that seem tricky, and when you're done, zip on ahead to the "Cracking the *ph* cryptic code" activity.

Whenever I talk about spelling chunks or spelling units, I'm talking about letters that naturally go together in words. Some of them are syllables (like the two syllables in *al-most*) and some will be blends (like the *str* in *strong*) or digraphs (like the *ou* in *loud*). A *spelling chunk* is any part of a word that your child needs to look at more closely or get more practice with.

Table 6-8	*ph* Words	
phone	Phil	phase
phantom	phrase	physical
philosophy	alphabet	elephant
hyphen	orphan	graph
photograph	autograph	geography
triumph		

Activity: Cracking the *ph* cryptic code

Preparation: Make a copy of the list that follows. If you're no good at cryptic clues, don't worry, neither am I, so the ones in this activity are pretty basic, but probably not so basic that you won't need to refer to the table.

Follow this step: Using Table 6-8, solve the following word puzzles.

1. This word appears four times (once on its own, three times inside other words).
2. This word has a car at the front.
3. A boy's name that starts with *T* is at the end of this word.
4. A boy's name is at the front of this word and it appears on its own, too.
5. A tiny animal is inside this animal.
6. The name of a number is at the end of this word.
7. You may see right through this word.
8. This word has *has* right in its middle.
9. This word has five letters. **Hint:** If you took *r* and *h* away you'd leave a *gap*.
10. Take the last three letters from this word and find a female chicken.

Answers: 1 — graph, 2 — autograph, 3 — phantom, 4 — philosophy, 5 — elephant (ant), 6 — phone, 7 — phantom, 8 — phase, 9 — graph, and 10 — hyphen.

Asking wh Questions

Wh appears in questions. *Why, when, which, what, where,* and the odd sounding one, *who*? Nothing is hard about *wh,* except that your child may write *where* when he actually means *were.* Show him that *were* isn't a question, and that being so, it starts with *w* not *wh.* All the other questioning words, including the weird word *who,* start with *wh.* (Why *who* isn't spelled *hoo* is one of life's many mysteries. My personal belief is that *who* ranks way up there with hair combovers (do they really think we can't tell?) and friends (so called) who put you on hold when you call them. (Really, is anyone *that* much of a VIP?) I digress! *Wh* is an easy digraph. Run through the questioning words with your child, point out the hazardous *where/were* thing and relate your exasperation with *who.* That's really all you need to do. Ask your child questions like, "Can you think of *wh* words that ask questions?" Share a whiteboard to jot them down. This activity need not take any longer than about five minutes.

Part III

Coming to Grips with Long Vowel Sounds

The 5th Wave · By Rich Tennant

I just don't think you can start good spelling habits too early.

In this part . . .

*L*ittle spelling rules open big doors for your child. This part of the book shows you three long-vowel rules that help the two of you uncover hundreds, maybe thousands, of new spellings. You get the cute Bossy-*e* rule, which helps your child hear the difference between words like *hop* and *hope* and jot down the long spelling before it's forgotten, and you hear the "When Two Vowels Go Walking, The First One Does The Talking" rhyme, which helps your child surge forward with words like *neat* and *nail*. Lastly, in words like *play, funny* and *shy,* I show you the different ways your child can jot down *y*-on-the-end.

Chapter 7

Putting a Firm Pen on Bossy *e*

In This Chapter

▶ Finding out how Bossy *e* gets its name

▶ Recognizing Bossy *e* words

▶ Getting to know when and where to use Bossy *e*

Although some things make life easier, they sometimes have drawbacks. Take cellphones, for example. They drive you crazy in the theater but, in general, make life easier. Loud car stereos dull your hearing but help you forget that all the trucks are passing you on the freeway. Clothes dryers are a glut on power but who wants to wait three days for a dry shirt or hang out their undies only to provide comic entertainment for every teenager in the neighborhood? And then there's my Bossy-*e* rule. Unlike these other conveniences that make life so much easier, it has no drawbacks. Talk about it; write it out; add it to words. Nothing goes wrong. You and your child can use Bossy *e* with impunity. No one's going to get crazy, deaf, or wet.

Bearing with Bossy e

When your child spells a word like *make* or *mine,* she hears a long-vowel sound in her mind. She says the word to herself, hears that she needs to write a long vowel, and then jots it down. One common way of spelling the long-vowel sound is to tag an *e* onto the end of words that otherwise have a short-vowel sound (like kit + *e* = kite). An easy way to remember how the *e* makes the other vowel have a long-vowel sound is to think of it as Bossy *e*. A Bossy *e* tells or bosses the earlier vowel into saying it's name, which is just another way of saying that the earlier vowel makes a long sound.

A short-vowel sound is the sound you hear in words like *mat, met, mit, cot,* and *cut*. A long-vowel sound is the sound the vowel makes when you pronounce it as its name, like *"ay," "ee," "eye," "oh,"* and *"u."*

Bossy *e* makes the other vowel say its name.

Your child can spell long vowels in other ways, too. The three most common ways are

- Using a Bossy *e,* like in *make, hike,* and *cone*.

- Combining two vowels (typically *ee, ea, ai,* and *oa*), and relying on the spelling adage: "When two vowels go walking, the first one does the talking." Check out how it works with words like in *mean, seem,* and *loan*. (I explain that adage more in Chapter 8.)

- Behaving like a vowel, like in *cry* (long *i*) and *happy* (long *e*). I explain more about *y* in Chapter 9.

The *when-two-vowels-go-walking-the-first-one-does-the-talking rule* applies to the vowel pairs, *ee, ea, ai* and *oa*. Some *ue* and *ie* words are in that group too, like *cue* and *tie,* but *oo* doesn't belong here at all. Words like *moon, book,* and *floor* all use the *oo* spelling, which I explain in detail in Chapter 11.

Spotting Bossy e Words

The idea of putting an *"e"* on the ends of words won't surprise your child. He sees so many words that end in *e* that he's already primed for spelling them. All that he really needs to remember when he spells Bossy *e* words is that the first vowel he uses is the long sound and the *e* on the end stays silent. (It probably does all it's bossing by glaring and fuming.) Table 7-1 gives you and your child an idea of just how prevalent Bossy *e* words are. Look through the words with your child and then home in on a column. Give your child a few minutes to look closely at the column, and then dictate any ten words for him to spell. Do the same with the other columns. When your child's done 50 words, I'd say he's earned a snack break.

Table 7-1 Bossy *e* Words

Long a	Long a	Long a	Long e	Long i	Long i	Long i	Long o	Long o	Long u
ace	game	sale	compete	bike	live	spine	bone	pose	brute
ape	gate	save	complete	bite	mice	stride	broke	prone	cute
bake	gave	scrape	Eve	bride	mile	strike	chose	robe	flute
base	grade	shade	Pete	crime	mime	stripe	code	rode	fume
blade	grape	shake	stampede	dice	nice	thrive	cone	role	fuse
blame	grave	shame	Steve	dime	nine	tide	cope	rope	plume
blaze	graze	shape	theme	dive	pile	tile	dome	rose	pollute
brave	hate	shave	these	drive	pine	time	doze	rope	rule
cake	lace	skate		file	pipe	tire	drone	slope	salute
came	lake	slave		fine	pride	twice	drove	spoke	
cane	lame	snake		fire	prime	vine	froze	stole	
cape	lane	spade		five	rice	while	hole	stone	
case	late	state		glide	ride	whine	home	stroke	
crate	made	stale		hide	ripe	white	hope	stove	
chase	male	take		hike	rise	wide	hose	those	

(continued)

Table 7-1 (continued)

Long a			Long i			Long o		
chose	mane	tale	hire	shine	wife	joke	wife	tone
date	mate	tame	hive	side	wine	lobe	wine	whole
drape	name	tape	ice	site	wipe	mope	wipe	woke
face	pale	trade	kite	slice	wise	nose	wise	
fade	pane	vane	lice	slide		note		
fake	pave	wade	like	slime		phone		
flake	plate	wake	life	smile		poke		
flame	rake	wave	lime	spice		pole		
frame	rate	whale	line	spike		pope		

Are you back from a break? Feeling refreshed? Good. The "Back to front and front to back" activity is a good way to ease back into Bossy *e* words. Your child has to figure out the word that's in a bit of a muddle and then write it out anew.

Activity: Back to front and front to back

Preparation: Grab your copy of *Teaching Kids to Spell For Dummies* (or make a copy of the list that follows) and some paper and a pen for your child to work with.

Follow these steps:

1. **Explain to your child that the words in the list are in a muddle.** In each word, the first letter has skipped to the end of the word or the last letter has skipped to the front.

2. **Have your child move either the first or last letters back to their original places for each word.**

3. **Have your child write down each corrected word.**

    1. ewad
    2. inew
    3. eslid
    4. epollut
    5. etrad
    6. hines
    7. dstampe
    8. okej
    9. haves
    10. lices
    11. oper
    12. elif
    13. efram
    14. akef
    15. eslim
    16. eskat
    17. pices

18. ecut

19. ecomplet

20. ridep

Answers: wade, wine, slide, pollute, trade, shine, stamped, joke, shave, slice, rope, life, frame, fake, slime, skate, spice, cute, complete, and *pride*

Spelling Bossy e Words

Here are a few ways to get your child to remember spelling patterns. You can have your child:

✔ Write words out a few times

✔ Unjumble the letters inside different words

✔ Sort words into groups

These methods are good ways to fix spelling images in your child's mind, but my favorite spelling practice of all is proofreading. When you dictate words to your child and get her to check her work or give her a piece of writing with errors in it to correct, you help her develop a proofreading habit that can prove useful her entire life. That said, the "Finding 18 errors" activity that follows is a proofreading exercise that focuses your child on Bossy *e*.

Activity: Finding 18 errors

Preparation: *Teaching Kids to Spell For Dummies* is good to have on hand for this activity.

Follow these steps:

1. **Read through "The Gruesome Story of the Greedy Ape" with your child.**

2. **Find 18 words that have either an extra *e* or a missing *e*.**

Give your child help when she needs it, but try not to muscle in when she can figure things out for herself. If you think this activity is too hard for your child, you can underline each incorrect word or jot down the number of errors to the left of the lines that have errors in them.

The Gruesome Story of the Greedy Ape

There once was an ap who likd to tast strang things. At first she loved toe munche on cak, graps and nutes, but then she wanted to try more foods.

She tried milkshaks. She tried chewing gume. She tried hote dogs. All the food was good. What else should she eat? The ape swallowed a whole potato. She munched three mangoes. She crunched up several cantaloupes. She saw a snak slid past her. She grabbed it and gobbled it down. She caught a pige grunting in the grass and swallowed him down whole. She chasd a bulle and shoved him down her throat. You cane guess what happened to her can't you.

By now, your child has warmed up for writing Bossy _e_ words pretty much from scratch. In the "Three Bossy _e_ quizzes" activity up next, you ask your child to spell three groups of words. They are the three most common kinds of Bossy _e_ words — words that have the _a-e, i-e_ and _o-e_ combinations.

You may be wondering why I don't include the _e-e_ combination in this activity. When your child spells the long-_e_ sound, he most often spells it with _ee_ or _ea_. I talk more about words with two vowels together in Chapter 8.

Activity: Three Bossy _e_ quizzes

Preparation: Make a copy of this activity or have your copy of _Teaching Kids to Spell For Dummies_ in front of you along with pen and paper.

Follow these steps:

1. **Have your child read the questions in each of the three lists —** "Words with _a_ and Bossy _e_ in them," "Words with _i_ and Bossy _e_ in them," and "Words with _o_ and Bossy _e_ in them."

2. **Have your child write the answers.** The first letter of each answer is provided.

   Words with _a_ and Bossy _e_ in them

   1. The opposite of cowardly: b

   2. You put a picture in this: f

   3. You eat this on your birthday: c

   4. A big pond of water: l

   5. Eat off this: p

   6. The biggest animal: w

   7. A slithering animal: s

   8. Soccer is a: g

   9. To get paint off a door, do this: scr

10. Your teacher gives you a gr_____ for your work

11. A gardening tool: r

12. When bread is no longer fresh it's this: s

13. Opposite of early: l

14. A horse has this: m

15. Open this to get into the garden: g

Answers: Brave, frame, cake, lake, plate, whale, snake, game, scrape, grade, rake, stale, late, mane, and *gate*

Words with *i* and Bossy *e* in them

1. A husband usually lives with his: w

2. This goes onto a wheel: t

3. Bees live here: h

4. Opposite of black: w

5. Look at a clock to tell the: t

6. A cut of cake: s

7. A number: n

8. Do this in a pool, off a board: d

9. Stealing is a c_____

10. Do this in a car: d

11. Do this with your mouth: s

12. Water gets to your house through this: p

13. Do this with your teeth: b

14. This is a long way to walk: m

15. Draw a straighter one with your rule: l

Answers: Wife, tire, hive, white, time, slice, nine, dive, crime, drive, smile, pipe, bite, mile, and *line*

Words with *o* and Bossy *e* in them

1. Your skeleton is made of this: b

2. A flower: r

3. Tie boats with this: r

4. You could fall down this: h

5. Tell your friend one: j

6. Water the grass with this: h

7. Cook on this: s

8. Have an ice cream c_____

9. Firefighters slide down this: p

10. Write this to a friend: n

11. You must crack this to understand a secret message: c

12. Skim one across the pond: s

13. This is on your face: n

14. This is the soft fleshy part of your ear: l

15. She had the lead r_____ in the play

Answers: Bone, rose, rope, hole, joke, hose, stove, cone, pole, note, code, stone, nose, lobe, and *role*

Your child never can get too much practice at writing Bossy *e* words, so here's "Thinking in threes," another spell-a-word-nearly-from-scratch activity. Your child has to hunt down and write out words from Table 7-1.

Activity: Thinking in threes

Preparation: Have pen and paper for your child to use and copy of *Teaching Kids to Spell For Dummies.*

Follow these steps:

1. **Have your child read the questions.**

2. **Have your child write three words that:**

    1. Start with *"pi"*

    2. Have *w* in them

    3. End with *"de"*

    4. Start with *"sh"*

    5. Have *"th"* in them

    6. Start with *"str"*

    7. Have *m* in them

    8. Have more than six letters

    9. Have three letters

10. Have "*on*" in them

11. Have "ate" in them

12. Have "*ide*" in them

Because you can answer the problems above with more than three answers, an answer key cannot be provided. Use your dictionary if you're questioning any of the answers your child provides.

"Joke" is a Bossy e word

"Joke" is a Bossy *e* word and that's all the excuse that I need to grace you with some of my (renowned) jokes in the "Joking around with Bossy *e*" activity that follows.

Activity: Joking around with Bossy *e*

Preparation: Make a copy of the four jokes that follow and have a highlighter ready for your child to use. The first three jokes have Bossy *e* words in them. The fourth joke is there just because I'm indulging myself.

Follow this step: Have your child read the four jokes that follow and highlight the Bossy *e* words.

Q: Why did the chicken cross the playground?

A: To get to the other slide.

Q: Did you hear about the two silkworms that had a race?

A: It ended in a tie.

Q: Where do mermaids go to see movies?

A: The dive-in

Q: Why do elephants never forget?

A: Because nobody ever tells them anything

You and your child have just navigated your way through an ocean (or thereabouts) of Bossy *e* words. You're nearly back at the dock, but before you tie your nautical knots, cast off your reliable galoshes, and do other oceanic end-of-day stuff, you can coast through the "Forming Bossy *e* pictures" activity just for the fun of it. You need a crew for this one but no nets or lifejackets.

Activity: Forming Bossy *e* pictures

Preparation: Poster paper or whiteboard, pens, and your copy of this book will do just fine for this activity, but have your copy of this book turned to Table 7-1.

Follow these steps:

1. **Choose up sides so that you have two teams.**

2. **Each player (in turn alternating between the two teams) selects a word from Table 7-1 and draws a picture of it (the word) on the paper or whiteboard for everyone to see.**

3. **Members of the opposing team try to guess what the player is drawing.** The person drawing the word picture is not allowed to talk while the other players call out what word they think the drawer is drawing.

Correct answers are worth a point. The first team to score ten points wins.

Table 7-1 includes many nouns (things), but you need to leave the ones that are easiest to draw, like plates, stripes, and a nose, for your child. Draw trickier words, like lame and tame, yourself.

Chapter 8

Taking Charge of Words with Two Vowels Together

In This Chapter

▶ Getting to know the four partnerships

▶ Taking special care with *ee* and *ea*

▶ Combing through similar spellings

My washing machine empties itself into a sink. Today I forgot that and flooded the entire laundry. I loaded the washing machine, turned the dial, and headed off, right past the clothes that were soaking in the sink — all primed to obstruct the flow from the machine. The sink overflowed and everything got drenched. The whole soggy mess was dismal. Despite years of socks and suds, I still haven't managed to appreciate the relationship between my washing machine and that sink. Digraphs are a bit like my laundry duo (machine and sink). They're pairs of letters (like *ai, oa,* and *ea*) that work together. This chapter helps you show your child the vowel digraphs in words like *drain, soak,* and *scream.*

Explaining the When-Two-Vowels-Go-Walking . . . Rule

The first thing you need to tell your child about the rule that I'm giving you here is that it really is useful. It applies to masses of words and comes with its own little rhyme. The rule is: When your child's writing a word with a long-vowel sound in it, one way to spell that sound is to write two vowels side by side — usually *ee, ea, ai,* or *oa*. If your child wants to make a long-vowel sound in this manner, he writes the vowel-pair:

✔ That starts with an *e* for a long-*e* sound (either *ee* or *ea*)

✔ That starts with an *a* for a long-*a* sound

✔ That starts with an *o* for a long-*o* sound

The rhyme for this two-vowel rule is, "When two vowels go walking, the first one does the talking (and says its name)."

Hearing Long-Vowel Sounds

Table 8-1 gives you examples of many words that use the four main vowel pairs. Scan through them with your child. Copy the page and have her highlight the vowels. Then take her through the "Listening up for long vowels," activity.

Table 8-1		Words with Two Vowels			
ee Pairs		*ea Pairs*		*ai Pairs*	*oa Pairs*
bee	seem	bead	neat	aid	boast
beep	seen	beak	pea	aim	boat
beer	sheet	beam	peach	bail	cloak
bleed	sleek	bean	plead	bait	coast
breed	sleep	beast	pleat	braid	coat
cheer	sleet	beat	reach	brain	croak
creek	sneer	bleach	read	chain	float
creep	speech	bleak	real	drain	goat
deed	speed	bleat	rear	fail	gloat
deep	steel	cheap	scream	faint	load
deer	steep	cheat	seal	frail	moat
fee	steer	clear	seam	gain	oat
feed	sweep	creak	seat	grain	road
feel	sweet	cream	shear	hail	roast
feet	tree	deal	sneak	jail	shoal
fleet	tweed	dear	speak	laid	soak
free	weed	dream	spear	maid	soap
freed	week	each	squeak	mail	throat

ee Pairs		ea Pairs		ai Pairs	oa Pairs
glee	weep	ear	steal	main	toad
greed		east	streak	nail	toast
green		eat	steam	paid	
greet		fear	stream	pail	
jeep		feast	teach	pain	
heed		freak	team	plain	
heel		gear	tear	raid	
keen		gleam	weak	rail	
keep		heal	wheat	rain	
meet		heap	year	sail	
need		hear	yeast	saint	
peek		heat		snail	
peel		leak		sprain	
peep		lead		stain	
queen		lean		strain	
reed		leap		tail	
reel		least		trail	
screen		meal		train	
see		mean		wail	
seed		meat		waist	
seek		near		wait	

To be able to properly spell these words, your child must first hear the long-vowel and recognize the spelling chunks associated with that sound. Kids who write words like *slep,* in place of *sleep,* more than likely do it because they hear that long-vowel sound but don't know the corresponding spelling chunk that makes the long-vowel sound. To make sure that your child not only the hears the long vowel but also uses the right spelling chunk, run through the "Listening up for long vowels" activity that follows. If she makes mistakes, continue doing this activity for a few days. Preparing a new list of words is easy.

Activity: Listening up for long vowels

Preparation: Make a copy of this list that follows and grab a pen or pencil.

Follow this step: Read the numbered list of words to your child and have her circle (or tell you) which word of each set of three is the two-vowel (or long-vowel) word.

1. kick — cream — cut
2. cheat — chin — chat
3. chop — shop — shoal
4. pain — pant — plant
5. stand — slap — sail
6. seed — send — sell
7. sleep — slip — slim
8. toad — tip — test
9. flick — flat — fleet
10. mast — man — main
11. bent — bead — best
12. road — romp — rest

Sorting Through Long and Short Sounds

After your child begins hearing the vowel sounds, it's time for him to start penning those pairs. Grab a whiteboard or poster paper, some bright-colored markers, and maybe some snacks for the "Four pairs of vowels" activity.

Activity: Four pairs of vowels

Preparation: You not only need your copy of this book (turned to Table 8-1) but also a timer or a watch to time a ten-minute break. You and your child probably should spend at least half an hour on this activity, but you can set your own time limit.

Follow these steps:

1. **Have your child write the four main pairs of vowels — *ee, ea, ai,* and *oa* — across the top of the whiteboard or paper in big bright letters.**

2. **Have your child write five words under each pair of letters so that she has four columns of five words each.**

3. **Have your child turn the paper or whiteboard over and take a ten-minute break.** Be sure to tell your child that you're taking the break to find out whether she can keep those vowel pairs in her memory.

4. **After the break, dictate random words from Table 8-1 for your child to spell on the blank side of the paper or whiteboard.** She can draw four columns again if she wants.

If you prefer, you can dictate the same words that your child already wrote down.

Whenever your child spells words in the course of her normal writing, she flits between long and short vowels (and other sounds). The "Changing between short and long vowels" activity up next mixes long- and short-vowel words so your child gets quicker and more comfortable using the two.

Activity: Changing between short and long vowels

Preparation: Make a copy of the following list of 14 statements.

Follow this step: Have your child find the misspelled word in each statement and then write the correct word. She needs to change short vowels to long vowels and vice versa.

1. Monkeys eet bananas.

2. Plants grow from seds.

3. If I kick you, you fel pain.

4. Orange pel doesn't taste good.

5. Cars drive on rods.

6. On ice, you must watch your steep.

7. Tomatoes are read.

8. You sleep in your bead.

9. Tods are like frogs.

10. A bunch of naval boats is a flet.

11. Flowers have petals and steams.

12. You play soccer on a tem.

13. Water is wheat.

14. I saw the sick lady fant.

Tall, outdoors type

The other day, when I was stuck in traffic, I noticed a big yellow crane standing outside a warehouse that had industrial machinery for hire. On the crane was a large sign. It read, "Tall, outdoors type seeks relationship."

Everyone has relationships. The letters that make a digraph are in a relationship. One letter is the extrovert, the other is the silent type, but it works for them. Tell your child about these vowel relationships. Explain that whenever he sees the two together (*ee, ea, ai,* or *oa*), they're interacting. The first one is the talker (it says its name), and the second one is quiet.

The next "Five up" activity is a nice change, because you need to throw a die to play. Each player must write four- and five-letter words, too, and that means your child probably will write double-vowel words.

Activity: Five up

Preparation: Grab one die and a shaker plus enough pen and paper for every player.

Follow these steps:

1. **Take turns rolling the die.** The first person to roll a one starts play.

2. **To start play, the player writes a one-letter word and rolls again. If the player gets:**

   A two: H writes a two-letter word and rolls the die again.

   A number other that a two: Play shifts to the next player.

   Players try to roll a one; then two; then three; then four; and then five, in order. If a player rolls an unwanted number (like three when a four is needed) play shifts to the next player.

3. **When the play comes back to the first player, he continues where he left off.** On second and subsequent turns, you don't have to start over and roll a one again.

Some important parts of the game: Each new word that a player writes must have at least one letter in it from the previous word. Players who roll sixes get to roll again. The first player to write five words and then roll a six, wins.

Spelling Long Sounds

Throughout this book, I tell you that your child has to hear sounds inside words, jot down possible spellings, and then recognize the right one. In the

"Sounds right; looks wrong," activity that follows, your child must choose the correct spelling from a group of words that all sound out the right way. Some words (like *mane*) are Bossy *e* words. You can flip to Chapter 7 to brush up on the Bossy *e* rule.

Activity: Sounds right; looks wrong

Preparation: Make a copy of the list that follows and have a pen or pencil ready for your child to use.

Follow these steps:

1. **Have your child circle or highlight the right spelling.**

2. **Ask your child (or tell him) what's so special about questions 11 and 12 (each has two correct spellings with different meanings).**

   1. creyp — creep — creap

   2. cheat — cheet — chete

   3. yeer — yere — year

   4. seet — sete — seat

   5. loaf — lofe — lowf

   6. flote — float — flowt

   7. fame — faym — faim

   8. speek — speak — speik

   9. trayl — trail — trale

   10. chain — chane — chaen

   11. mane — main — mayn

   12. lain — lane — layn

ee and ea Words

The sounds of *ee* and *ea* are the same. The best way for your child to get better at choosing the correct spelling is to spell *ee* and *ea* words often. The next "Pairs of vowels" activity asks your child to choose between *ee* and *ea* spellings. If your child isn't sure which to choose, have her write out the two options. If she still isn't sure which is right, tell her the answer and save the word to look at again later.

Activity: Pairs of vowels

Preparation: Make a copy of the list that follows and have pen or pencil ready for your child to use.

Follow these steps:

1. Have your child solve the riddle that follows.

2. Have your child circle the 15 correct spellings in the list that follows the riddle.

3. Have your child tell you why the words from 13 on are special and what each word means.

Riddle:

Q: What's gr_ _n and has two legs and a trunk?

A: A s_ _sick tourist

1. stream — streem

2. screem — scream

3. teach — teech

4. speech — speach

5. weed — wead

6. year — yeer

7. bleach — bleech

8. weep — weap

9. dreem — dream

10. feel — feal

11. green — grean

12. creem — cream

13. beech — beach

14. cheap — cheep

15. real — reel

16. seem — seam

17. steel — steal

18. week — weak

19. read — reed

20. see — sea

Answers: Stream, scream, teach, speech, weed, year, bleach, weep, dream, feel, green, cream, beech and beach (a tree and a seashore), cheap and cheep (inexpensive and a bird noise), real and reel (not fake and a spool of sorts), seem and seam (how something feels and where two pieces of cloth are stitched together) steel and steal (metal and taking without permission), week and weak (seven days and not strong), read and reed (what you do with a book and a hollow grass), and see and sea (what you do with your eyes and a large body of water).

A Mix of Long Sounds

For a finale of two-vowel words, I've put together the "Two-vowel word quiz." Have your child grab a watch or timer and try to answer the questions within five minutes. Tell your child that you're not sure whether the quiz is a bit tricky for him, but maybe he'd like to give it a try just the same.

Your child enjoys a little competition. If you talk up the task, he can feel especially proud when he succeeds at it.

Activity: Two-vowel word quiz

Preparation: Grab some paper, a pen, and make a copy of the questions that follow.

Follow this step: Leave your child to it! The only instruction is that your child needs to answer these riddles by writing write single-word answers.

1. Begins with the same four letters as *please*. Means to beg.

2. An animal. Rhymes with coat.

3. This is in your skull. It controls all that you do.

4. The letters and flyers that are delivered to you.

5. A small stream. Starts with the third letter in the alphabet.

6. You do this in your sleep. Starts with the same letter as *dog*.

7. You sail in this. Rhymes with *oat*.

8. This animal moves *very* slowly.

9. This kind of vehicle runs on tracks.

10. A juicy fruit. Rhymes with *teach*.

Answers: Plead, goat, brain, mail, creek, dream, boat, snail, train, and peach.

Whew! Time for some comic relief. Tell your child this joke and be sure to cajole him into saying that it's *very* funny. (My kids are *so* ungracious about my roaringly funny jokes!):

> While out shopping, a tortoise has her bag stolen by a snail. A police officer asks her whether she saw the assailant. "Sorry." she says, "It all happened so fast!"

Copy-Cat Vowels

Some spelling chunks are simple. They always look and sound the same. Others take a bit more getting to know. After your child grows completely comfortable with the *ee, ea, ai* and *oa* spelling chunks, you can show her spellings that either look the same as those chunks but sound different or sound the same as those chunks but look different. After you get going, you'll see that it isn't as hard as it sounds (or looks).

When I talk about spelling chunks or spelling units, I'm talking about the spelling bits that make up words. They can be syllables (like the two syllables in *al-most*) or blends (like the *str* in <u>*str*</u>*ong*) or digraphs (like *ee, ea, ai,* and *oa*).

i before e

The three most common ways for your child to spell the *ee* sounds are

- ✔ *ee* as in: cheer, heel, weed, peer, sneer, sheer, seem, feet, and seed.

- ✔ *ea* as in: hear, teach, fear, team, year, dear, weak, clear, near, read, plead, and stream.

- ✔ *e_e* (read *e* blank *e*) as in: here, severe, adhere, hemisphere, interfere, mere, sphere, sincere, these, atmosphere, stratosphere, scene, and Pete. (I talk about this Bossy *e* spelling in Chapter 7.)

In words like *please, breeze,* and *cheese,* your child uses the *ea* or *ee,* and *e_e* spellings.

Spellings like *meet* and *meat* use the when-two-vowels-go-walking-the-first-one-does-the-talking rule, and spellings like *Pete* use the Bossy-*e* rule. A fourth way for your child to spell the same sound is with *ie,* remembered with the rhythm; "*i* before *e* except after *c.*" Table 8-2 gives you heaps of *ie* words. Have your child *piece* them together, *believe* in them, and *shriek* if he likes. Next up I give you the "Spelling buddies activity," a simple looking-and-writing activity that goes with Table 8-2 so your child can take a careful look at how the words are pieced together.

Table 8-2		*ie* Words
believe	shriek	shield
frontier	chief	relieve
pierce	grief	niece
piece	cashier	thief
relief	field	diesel
siege	pier	brief
belief	wield	yield
achieve	retrieve	friend

A spelling mnemonic, or memory jogger, that kids like to use for *friend* is "A *friend* stays to the *end*."

Activity: Spelling buddies

Preparation: Open your copy of *Teaching Kids to Spell For Dummies* to Table 8-2, and have a pen and piece of paper ready for both you and your child.

Follow these steps:

1. **Together with your child, write out the words from Table 8-2.**

2. **Point out the features of each word so your child remembers them better.**

   Let your child do the talking but add your five cents worth whenever you see something that she misses. Here's how your dialogue may go for *piece* and *diesel*.

   - **For piece:** "Here's the *ie* part, and *ce* goes on the end to make the *s* sound."

   - **For diesel:** "There's an *s* in this word to make the *z* sound. The ending is "*el*" (not *al* or *le*)."

With "diesel" the *s* can make either a *z* or an *s* sound depending on your dialect.

Except after c

The words in Table 8-2 use the *i*-before-*e*-except-after-*c* rule. You probably learned this rule when you were a kid and still use it today. Table 8-3 shows words that make use of this really useful rule, but happen to fall under the except-after-*c* part of the rule. Do the "Spelling buddies" activity, using the Table 8-3 words and then dictate a few for your child to spell. Repeat the same routine with all the tables in this chapter and take a lot of fun breaks. The nearby "Moving, throwing, and banging" sidebar isn't a bunch of house-moving horror stories, but it is a description of neat games you can easily fit in between your spelling sessions.

Table 8-3	*i* Before *e* Except After *c*	
receive	ceiling	receipt
deceit	conceive	conceit
deceive		

Words that follow the when-two-vowels-go-walking rule rather than the *i*-before-*e* rule are *tie, pie, lie,* and *die*. All have the long-*i* sound (that you expect with the when-two-vowels-go-walking rule), rather than the long-*e* sound that you hear in words that adhere to the *i*-before-*e*-except-after-*c* rule.

Eight neighbors

After your coming to grips with the *i*-before-*e*-except-after-*c* rhyme and cadence and how it works, you'll want to show your child a last addition to the rhyme:

i before *e* except after *c*, except when you hear "*ay*" like in *neighbor*

The part about when you hear long-*a* helps your child spell words like *eight*, weigh, and *neighbor*. Table 8-4 gives you these *ay*-sounding words.

Table 8-4	Words like *Neighbor* and *Eight*	
neighbor	eight	reins
reign	vein	weigh

weight	freight	beige
sleigh		

e before i

Earlier in this chapter, I said that I'd introduce you to some words that take a bit of getting to know. Well here's the pick of the bunch. Table 8-5 gives you a group of words that has the *ee* sound spelled as *ei*. It reverses the usual *i*-before-*e* rule. Your child must watch out for this *weird* bunch of words so have him read through Table 8-5 and home in on the vowels.

Table 8-5		*ei* Words
seize	weird	neither
either	*leisure*	*caffeine*

A handful of words have their own unique sound for *ei* and *ie*. The group that you're on your guard for here is: *foreign, their, forfeit, soldier, height,* and *view.*

Oh my gosh, these *e*'s and *i*'s can get confusing! I've given you the rules (and the words that are outcasts from the rules!), because they're handy to know. But remember that it's easier just to forget the rules and simply give your child plenty of practice at writing out the words. Writing out words more often enables your child to get better at jotting down his options (is it *soldier* or *soldeir*?) and spotting the right one.

If your child is grappling with whether to write *ie* or *ei,* his best bet is to opt for *ie,* because it's more common.

These games give your child a physical and mental break between bouts of spelling. You can do any activity to give your child that break, but don't forget to do something. Your child's attention span for serious concentration is only about 20 minutes (and yours is just about the same).

Dreadful bread

You're past the tricky part! The next words that I give to you won't require any cerebral gymnastics, and none of these words are isolated words either, so that makes the going much easier. Your child gets to spell word families, and that's always a plus for helping her remember the spellings.

Moving, throwing, and banging

When my kids were little, I read them stories by Enid Blyton. One of the stories featured a fearsome character called Dame Slap-A-Lot. You can guess what Dame Slap-A-Lot did to kids who didn't use their manners or show her respect. After that story, I often chased my kids around the house slapping my hands together menacingly and declaring myself to be Dame Slap-A-Lot. I miss Dame Slap-A-Lot. Anyway, you may be wondering where the activities have gone and why I'm waxing nostalgic about Dame Slap-A-Lot. The thing is, I don't give you a lot of spelling activities in this chapter, because the best way you can help your child remember these fairly hard spellings is to have him look closely at them and write them down several times. That's the number one thing to do, and dictating ten words for your child to spell every night is a great idea, too. But where's the fun in that (and there's *still* no explanation for Dame Slap-A-Lot)? Ah ha. I don't give you a lot of spelling activities in this chapter, but I *do* provide you with games you can play with your child between bouts of spelling. And I get around to Dame-Slap-A-Lot right now: Here are two games that will cast you in the role of Dame Play-A-Lot, who is much more socially acceptable, but not half as much fun, as good old Dame Slap-A-Lot. Don't forget to include game breaks, because they can make the difference between your child persevering with spelling exercises, or not.

Beanbag toss

You can set up this throwing game at a moment's notice. Use a cardboard box as the receptacle for your tosses and set a starting line for each participant. Throw objects into the box and see who gets the biggest number of hits. Play three rounds, throwing things like coins, plastic eggs (left over from Easter), or socks stuffed with rice. If you want to get really fancy, you can buy actual beanbags (or use beans in place of rice). If this game sounds pedestrian, wait until you're evenly matched with your child! You'll get revved up and demand any number of bonus rounds and replays. It depends on how poor of a sport you are.

Bang!

An easy clapping game that girls in particular love, Bang is a game I play with my daughters to fill times when we have to wait someplace. We usually end up showing other entranced girls how to play. Standing and facing each other, each player claps four claps at the same time to begin. Now (together) do two quick claps (these two immediately follow your initial four claps, making a total of six beginning claps) and then choose from one of these hand actions (similar to the game "Paper, rock, scissors").

- ✔ Point both thumbs up
- ✔ Point both thumbs down
- ✔ Point both thumbs to your left
- ✔ Point both thumbs to your right

If you each chose a different action, keep going with two claps and then an action. Whenever both players choose the same action, point your forefingers at your opponent and shout, "Bang!" like a gun. You're trying to be quickest on the draw, the first to shout "Bang!" Keep going and get faster!

This word family uses the *ea* spelling chunk to make the short-*e* sound (like in *bed*). Some common words in this bunch are dead, head, and bread. Table 8-6 shows the rest of the family.

It just so happens that in this bunch of words are a few *homographs* — words that have two meanings for the same spelling. *Read* is a homograph (you can have "I will read" or "I read it yesterday") and so is *lead* (you can have the kind that's heavy and the lead-role-in-a-play kind). Oh, and *breath* is a word that isn't to be confused with *breathe* and *weather* isn't the same thing as *whether or wether* — *baah!* Did I say there'd be no cerebral gymnastics involved with this table? Maybe I should've allowed for the odd somersault!

Table 8-6	*ea* Words, like in *Head*	
bread	head	lead
read	dead	thread
dread	dreadful	ahead
instead	forehead	breath
death	feather	weather
heather	leather	meant
leant	health	wealth
stealth	jealous	zealous
endeavor	realm	breakfast

Chairs and stairs

You and your child cruised through words like *raid, maid,* and *sail* earlier in this chapter. Now it's time to take your child through the *air* family of words. Although this family shares the *ai* spelling chunk with the when-two-vowels-go-walking words, on closer inspection, you don't just have *ai* but rather the complete word *air.* Table 8-7 shows you the ever-so-easy *air* family

Table 8-7	*air* Words	
air	hair	stair
pair	fair	chair
repair	despair	affair

(continued)

Table 8-7 *(continued)*

flair	aircraft	aircrew
airfield	airline	airstrip
airport	airway	airtight
airman		

Scared of bears

When your child wants to write *air,* he probably jots it down with ease. Many words have *air* in them, so he's familiar with that spelling. However, you can spell the same sound in other ways. The most common alternative to *air* is *are.* Table 8-8 gives you some *are* words, and after that, I show you two more options, *ear,* like in *bear,* and *aer,* like in *aerosol.*

Table 8-8	**Words like *Square* and *Bare***	
dare	rare	bare
share	stare	glare
spare	scare	square
snare	beware	aware
declare	care	prepare
compare	mare	hare
fare	flare	scare
blare	ware	beware

The little group of words like *bear* is in Table 8-9.

Table 8-9	**Words like *Bear***	
pear	bear	tear
wear	swear	

And the *aer* bunch is in Table 8-10.

Table 8-10	*aer* Words	
aerosol	aerobatics	aerodynamics
aeronautical	aerodrome	aeronautics
aerated	aerial	aerialist

Teachers have things to smile about

You're nearly halfway through this book. You've spelled many words with your child, and you've put many activities under both of your belts. You're doing a good job. You deserve some teacher perks. Now what in the world can I give you in this simple book that qualifies as a teacher perk? Read the rest of this sidebar and you'll see. One benefit of teaching is that kids give you plenty of stuff to smile about.

Kids' Letters to God:

Dear God...

On Halloween I am going to wear a devil's costume, is that all right with you?

Is it true my father won't get into Heaven if he uses his bowling words in the house?

Did they really talk that fancy in Bible times?

Is Reverend Coe a friend of yours or do you just know him through the business?

I know all about where babies come from. I think. From inside mommies, and daddies put them there. Where are they before that? Do you have them in Heaven? How do they get down here? Do you have to take care of them all first? Please answer all my questions. I always think of you.

Please put another holiday between Christmas and Easter. There is nothing good in there now.

Why is Sunday school on Sunday? I thought it was supposed to be our day of rest.

I keep waiting for spring but it never comes yet. Please don't forget.

If you watch in church on Sunday, I will show you my new shoes.

We read Thomas Edison made light. But in Sunday school, they said you did it. So, I bet he stole your idea.

Thanks to Kevin at `www.emmitsburg.net/ humor/index_list/kids_index.htm.`

Chapter 9

Writing *y* Instead of *a, e,* or *i*

. . . .

In This Chapter

▶ Introducing the other uses of *y*

▶ Understanding when to use *y*

▶ Practicing words like *may, misty, my,* and *mystery*

. . . .

Without a shopping list, I may as well not go to the grocery store. Without one, there's simply no way that I'll manage to take back the library books en route, have my coffee in hand *and* my sunglasses propped on my head, mail my letters, pay my bills (at the ATM) and *still* remember to pick up whatever it was that prompted me to set off in the first place. Your child, however, isn't so memory challenged (or busy!). The very idea of telling her about the many faces of *y* may tire *you,* but she'll get the hang of it in a flash and have energy left over. She'll spell words like *cylinder* and *mystery* in no time at all (and still remember to sneak ten feet of bubble gum into your shopping cart and argue about who steers).

Getting Used to the Different Sounds of *y*

People call *y* things like the "other vowel," the "pretend vowel," and the "almost vowel." When your child spells words like *yellow* and *yam,* he hears the straightforward *y* sound that he learned when he was first introduced to letters. When he spells words like *play, happy, cry,* and *system,* things are a bit different; he hears a vowel sound but writes a *y.* This chapter leads you through the four "other vowel" uses of *y.*

Hearing It; Spelling It

Hear it; spell it. That's what spelling's basically all about. Your child hears a word in her head, breaks it into chunks of sound, and if she's lucky, remembers exactly how to write those chunks of sound. Mostly she tries out a few ways before she gets it right. Some chunks are easy. She only ever writes the *ch* sound as *ch*, she only ever writes the "*tuh*" sound as *t*, and with blends like *str* and *cl*, what she hears is what she gets. Other chunks are more difficult.

Vowel sounds are always tricky, Your child can write the same vowel sound in a few different ways. The way that I talk about in this chapter is the *y* way. When your child hears the long-*a* sound in words like *play*, she spells it as *ay*; when she hears long-*e* on the end of a word like *silly*, she spells it with a *y*; when she hears a long-*i* sound on the end of a small word like *by*, she spells it with a *y*. and when she hears a short-*i* sound in the middle of a word like *system*, she uses a *y* there, too.

y Sounding Like Long a (day, say, and play)

The "*ay*" family is a cinch. Your child sees *ay* words all the time, and the sound-to-spelling step is a straightforward one. He'll whiz quickly through the words in Table 9-1. Have him read the words to you, dictate a few for him to spell, and then zip ahead to Table 9-2.

Table 9-1	*ay* Words	
bay	day	Fay
gay	hay	Jay
Kay	lay	may
pay	ray	say
way	play	stay
tray	clay	pray

y Sounding Like Long e (happy, funny, and silly)

Okay, it's this simple: When your child hears "*ee*" on the end of words of two syllables or more, she jots down a *y*. The *y* makes the "*ee*" sound. In Table 9-2, I give phonetically regular words for your child to warm up on. Have her cast her eyes over them and then move forward with the activities that follow.

Phonetically regular words are words that your child spells just the way they sound. He doesn't have to play with spelling options, because what he hears is what he gets. All the words in Table 9-2 have simple short-vowel sounds, and the only spelling feature that deviates from the rule is double consonants (in words like *bunny* and *cherry*).

Table 9-2	Easy Words That End with *y*	
berry	body	bumpy
bunny	cherry	chilly
copy	dizzy	empty
entry	family	funny
granny	happy	holly
hurry	jolly	lanky
lumpy	marry	merry
milky	nanny	plenty
silly	skinny	sloppy
sorry	spotty	sunny
ugly	very	windy

Activity: *y*-at-the-end quiz

Preparation: You need this book open to Table 9-2 and paper and pencil.

Follow this step: Read the clues to your child. Have her find the answers from the table and write them out.

1. Two words that mean happy *(Answer: happy and merry)*
2. Thin *(Answer: skinny)*
3. Not smooth *(Answer: lumpy or bumpy)*
4. Three words to do with the weather *(Answer: chilly, sunny and windy)*
5. Opposite of full *(Answer: empty)*
6. Apologetic *(Answer: sorry)*
7. Where you go in *(Answer: entry)*
8. Unattractive *(Answer: ugly)*
9. What the bride and groom do *(Answer: marry)*
10. You can eat this *(Answer: berry)*

Activity: Half and half

Preparation: Have a copy of Table 9-2 and paper and pencil.

Follow these steps (suggested dialog is in quotations):

1. **Give your child these instructions: "Find all the words that have a double letter."**

2. **Say, "Draw a line down between the double letters so that you split each word into two parts."**

3. **Say, "Give me your sheet so I can read you the first part of each word. See if you can write the whole words from hearing just the first parts."**

If all words were made of regular short-vowel sounds, spelling would be a pretty dull business (and this would be a slim book). But spelling takes some strategizing. When your child spells, he'll have stretched-out sounds to figure out and, at times, some downright strange spellings to get comfortable with. Table 9-3 leads your child through words that have *y* on the end and tricky (but not too tricky) spelling features. I've underlined the spelling chunks that your child needs to watch out for. Have him read through the words, checking out the underlined parts, and then move on to the activity.

Table 9-3	More Words That End with *y*	
b<u>a</u>by	cl<u>ou</u>dy	cr<u>a</u>zy
cr<u>ee</u>py	d<u>ir</u>ty	en<u>e</u>my
fan<u>c</u>y	l<u>a</u>dy	m<u>a</u>ny
nasty	p<u>ar</u>ty	p<u>o</u>ny
pr<u>e</u>tty	prop<u>er</u>ty	thi<u>rs</u>ty
t<u>i</u>ny	w<u>ea</u>ry	w<u>o</u>rry

Activity: Sorting sounds into groups

Preparation: Open *Teaching Kids to Spell For Dummies* to Table 9-3.

Follow these steps:

1. **Ask your child to read through the words and look at the underlined parts.**

2. **Have her write groups of words in the groups I give, looking at the numbers in parenthesis to see exactly how many words to find.** Do this activity as a partnership so you make sure that your child succeeds. The groups include

- Long-*a* sound (3) *(Answer: baby, lady, crazy)*
- Long-*e* sound (2) *(Answer: creepy, weary)*
- Long-*i* sound (1) *(Answer: tiny)*
- Long-*o* sound (1) *(Answer: pony)*
- *ar* words (1) *(Answer: party)*
- *ir* and *er* words (3) *(Answer: dirty, property, thirsty)*
- *ou* words (1) *(Answer: cloudy)*
- *cy* words (1) *(Answer: fancy)*
- Leftover easy words (1) *(Answer: nasty)*
- Leftover hard words (4) *(Answer: pretty, enemy, many, worry)*

For the last two questions your child makes his own decision as to which word is easy and which four words are hard. It's fine to arrive at different answers to the ones I give.

Many of the words that your child finishes off with a *y* have the *-try* or *-ly* spelling chunks (endings). Table 9-4 gives you a bunch of challenging *-try* and *-ly* words. Look over the words, and then take your child through the two activities that follow. The first one is a look-and-spell drill, the second, because you both deserve it, is pure fun.

Table 9-4	*-try* and *-ly* Words		
Words Ending with -try	*Words Ending with -ly*		
c<u>o</u>untry	*boldly*	gr<u>a</u>vely	shapely
entry	bravely	h<u>a</u>stily	simply
gently	br<u>ee</u>zily	helpfully	sin<u>c</u>erely
gh<u>o</u>stly	cl<u>e</u>arly	hugely	stran<u>g</u>ely
hotly	dangerously	lamely	t<u>i</u>mely
industry	ea<u>s</u>ily	mildly	tr<u>u</u>thfully
pantry	fan<u>c</u>ily	ni<u>c</u>ely	w<u>i</u>dely
p<u>ou</u>ltry	g<u>e</u>nerally	pl<u>a</u>inly	wildly
puppetry	gra<u>c</u>efully	r<u>ea</u>lly	wi<u>s</u>ely
sentry			
tapestry			
wintry			

It's okay for your child to add *-ly* onto words that already end with *l* (like *general*) and hence have a word that has two *l*'s (*generally*). Words that end with *-ful* are the same. Although *full* gets shortened to *-ful* on the ends of words like graceful and helpful, your child uses two *l*'s again in words like gracefully and helpfully. Okay?

Activity: See it, say it, spell it

Preparation: Open this book to Table 9-4 and have paper and pen ready.

Follow these steps:

1. **Take a look at Table 9-4 together, noting the underlined spelling features (the underline means something tricky is going on).** If he wants to, have your child say the words out loud and comment on the spelling.

2. **Have him jot down any words he thinks are especially prickly.**

3. **Have him write a column of numbers from 1 to 20.** Dictate random spellings. If he spells word one correctly, he crosses off number two (because he won that space). Dictate a random spelling for number 3.

4. **Have your child keep crossing off bonus numbers for correct spelling, but he must add a number to his list for incorrect spellings.** If he makes no spelling errors, he ends up having spelled ten words.

The next activity is one of my favorites. It's fun, and if you have other kids wandering by, they'll want to offer their spelling suggestions. Your child spells words to get points, and because long words earn her more points, she'll want to collaborate and brainstorm with you or with siblings or friends to spell words like *constitutional*. Players compete for points, but even so, you play this game just for the happy interaction.

Activity: Toothpicks

In this activity, I ask you and your child to shake toothpicks (or golf tees) in a paper bag. Shake them well so that they lay flat; otherwise, you can end up with a pricked finger or even a splinter. Ouch!

Preparation: You need a package of colored toothpicks (or cocktail sticks) and a brown lunch bag. On plain paper write "Toothpicks." Have pen and paper for each player.

Follow these steps:

1. **In the bag put ten yellow, ten blue, and five red toothpicks.**

2. **Take turns picking a toothpick without looking in the bag as your opponent holds the bag, and vice versa.**

- If you choose a yellow toothpick, you score nothing, and it's your opponent's turn.

- If you choose a blue toothpick, you write a word beginning with the first t in "toothpick." Each time you get to write a word, you go through the letters in "toothpick" in order crossing each letter off after it's been used. You score points for your word, according to the number of letters in the word (five letters equals five points) you write.

- If you choose a red toothpick you score five points (and don't have to write anything) and play goes to your opponent.

3. **Continue taking toothpicks and spelling the longest words you can, until all the toothpicks are gone or all the blue and red toothpicks are used.**

Highest score wins.

This game doesn't have to be called "Toothpicks." Use any word that you want, but make sure that you have the same number of blue toothpicks as the number of letters in your chosen word. If you have marbles or buttons or other items that can be used rather than toothpicks, simply make the game fit your resources. Oh and by the way you can choose your own colors (in case you think it's unfair that I left out all the green toothpicks). You can also use markers on plain wood toothpicks.

Activity: Coffee for the jockey and me

Preparation: Open this book to Table 9-5.

Follow this step: Did you spot it? Three "ee" sounds are in the name of this activity, and not one of them is spelled with just *y*. You may think that you had the whole "*ee*" thing covered by now. Well you have, almost. Your child spells the ending "*ee*" sound with a *y* most of the time. But sometimes she uses *e, ee,* or *ey*. Table 9-5 gives you a few examples to run through so your child remains unruffled when dealing with *trees* or *turkeys* or any other "*ee*" sound at the end of words where *y* isn't featured. When you're ready, have your child try to spot and circle the correct spellings in this list.

1. agre — agree — agrey

2. mone — monee — money

3. coffe — coffee — coffey

4. me — mee — mey

5. se — see — sey

6. refere — referee — referey

7. hocke — hockee — hockey

8. fre — free — frey

9. journe — jouirnee — journey

10. hone — honee — honey

Table 9-5	Spelling the End "*ee*" Sound with *e, ee,* or *ey*	
Spelling "ee" with e	*Spelling "ee" with ee*	*Spelling "ee" with ey*
me	tree	key
he	bee	turkey
she	see	money
we	free	monkey
be	agree	jockey
	knee	donkey
	coffee	valley
	referee	hockey
	refugee	barley
	amputee	honey
	employee	chimney
	absentee	journey

y Sounding Like Long *i* (*my, by, and cry*)

This spelling rule is just about as easy as it gets. Your child hears words like *my, by,* and *cry* and spells the long-*i* part on the end with a *y*. The only thing he really has to think about is whether he's dealing with a *y* spelling or another way of spelling that sound, as in the words *sigh* and *lie*. Table 9-6 shows short words like *my*, Table 9-7 has longer words like *supply*, and to give your child a challenge, Table 9-8 shows tricky words like *cycle* in which *y* fits in the middle. Look over the tables with your child, and then scoot to the activity that follows each one.

Table 9-6	_y_ on the End of Short Words	
by	cry	dry
fly	fry	my
pry	shy	sky
sly	spry	sty
try	why	

The words in Table 9-6 are pretty easy. After your child reads them to you, you may simply want to dictate a few for her to spell. Alternatively, you may want to stretch your legs. You can play the License plates game by grabbing a notepad and pen (and by the way, your child) and walking or driving slowly around the block. If you drive, you need to take at least two kids with you, because it isn't safe for you to drive _and_ play at the same time. Okay?

Activity: License plates

Preparation: You need a notepad and pencil for each player.

Follow these steps:

1. **On the notepads, draw spaces for ten three-letter words.**

2. **For each word, draw three squares, one for each letter of the word you're going to write there.**

3. **Each player fills in three end squares with a _y_ so that she has to write a word ending with _y_ there.**

4. **Players take turns calling out three letters from a license plate.**

5. **Each player writes all three letters in any space on her pad and then tries to make words.**

The first player to make five words wins, or the player with the most words when the pads are filled wins. It's your choice.

You can adapt License Plates in a few ways:

✔ Play without filling in the _y_'s.

✔ Make your words four- or five-letters long so your child must spell blends and long-vowel sounds.

✔ Fill in other letters before you start, like _ee_ or _ea_.

✔ If the license plates in your state use mostly numbers give your child free letters or whole endings like *ean, eat, ey,* and *ash* that he can add onto with the few letters that he spots.

After your child gets the idea of words like *my, shy,* and *cry,* longer words with the same long-*i* endings don't seem so weird. Have her read through the words in Table 9-7 and take down a mental (or paper) note of the harder words. My choice of hard words includes *qualify, unify,* and *beautify,* but your child may have others in mind. When she's ready for you to run some words past her, head to the "Finishing words" activity.

Table 9-7	*y* on the End of Long Words	
multiply	reply	supply
occupy	qualify	magnify
unify	classify	horrify
purify	justify	notify
beautify	glorify	deny

Activity: Finishing words

Preparation: Open *Teaching Kids To Spell For Dummies* to Table 9-7 and have pen and paper ready.

Follow these steps:

1. **Spell the first part of each word to your child.**

2. **Have her guess what the word is and finish spelling it.**

Give clues if you need to, but if the odd word's too hard to guess, simply tell your child that word so she can get on with the spelling.

In Chapter 16, I talk about adding endings like *-er* and *-ing* to words, but you may want a quick preview about words that end with *y.* When your child adds endings to words that end with *y,* this spelling rule can help her. She changes *y* to *i* when adding any ending, except *-ing.* You can see this rule at work in words like occupied, occupies, and occupying

In Table 9-8, I give you some pretty tricky words. The best thing for your child to do with long or scary-looking words is to break them into manageable pieces. I talk about breaking words into syllables in Chapter 15, but for now you just need to help your child chop up the words in Table 9-8 and highlight the *y* masquerading as *i*. The "Marking up words" activity takes you and your child step by step through this marking and chopping-up process.

Table 9-8	*y* in the Middle	
cycle	style	rhyme
hype	nylon	type
pylon	cyclone	hyena
hydrant	dynamic	dynamite
cyclist	asylum	hydraulic
tyrant	typhoon	psychology
python	hydrogen	hygiene
paralyze		

Activity: Marking up words

Preparation: Make a copy of Table 9-8, and be ready with highlighter pens.

Follow these steps:

1. **Ask your child to highlight the *y* that's making the long-*i* sound in each word.**

2. **Ask him to break every word into parts, or syllables, putting the breaks where he thinks they need to go.**

3. **Ask him to underline, circle, or mark (with a new color), any special spelling features, such as the soft *g* and *ie* in *hygiene* or the silent *p* in *psychology*.** Some words have many marks on them, because they're hard.

4. **Have your child grade (or number) the five hardest words, from one to five, with one being the hardest word.** Can he spell them all back to you without looking at the table again?

When your child identifies hard bits inside a word, it helps her recall the whole spelling later. Anytime she comes across tricky words, help her break them up and mark the hard bits (it's fun to call them "putrid parts" or "barfy bits," or any other vile term that helps your child remember).

y Sounding Like Short i (Mystery and System)

Here's the last vowel sound that your child will write with a *y* — short *i*. In words like *crypt* and *cylinder*, and in plenty more words, too, she'll jot down a conspicuous *y*. To get friendly with this kind of word, she needs to get into a marking and chopping-up mode. If she examines each word in Table 9-9, breaks it up, and then jots it down again, she soon gains a feel for smooth-flowing spelling. Help her mark and chop the words, and then dictate a few of them for her to write from scratch. After all that, present your child with the quiz that I give you next.

Table 9-9	Words Like *Mystery* and *System*	
crypt	cryptic	cylinder
cymbal	crystal	cyst
dyslexia	gymnastics	gypsy
hymn	hypnotic	lymph
lynch	mystery	myth
Olympic	oxygen	pygmy
symbol	sympathy	syrup
system	typical	tyranny

Activity: y Quiz

Preparation: Use the words in Table 9-9, a pen, and paper for this activity.

Follow this step: Read these questions and statements out loud to your child, and have her write her answers.

1. Write a word that begins with *hyp*. *(Answer: hypnotic)*

2. Something that you breathe in begins with *o*. *(Answer: oxygen)*

3. Begins with *o*, the name of the international games competition that takes place every four years. *(Answer: Olympics)*

4. Begins with *mys*, it's a kind of puzzling story. *(Answer: mystery)*

5. A sport that begins with *gym*. *(Answer: gymnastics)*

6. Pour this on your pancakes. Begins with *sy*. *(Answer: syrup)*

7. A kind of tomb or grave. Begins with *cr*. *(Answer: crypt)*

8. A kind of clear, expensive glass. Begins with *cr*. *(Answer: crystal)*

9. If you are sorry for someone, you have *sym*. *(Answer: sympathy)*

10. Average, usual, normal. Begins with *typ*. *(Answer: typical)*

Shiny and pricey

Strange things happen with the spell-checker on my computer, especially when I type in words like "shiney" and "shiny" and "pricey" and "pricy." I'm allowed to keep both "pricey" and "pricy," they're both acceptable spellings, but I can't have "shiney." Hmm. How about "lacey" and "lacy"? My computer hasn't shown me a red squiggly line, so I can keep both of them. How then should you give your child the scoop on spelling words like shiny, pricey and pricy, and lacey and lacy? Tell him two things:

1. When you add a *y* ending to a word that ends with *e* (*shine*, for example), drop the *e* and you'll most likely be right — in other words, shiny. You can spell some words either way (pricey pricy; boney bony; nosey nosy; and whiney whiny) but the *y*-only way (not the *ey* way) is the most common.

2. Whenever you're not sure of a spelling, any spelling, try out your options. Write down the possibilities and go for the one that looks best. (Or, type it and use your spell-checker or better still a (much more reliable) dictionary!).

The following table shows a bunch of words that your child just chops the e off of and adds *y* onto to make nice adjectives (describing words).

bone	flake	grime
haze	nose	shade
shake	shine	snake
stripe	wave	whine

Part IV
Using Word Families

The 5th Wave   By Rich Tennant

"That's why spelling well is important. Kyle launched a search for 'fertilizing practices', but mistakenly typed in 'fertility practices'."

In this part . . .

Don't you just hate spelling books that give lofty, long-winded accounts of a few hundred rules and a few (hundred) more exceptions? They talk about things like "unaccented sounds" and advise you to do all kinds of nasal gymnastics. Well, if you've ever felt suffocated by that sort of stuff, here's a breath of fresh air. This part of *Teaching Your Kids to Spell For Dummies* tells you all about word families and sight words and silent and soft letters in simple terms. I explain everything in down-to-earth, practical tones and give you so many tips and words to spell that your child need never, or almost never, go wrong.

Chapter 10

Getting Into Word Family Mode

In This Chapter

▶ Inspecting the spelling chunks inside words

▶ Finding word families

▶ Getting to know the easiest word families

▶ Introducing "schwa"

1 just spent my first winter in a place that gets plenty of snow. I did pretty well with boots and gloves and gravel and salt but had a shaky start with clearing snow from my front path. In fact, it was my husband's fault. He had the bright idea that we could buy a garden shovel for use with both winter snow and summer soil and hence save a hefty five or so dollars on a proper snow shovel (only wimps need them anyway). Each morning I shoveled. When I could barely lift my arms and needed help turning my head, I bought a snow shovel. The spelling information that I provide in this chapter is like I'm handing you a snow shovel (readers in hot climates may need to visualize). I introduce you to the idea of teaching your child not one word at a time (that's the garden shovel way) but whole families (ta-da; the snow shovel!).

Looking at What's in a Word

Your child must hear words in his mind, and then write them in chunks of sound to be able to spell words. The more practice he gets at writing chunks of sound, the better he gets at spelling. After he can spell *bank*, for example, he can easily spell *thank, sank,* and *drank*. These words form the *ank* word family.

When spellings don't match sounds in the usual way (like in the word *who* — which you'd expect to be "*hoo*"), your child has to recall the visual pattern of the word. He has to say the word in his mind, recall that it's spelled in a strange way, and then jot down his options. After all that, his visual memory must kick in so that he recognizes the correct spelling from the possibilities that he thinks about. I talk more about unusual words like *who* in Chapter 12.

Introducing Word Families

Word families are groups of similar words. Each word in the family has the same chunk of sound in it, spelled the same way. When your child is comfortable with word families, she builds a bigger repertoire of spellings than she'd otherwise have if she tried to remember every isolated individual spelling.

There are an awful lot of word families. Words like *at, bat,* and *cat* are part of a family and so are words like *pretentious, infectious,* and *conscientious!* This chapter gets you and your child started on the easier families, the ones that are spelled in a phonetically regular way (meaning they sound out easily) with short vowel sounds.

The spelling chunks (like at, ank and ick) that I introduce you to in this chapter have a technical name. They're called *phonograms.* Many books give you word lists of phonograms, and to convince you of how common the phonograms are, they offer impressive statistics. They tell you things like 20 phonograms appear in a zillion cool words.

Getting Friendly with Simple Families

The tables in this chapter are chock-full of straightforward, one-syllable words, but here and there you come across a soft or silent letter. You can flip to Chapter 14 to brush up on soft letters, and Chapter 13 gives you the lowdown on silent letters. You see blends like *sn* and *spl* here too and the consonant *digraphs* (two letters making one new sound) *ch, sh,* and *wh.* To delve deeper into blends you can turn to Chapter 5 and for more on consonant digraphs you can skip to Chapter 6.

Exploring what's with *wh*

Every time I call *wh* a consonant digraph, I flinch. You see, most spelling books call *wh* a digraph, so I feel obliged to let you to know that. But (and this is a fairly big but), I personally don't think that *wh* counts as a digraph at all. A digraph is a new sound made by two letters, like *ch, sh,* and *th.* I simply don't believe that *anyone* (except perhaps flaky time travelers who lurch into the present from ye olde tymes without first having swatted-up on the local tongue) says *wh* any differently than they say *w.* That being so, it's my contention that *wh* just doesn't cut it as a digraph. I hope that I haven't completely confused, not to mention bored you with this sidebar, but the *wh* digraph thing grates with me. I'm quite done now, though, it's out and I can get on with my life again.

Wondering about words of Winkdom?

On my gosh! How much fun can one person stand? I just discovered the North American Tiddlywinks Association. I'm in a happy daze. Were you aware that in the United Kingdom there is an English Tiddlywinks Association *and* a tiddlywinks society at each of the la-di-da universities, Oxford and Cambridge? Hmm, I bet you weren't. Neither was I. But now I am and what's more, I've learned some words that I'm ranking way up there among my absolute favorites. Who, for heavens sake, wouldn't fall in love with tiddlywinks terms like squidger, squopping, and boondocking? Do yourself a favor and log on to the Internet at home or race to the library and kick off any users whose intentions are less serious than your own (being polite about it, of course), and go to www.tiddlywinks.org.

Ball and Jacks

You need to buy the stuff for this game but it costs hardly anything. Avid players tell me that metal jacks are best. Jacks are little three dimensional stars, and the ball is a little one that fits easily into your hand. To play, you throw the jacks on to the playing surface; then bounce the ball, and before catching it, pick up the jacks. True of all these games, you have to spend quite a bit of time getting familiar with the moves before you gain an affection or knack for playing it.

Marbles

Marbles can be played in a few different ways. The best way to get started is probably to ask a dad or granddad to demonstrate. If neither is available, nor ever got recruited into the marble mob as a kid, you can get information from the Web site mentioned in the introduction to this sidebar.

Chinese jump-rope

This game is easy to set up but tricky to explain. You need three players. Two of them serve simply as human stands whose job is to stand facing each other with their legs at hip's width apart and a loop of elastic stretched around them both at their ankles. The third player jumps on and off the elastic, doing tricks of increasing difficulty. When the jumper makes a mistake, she takes over from one of the stands. Entire books have been written about this game, but you can get plenty of ideas from the Games Kids Play Web site.

Hula-Hoop

A girl in my daughter's class can hula hoop for 19 minutes. She can hula in the usual midriff position and on her arms, legs, and neck, too. She sounds pretty elastic to me, but then I'm a three-minute hula hooper at best. Hula hooping is keeping a plastic hoop, about three feet in diameter, twirling around your waist by gyrating your hips. After you buy a Hula-Hoop, you can use it for a few different games. Throw it over bottles and boxes; buy some doweling and run around the garden doing the hoop and stick thing you see kids doing in museum videos; sit in the hoop and tell your kids you're in quarantine so they need to keep their distance for an hour or two.

And now, I'm off to assuage my mother-who-lets-her-kids-vegetate-in-front-of-the-TV guilt by offering myself up for a strenuous game of Tiddlywinks. (I'd opt for the jump-rope, but I need full use of my legs tomorrow).

A smorgasbord of spellings is in front of you in the seven upcoming tables and you'll want your child to spell words from each of them. Even if you consider the words in these tables easy, making sure that your child can spell them is a good idea, because big words are made by the joining up of little words or spelling chunks like the one in these tables. How can you stop your child from thinking it's all too easy? My solution is to give you a spelling folder in this chapter. Your child can use the folder with words from this or any other chapter. Whenever you're both ready for a change from the spelling folder, you can play games, such as card games like Go Fish, board games like Connect Four or Chutes and Ladders, and throwing games, like launching balls into a hoop, dropping beans into a bottle, or tossing plastic eggs into a box.

Introducing the Spelling Folder

The spelling folder that I introduce you to now is dear to me. I own several dog-eared folders, some of which are adorned with photos of the kids to which they once belonged. The word folder is a neat way to keep track of your child's spellings and get him to practice for a short time each day.

Activity: Spelling folder

Preparation: Pick up one manila folder, some sticky tape, scissors, and some poster paper or thin cardboard (old birthday cards work well). Stickers and colored markers are optional extras.

Follow these steps:

1. **On the front cover of the folder, have your child write "Spelling."**

2. **On the inside left cover, have her tape a large pocket and write on it, "Done".** She makes the pocket by laying down a birthday card (about 6 inches wide and 4 inches high) and taping down three sides of it, leaving the top open.

3. **On the inside right cover, she needs to make six small pockets in two columns of three.** She numbers them 1 to 6 with the bottom left pocket being number 1, the bottom right pocket being 2, middle left 3, middle right 4, top left 5 and top right 6. These pockets are sort of a ladder that your child moves his words (written on small pieces of paper) up. She plays spelling folder games (which I describe next) with ten words, and then puts them into pocket 1. Later she takes out the words, plays the games again and then puts them in pocket 2. Later still (maybe the next day) she takes the same words out, plays the games with them and puts them in pocket 3 and so on until all the words have been in all six pocket s and are done. The big "Done" pocket is the final resting place for your child's words after they've moved through the six small pockets).

4. **When your child makes the folder, she can decorate it.** Give her complete charge of the folder, scribbling and drawing on it exactly as she likes.

5. **When she's done creating her folder, have her find ten words to use with it.** Find the words from any of the tables in this chapter or from other chapters. Among those words will be some that she can't yet spell (you'll know from examining the words with her and giving her dictations). Have her write each of the ten words on a small bus-ticket sized piece of paper.

6. **Do spelling-folder games with the ten words.** The games are as follows:

   • **First spell:** Have your child bring her folder to you. She hands you the words and you call them out for her to write.

   • **Random mix spell:** She takes the words, spreads them outface-down and mixes them up. She then hands you one word at a time, without looking. You call out the word, and she writes it down.

   • **From the deck spell:** She stacks the words in a facedown deck. You take words from the top of the stack, calling out each of them. She writes them.

   • **From the hand spell:** You hold the words like a hand of cards. She pulls words out without looking, and you tell her what she took. She writes the words.

7. **After completing these four spelling games your child has definitely had good spelling practice.** She puts her words into pocket 1 to be used again the next day. Follow this routine every night for a week, and then put the words you've used into the big "Done" pocket, and get ten new words. Try a total of about ten weeks of this activity and then give the spelling folder a break or permanent retirement.

The spelling folder gives your child an intensive, but fun, blast at tricky spellings. To be sure that your child doesn't get through the six pockets only to forget his spellings later on, ask him every now and then to spell a couple of words from the "Done" pocket.

Sailing Through One-Syllable Word Families

You and your child can zip through the one-syllable word family tables (10-1 through 10-7) with relative ease. They'll take you to the section about schwas, where things get meaty. Have your child read the words in the tables and spell a few that you dictate. Pop some of them into the spelling folder to practice through the week. When you decide that your child has a good handle on these words, use the spelling folder with words from any other table in this book. And, of course, play the regular nonspelling games whenever you and your child are feeling perky or in need of a change of pace before you settle back down to spelling.

Table 10-1	*at*, *an*, and *ap* Words	
at	*an*	*ap*
at	an	cap
bat	ban	chap
brat	bran	clap
cat	can	gap
chat	clan	lap
fat	fan	map
flat	man	nap
hat	pan	rap
mat	plan	sap
pat	ran	scrap
rat	scan	slap
sat	span	snap
scat	tan	tap
splat	than	trap
that	van	zap

Table 10-2	*ack*, *ank*, and *ash* Words	
ack	*ank*	*ash*
back	bank	ash
backpack	blank	bash
black	clank	cash
crack	crank	clash
Jack	drank	crash
lack	frank	dash
pack	plank	flash
quack	prank	gash
rack	rank	gnash

ack	*ank*	*ash*
sack	sank	lash
shack	shrank	mash
slack	spank	rash
smack	stank	sash
snack	tank	slash
stack	thank	smash
tack	yank	splash
track		stash
whack		thrash
		trash

Spelling chunks like *ell* and *ill* are common. When your child writes a single-syllable word ending with *l, f,* or *s,* he nearly always needs to double that last letter. You can see this double-letter rule at work in words like *hill, bell, doll, huff,* and *hiss.*

Taking tips from Dr. Seuss

A few lines back, I said that I'd only give you the spelling folder activity in this chapter. Well I started off with that in mind, but then other things, specifically Dr. Seuss-type things, crept into the picture, too. If you have a young child, you'll find that the Dr. Seuss books *Hop on Pop-Up* and *The Cat in the Hat* fit perfectly with showing him simple word families. In Dr. Seuss style, you and your child can compose your own poetry made from simple word families. Here are some fill-in-the-gaps poems to start you off:

A poem of *at* words

I saw a _____

On a_____

It was_____

What do you think of _____?

A poem of *an* words

Have a _____.

Get a _____.

Take a _____,

If you _____

A poem of *ap* words

Set a _____.

Sit on a _____.

Sleep in a _____.

Take a _____.

Table 10-3	*ell*, *ent*, and *est* Words	
ell	*ent*	*est*
bell	cent	best
cell	bent	chest
fell	dent	crest
sell	lent	nest
shell	rent	pest
smell	sent	rest
spell	spent	test
swell	tent	vest
tell	vent	west
well	went	
yell		

Table 10-4	*it*, *ip*, and *in* Words			
it	*ip*		*in*	
bit	chip	ship	bin	tin
fit	clip	sip	chin	twin
hit	dip	skip	din	win
kit	drip	slip	fin	
knit	flip	snip	grin	
lit	grip	strip	in	
pit	hip	tip	kin	
quit	lip	trip	pin	
sit	nip	whip	shin	
wit	rip	zip	thin	

Table 10-5		*ick, ill, ing,* and *ink* Words	
ick	*ill*	*ing*	*ink*
brick	bill	bring	blink
chick	chill	cling	clink
click	drill	fling	drink
flick	fill	king	ink
kick	frill	ring	link
lick	gill	sing	mink
Mick	grill	sling	pink
Nick	hill	spring	rink
pick	ill	sting	shrink
prick	Jill	string	sink
quick	kill	swing	slink
Rick	mill	thing	stink
sick	pill	wing	think
slick	sill		wink
stick	skill		
thick	spill		
tick	thrill		
trick	will		
wick			

Table 10-6	*ock, og,* and *op* Words	
ock	*og*	*op*
block	bog	bop
clock	cog	chop
dock	clog	cop

(continued)

Table 10-6 *(continued)*

ock	og	op
flock	dog	crop
jock	flog	drop
knock	fog	flop
lock	hog	hop
mock	jog	mop
rock	log	plop
shock	slog	pop
smock		prop
sock		shop
unlock		slop
		stop
		top

Table 10-7		*ug, uck, ump,* and *unk* Words	
ug	**uck**	**ump**	**unk**
bug	buck	bump	bunk
drug	chuck	chump	chunk
dug	cluck	clump	drunk
hug	duck	dump	dunk
jug	luck	jump	flunk
lug	muck	lump	funk
mug	pluck	plump	hunk
plug	puck	pump	junk
rug	struck	rump	shrunk
shrug	suck	slump	skunk

ug	*uck*	*ump*	*unk*
slug	truck	stump	spunk
smug	tuck	thump	stunk
snug	yuck	trump	sunk
thug			trunk
tug			

Taking the Stress Out of Schwas

You've probably read this title and thought, "What in the world is a schwa?" Well a *schwa* is a pompous sort of a word for a vague sort of a thing. So you see there's nothing for you to worry about! Know that a schwa is a vowel. The word "schwa" is the name given to vowels that make a sort of indistinct "*uh*" sound that you barely pronounce. To get the feel of what the indistinct sound of a schwa is, say these words to yourself, with normal pronunciation, and listen for that lazy "uh" last sound: *doctor, teacher,* and *collar.* Now say *again* and *around,* and listen for the first sound. Do you hear that "uh" sound again? You do? Great! That sound is a schwa.

The schwa sound "*uh*" can be spelled and indicated by any of the five vowels. Whenever your child writes a schwa, it will be in the unstressed part of a word. Table 10-8 shows you a bunch of words that have schwas in them. You'll notice that the schwa *u* isn't a big deal, because your child hears and writes short *u* ("*uh*"), but when he hears "*uh*" in a word like *agree,* he has to remember that this particular "*uh*" is spelled with an *a.* After Table 10-8, I talk about ways to tackle the spelling of "*uh.*"

Table 10-8		**Schwa Sounds**		
Schwa a	*Schwa e*	*Schwa i*	*Schwa o*	*Schwa u*
above	kitten	clarity	button	abacus
about	kitchen	finality	lemon	census
along	listen	futility	lesson	chorus
agree	quicken	quality	melon	focus
among	sicken	security	reason	genius

When your child tells you that she "brung" her book home, you probably correct her, telling her that she *brought* her book home. That, of course, is helpful for your child. But what if when she's writing the word "listen," she says *lis-ten* (pronouncing the silent *t*) either to herself, or even out loud, to help with remembering the right spelling. Is that a good thing or not? Some people say that you shouldn't encourage kids to purposely mispronounce words just so they can remember how to spell them. Others say, "What the heck, whatever works is fine." As long as your child knows the correct pronunciation of a word like *listen*, and what it means, I don't see anything wrong with her using any kind of self-talk she wants to make spelling easier. In time, she won't need to use those strategies, but until then, she has plenty of words to get used to, so memory joggers of any kind can make her life easier. With that in mind, read through the words in Table 10-8 with your child and ask her to break them up and pronounce them in ways that feel right. Dictate some for her to write and give her great big hints for spelling the hard words, like *genius*, if she wants you to.

If your child needs help spelling some words, by all means, help him. If you make him spend ages figuring words out for himself, he'll feel resentful and think of spelling as a punishment or endurance test. Let him figure parts of words out. Tell him the tricky parts that he can't work out. Have him write down and save any tricky words. Help him practice spelling them several more times over the span of a few nights.

In dictionaries, you'll find that the sound of the schwa is indicated. Look for an upside down and left facing lower case *e,* just like this: *ə*.

Schwa at the beginning

Thinking about schwa sounds can be mind boggling. I recommend that you don't worry so much about the whys and wherefores of the schwa and instead just point out to your child that some kind pronunciations are fairly sloppy. The next group of words shows you what I mean. All the words in Table 10-9 start with schwa *a*, pronounced as indistinct, indifferent "*uh*." Have your child read the words. She can pronounce that lazy, drawled "*uh*" sound as solid, short *a,* if it helps her remember the spelling. Dictate a few words for her to spell.

Table 10-9	*Around* and *about* Kinds of Words	
again	afraid	asleep
appear	appoint	amiss
announce	along	agree
around	alarm	arrive

appeal	above	among
apart	apply	attend
arrest	anoint	approve
away	alone	ago
attempt	approach	applause
arrange	about	across
another	attention	apology
apostrophe	anonymous	

Schwa at the end

Your child will come across a particular bunch of schwa words quite often — words that are spelled with a schwa a on the end. Words like *idea* and *camera* come under this lazy-*a* ("uh")-on-the-end category and a whole bunch of names of countries do, too. Table 10-10 shows you the words that I'm talking about. After you've looked them over with your child, you may enjoy the geographical detour that I outline in the next activity.

Table 10-10	*Camera* and *Canada* Kinds of Words	
extra	banana	idea
area	criteria	bacteria
doctor	teacher	collar
camera	inertia	malaria
sofa	ammonia	insomnia
delta	anemia	famous
lemon	Canada	Zambia
Asia	America	India
Russia	China	Africa
Alaska	Australia	Austria
Indonesia	Venezuela	Antarctica

Because many schwas are in the names of countries and continents, you can practice spelling them with your child by taking him on a cartographical diversion into labeling maps. Relate places on maps to your ancestors or living relatives, or describe to your child how other kids live in different parts of the world. The next activity gives you a chance to flex your latitudes and wow your child with your worldliness.

Activity: Spelling continents

Preparation: You need an atlas, Internet access, or a good visual memory of the continents for this activity.

Follow these steps:

1. **Draw a simple map of the continents with your child.** A good way to share the drawing chores between you and your child is for you to pencil in the lines while your child traces over them with markers.

2. **Have your child label the continents and point out the "*uh*" spellings on the ends of America, Africa, Asia, Australia, and Antarctica.** If your child enjoys this activity, add the names of the oceans and any other features that you feel like including.

A snippet of information that can help your child to grasp the idea of continents is to tell him that if he flew up in a rocket and looked down on the earth, he'd be able to see all those shapes that he's drawing.

A couple of handy Websites for maps, continents, and flags are www. enchantedlearning.com/geography/continents/ and www.plcmc.org/ forkids/mow/ (*mow* stands for maps of the world).

Schwa in the middle

The next table is not for the fainthearted. It has big words in it and each of them has a schwa sound somewhere in the middle. The schwa sound can be hard to detect, and you may not think any exists at all, but regardless of whether you hear one in there, these words definitely give your child a challenge. Have your child take a good look at Table 10-11, (I underline the schwas) and then try putting a few of the words into the back-to-front activity that I give you next.

If you pronounce the schwas in this table as something other than "uh" don't worry; that's what schwas are like. Some of us pronounce them clearly, just as they're spelled, while other of us do the "uh" thing. (You can debate what counts and what doesn't count as a schwa for a long and fruitless time!)

Table 10-11	Schwa Words for a Challenge	
brav**e**ry	pent**a**gon	flex**i**ble
ad**a**mant	om**i**nous	just**i**fy
hel**i**copter	popular	emanc**i**pate
omnip**o**tent	cel**e**brate	c**o**ntrol

The game that I provide for you here works well with any word. Play it any place, any time, because all you have to do is spell out a word backward to your child.

Activity: Spelling back to front

Preparation: None

Follow these steps:

1. **Spell out a word to your child backward. (d-a-r-w-k-c-a-b)**

2. **Do the same thing once more, and then ask him to spell it back to you in its real, right-way-around form.**

Be extra clever with this activity by throwing in a palindrome such as *radar* or *racecar*!

You may be surprised to find (like I have) that you're not half as good at this game as your kids are. I was horrified to discover that in back-to-front terms even simple words are beyond me. My kids (rather heartlessly) exclude me from this game now because I only hold everyone up.

Chapter 11

Guiding Her Pen to Bigger Word Families

In This Chapter

▶ Recognizing distinctive spellings like *all* and *ight*

▶ Getting the hang of vowel+*r* spellings

▶ Finding out about two vowels+*r*

▶ Practicing hard spelling patterns like *augh*

Anyone who knows anything about spelling will tell you that word families are important. In this chapter I introduce you to the key word families. I start you off with the easiest ones, like the *all*s and *alk*s, move you through the sound-alikes, like *er* and *ir*, and point out the look-alikes, with words like *book* and *boom*. Some of the really tricky words, like *thought* and *enough* are here in this chapter, too. With all these words to choose from, you're sure to find some that your child asks questions about at one time or another.

The Distinctive-Looking all and alk Families

After your child has the hang of simple word families, such as the *ell (bell, sell, smell)* and *ink (brink, shrink, pink)* families, she needs to come to grips with common but more complex word families. Start her off gently with the distinctive-looking *all* and *alk* families that I show you in Table 11-1. She's written some of these words hundreds of times already, so you probably only need to dictate a few of them for her to rev up on.

Table 11-1	*all* and *alk* words
all	*alk*
all	balk
ball	chalk
call	stalk
fall	talk
gall	walk
hall	
mall	
small	
stall	
tall	
wall	

Renegade words can disrupt your flow. You show your child a bunch of words that follow a logical, predictable pattern, and you look all knowing, and then he thinks of a word that's spelled with the same pattern that you're showing him but doesn't sound a bit like the others. Renegade words of the *all* family are *shall* and *balloon*. There, now you won't be caught unaware.

When your child spells words like *almost, although,* and *altogether,* he only has to use one *l*.

Being Savvy with Vowel+r Words

Okay, this is where you and your child need to roll your sleeves up for vowel+r words. Here I tell you about a whole bunch of words that fit a vowel+r spelling pattern. Although the term "vowel+r" may sound cumbersome to you, this group contains so many words that I have to use the umbrella term "vowel+r" to fit them all in. Don't be scared, there are easier and harder ways of looking at these words and I'm taking the harder, oops I mean easier, way. Here is the easy explanation of vowel+r:

When you put each of the five vowels in front of *r* you make five spelling chunks. Easy so far, right? Your child uses the *ar, er, ir, or,* and *ur* spellings all over the place, and if you're really on the ball, when you read those chunks, you notice that *or* and *ar* are separate spellings for separate sounds whereas *er, ir,* and *ur* are three separate spellings for the *same* sound. Which means that when your child wants to spell a word with the "*er*" sound in it; she has to do a mental, or on paper, check of *er, ir,* and *ur* to see which one fits. The more practice she gets, the better she can remember or spot (from her jotted-down possibilities) the right spelling. So now, of course, you know just what to do: Give your child plenty of practice with plenty of words so she can make plenty of progress.

The words in the vowel+r family aren't all that hard; just wait until you see what's coming later! This activity is a plain, practice — and practice — again one just like you'd see happening in any spelling class. I'm saving quizzes and stuff for further into the chapter, when the going gets a little harder. For now, here are some basic spelling routines.

Activity: Looking, marking, and writing (then doing it some more)

Preparation: Open this book to Table 11-2, or make a copy of it so your child doesn't mark the book, and grab your highlighting pens, regular pen, and paper.

Follow these steps:

1. **Have your child read the *or* column and mark any unusual or tricky-looking spelling chunks.** Make sure he includes any words he thinks he may otherwise forget.

2. **Dictate a few words from the column for him to write.** Include the words he's marked.

3. **Repeat Steps 1 and 2 with the next (*ar*) column, and then dictate a mix of words for your child to spell from the two columns (*or* and *ar*).**

4. **Explain that the next three columns have different spellings that nevertheless sound the same.** Lead your child through each column, just like you did in the first two steps, and then walk him through a mix of spellings from all three columns.

5. **Take a break! Congratulate yourselves.**

You systematically and thoroughly took on a lot of spellings, and should now be pretty accomplished with your *r*'s.

Table 11-2		Words with Vowel+*r*		
or	*ar*	*er*	*ir*	*ur*
		(er ir and ur all sound the same)		
born	art	clerk	bird	blur
chore	barge	fern	birth	burn
core	barn	germ	chirp	blurt
cork	car	her	dirt	burst
corn	card	herb	firm	curb
for	cart	herd	first	church
force	charge	jerk	flirt	churn
fork	charm	nerve	girl	curl
horn	chart	perch	shirt	curse
horse	dark	perk	sir	curve
north	dart	person	skirt	fur
or	far	serve	stir	hurl
order	farm	stern	third	hurt
pork	hard	swerve	thirst	nurse
port	large	term	thirty	purse
score	mark	verse	whir	spur
shore	marsh		whirl	spurn
short	park			spurt
sore	part			squirt
snore	scar			surf
sort	shark			surge
sport	sharp			turn
store	snarl			urge
storm	spark			
swore	star			

or	ar	er	ir	ur
thorn	starve			
tore	yard			
torn				
wore				
worn				

Recognizing other ways of using or and ar

Did I mention that you encounter a few thinker spellings in this chapter? I did? Good. Here's where they begin. In this section, I show you the other ways of using *or* and *ar*. I give you words like *worm* and *warm*. They're the kind of thinker spellings that easily trip up your child unless you give him due warning. Take your child through Table 11-3. Hang out with all those *or*'s and *ar*'s for a while. If you can think of other words that don't start with *w*, you're way ahead of me.

Table 11-3	Using *or* and *ar for* other sounds
or ("er")	*ar ("or")*
worm	war
work	warm
world	ward
worse	warn
word	warmth
worth	
worst	
worsen	

Daffodils and dishes

I don't lead an edge-of-your-seat sort of a life, so I look forward to bulb-planting time. This year, while I was doing my horticultural best, my daughter invited a friend over. They cooked muffins, cookies, flavored rice, ravioli, and in fact, as they pointed out, anything that came in a packet. They laid the table with several cloths. They didn't scrimp on plates. They lighted candles. They used a lot of side dishes, and there were more than enough wineglasses. It was a feast. Of course, I really had no business to be looking at the dirty muffin tins, the pots and pans with inches of rice stuck to every surface, the egg

shells, oily measuring jugs, and sugary goo hardening on my countertop. The whole scene looked like one thing to me and something entirely different to those kids. That's how spelling can be. Your child doesn't see spellings like you do, because she's had less experience. Until someone (like you) shows her words like *talk* and *tight*, she quite reasonably writes things like *tawk* and *tite*. Show her the right spellings. Explain that she can develop an eye for spotting what's right. If you pass the dishwasher or broom, you may want to casually point them out, too, as equipment to include in the next kitchen extravaganza.

Moving ahead to two vowels+r

Time to turn the heat up a tad. Here I introduce you to not one but two vowels in front of *r*. They look a bit much at first, but remember that you don't have to race through every table in one go.

This chapter is challenging, so take your time. Have your child spell the same column (mixed around) a few times before moving forward to the next words. Make sure he's good and ready before you progress. Being thorough is better than being fast, because the last thing you want is your child forgetting words that he thought he had firmly under his belt.

Table 11-4 shows five bunches of words with two vowels+r. Your child won't anticipate these spelling patterns until he 's gotten used to using them, because after all, who expects to write *earn* for a word that sounds like *urn* or *heart* for a word that should reasonably be *hart*? Your child obviously needs to take a good look at these words and put plenty of mileage on his pen. Have him look at a few words, cover them over one at a time, and jot each one down for himself. Then direct him to the activity that follows Table 11-4.

When you look at Table 11-4, you see a strange thing going on. Earlier your child shimmied through different spellings of the "*er*" sound (*er, ir,* and *ur*), and now, with two vowels+r she's faced with three different spellings for "*or.*"

I provide you with pronunciation (in parenthesis) as I hear it. If you pronounce words differently, that's no problem. Your child attaches spellings to whatever pronunciation he uses, which is probably the same as yours.

Table 11-4		*r* after Two Vowels		
ear ("er")	*ear ("ar")*	*our ("or")*	*oar ("or")*	*oor ("or")*
earn	heart	course	boar	door
pearl	hearth	court	soar	floor
earth		four	oar	
search		pour	roar	
yearn		fourth	coarse	
early		source	hoarse	

Activity: Finding an *our, oar,* or *oor* match

Preparation: Make a copy of the list of questions that follows.

Follow this step: Have your child write the answers to the questions. Give him clues whenever he needs some.

1. "Of c_____!"
2. When you have a sore throat, your voice is h_____.
3. A place for judges and lawyers.
4. Another kind of "sore," like a bird does.
5. Use this in a boat.
6. A lion makes this noise.
7. Another kind of "sauce" that means where a thing comes from.
8. The number after three.
9. You have pores in your skin, but you ____ your drink.
10. A male pig.

Answers: course, hoarse, court, soar, oar, roar, source, four, pour, boar

Activity: Finding an *ear* match

Preparation: Make a copy of the list of questions that follows.

Follow this step: Have your child write the answers to the questions, helping him with clues whenever he needs them.

1. Opposite of late.
2. A valuable stone.

3. An organ in your body.

4. Our planet.

5. To look hard.

6. To want.

7. You may ____ money for doing a job.

8. The place in front of a fire.

Answers: early, pearl, heart, earth, search, yearn, earn, hearth

Igh and ight Words

Words that end in *igh* and *ight* can be scary for your child. It's hard for her to remember about *gh* being silent and *i* making its long sound. You may decide that if ever there were a good time for a *mnemonic* (memory jogger), it's now. Here's a mnemonic to help your child remember at least the *ght* spelling chunk of words like *bright* and *sight:* Words like *fight, might,* and *tight* are (in true Harry Potter style) *great hairy twit* words. I know that isn't exactly elevating, but a lot of the things that your child remembers best aren't! Run the great hairy twit sentiment past your child to find out how she feels about it. If she thinks it'll stick in her mind, try her on a few dictated words to see if it works. If she isn't keen on it, have her think up her own mnemonic. See Table 11-5 for examples.

Giving your child free rein to make up her own mnemonics may not be right for you. She may discover a knack for finding unsavory phrases that set your cheeks on fire. If she does, it's a pretty safe bet that she'll never forget them either, and then you'll have to weigh her improved spelling against the affront to your sensibilities!

Table 11-5	*igh* and *ight*	
igh ("eye")	*ight* ("ite")	
thigh	blight	light
high	bright	might
sigh	fight	night
	flight	right
	fright	sight
	height	slight
	knight	tight

Eight, Ought, and Aught

You simply cannot get away from the fact that the words in this section are hard. Your child must remember a strange bunch of letters to be able to write words like *taught* and *weigh* and can be forgiven for wondering why they're not spelled *tawt* and *way*. The explanation for the hardest part of these words, the *gh* part, is that *gh* is a silent spelling chunk. Your child must write it, but he won't hear it. Pretty tricky, huh? To make things easier, I suggest a couple of mnemonics They have sort of medical and moralistic themes, but hey, here's your chance to help your child with spelling *and* get a handle on his personal hygiene. Besides, *you* try finding mnemonics for these spellings; it isn't easy.

To remember the arrangement of letters in words like *eight* and *weight* tell your child: "Eight itchy gnomes have ticks."

For the itchy gnome mnemonic to work, your child needs to remember that *eight* starts with *e*. The payoff is that "eight" reminds him that the words that fit this mnemonic rhyme with eight. He needs to remember the silent g in *gnome* too, but that's pretty easy if he pronounces the spelling phonetically as "guh-nome." (Is there no end to this inventiveness?)

To bring words like *thought* and *brought* to mind, tell your child that "Only ungrateful girls hate toys." While she has these thought-provoking tick and toy messages still in her mind, zip ahead to the activities.

Activity: Eight itchy gnomes have ticks

Preparation: Open this book to Table 11-6, and have your highlighter pens, regular pen, and paper ready.

Follow these steps:

1. **Remind your child that, "Eight itchy gnomes have ticks," and then ask her to highlight the *eight* part of the words in the table.** (Tell your child to just remember that *weigh* doesn't need a *t* on the end, which is easy to remember because you don't hear the *t*.).

2. **Now give your child these clues so that she writes out the words.**

   1. A number.

   2. You see your ____ when you stand on scales.

   3. You _____ yourself when you stand on scales.

   4. You ride this on the snow.

   5. The goods that boats, trains, and trucks carry.

Hooked on mnemonics

You can pose the figuring out of mnemonics as a problem for your child to solve. When I asked my own daughter to think up a saying for helping remember *ought*, she was hooked. She tried new mnemonics for 15 minutes at the height of birthday party preparations. (I'm not obsessive; I spent an hour, or so, pondering this on the day of my daughter's party.) She came up with forgettable things about gibbons then made a dramatic exit. "I have to do like a million things because it *is* my *birthday* Mom," she remonstrated. But, ah ha, I knew that she really *couldn't* think up a better mnemonic that mine!

Activity: Only ungrateful girls hate toys

Preparation: Open this book to Table 11-6, and have your highlighter pens, regular pen, and paper ready.

Follow these steps:

1. **Remind your child that, "Only ungrateful girls hate toys," and then ask her to highlight the *ought* part of the words in the table.**

2. **Now give her these clues so she can write the answers.**

   1. He _____his dog to school.

   2. The soccer team _____a good fight.

   3. She _____ a new bag.

   4. He _____about the problem.

   5. She _____to take more care.

   6. The prince _____his true love far and wide.

Table 11-6	*eigh, ought,* and *aught*	
eigh ("ay")	*ought ("awt")*	*aught ("awt")*
freight	ought	taught
weight	brought	caught
sleigh	fought	
eight	thought	
weigh	bought	
	sought	

And what about *taught* and *caught*? Strange words, aren't they? Tell your child that you'd have to be mad not to think these two have a sneaky kind of spelling. Ask her how she'll remember them. Will she start off with the "Only ungrateful girls hate toys," mnemonic and then remember to change the *o* to an *a*? Or what?

You've probably heard the terms "child centered" learning and "active" learning. They describe how your child learns best when he actively figures stuff out for himself. When you get your child to figure out his own spelling mnemonics you facilitate child-centered and active learning (and he remembers his own mnemonics better than yours, provided that his make good sense to him.) The word "facilitate" is apt here. When teachers set up child-centered activities they describe their role as that of facilitator.

Enough and Some

Just so you know, this chapter gets easier after this section. A few words here may have your child volunteering to clean her room rather than cranking her spelling skills up a notch, but reassure her that there's no need to be rash. When she breaks these words into chunks, she can speed through them, and although she may not realize it, she understands a few of those chunks already. The next activity takes you and your child one step at a time through the sizzlers in Table 11-7.

Table 11-7	Words like *enough* ("*u*") and *some* ("*u*")	
ou ("*u*") words	*o* ("*u*") words	
enough	some	other
rough	love	oven
thorough	cover	done
encourage	none	tongue
courage	money	discover
tough	mother	smother
double	dove	above
flourish	shovel	stomach
young	among	nothing

(continued)

Table 11-7 *(continued)*

ou ("u") words	o ("u") words	
couple	front	wonder
nourish	brother	
touch	glove	
country	come	
trouble	honey	
cousin	Monday	

Activity: Colors and chunks

Preparation: Make a copy of Table 11-7, and grab some color highlighter pens.

Follow these steps:

1. **Starting with the *o* words, ask your child to find all the words that have only one spelling chunk (or syllable).** Tell him that he has to find nine words, and one of them is tricky, so watch out. The words are *some, love, none, dove, front, glove, come, done,* and *tongue:* tongue is the tricky one.

2. **Have your child color all the words in the same color then dictate them for him to spell.**

3. **Tell your child that all the *o* words that remain have two chunks, except for one.** Ask him which one it is. (The answer is *discover.*)

4. **Have your child color the two-chunk words in a new color, and the three-chunk word in its own color.**

5. **Ask him which words are easy, hard, or strange.** Help him take a good look at the words, and then dictate them for him to spell. Give clues and help whenever he needs it. Encourage your child to try spelling the hardest words of all again until he's conquered them soundly.

6. **Go through the same careful, systematic routine with the *ou* words.**

You want your child to get the message that all spellings can be brought under control. The trick is to group them, tackle a few at a time, and use plenty of colors! The most important thing of all for you to remember is to keep your tone positive and your message one of, "Don't worry, we can crack this."

Swooping In on the Two oo's

The *oo* sound of *boot* is the easiest *oo* spelling with which to start your child's spelling voyage. Many words are in this group, and your child can easily hear and then spell that nice long sound. Conversely, the sound in *book, look,* and *took* isn't a bit like the nice long one in *boot,* but the words in the *book, look,* and *took* family are just as common, so with a bit of practice, your child can quickly and easily come to grips with them, too. Have him watch out for words like *door* though. Only a handful of *door*-type words (where the *oo* spellings has an *aw* or *or* sound depending on your accent) are out there. Lead your child through all three families in Table 11-8 with the "Colors and chunks" activity. Remember that speed isn't important but thoroughness and cheerfulness are.

Table 11-8		b*oo*ts, b*oo*ks, and b*oo*rs	
oo like in boot		*oo like in book*	*oo like in door*
boo	moose	book	boor
boom	noon	brook	door
boot	noose	cook	floor
broom	pool	crook	moor
cool	room	foot	indoors
coop	scoop	good	outdoors
croon	scoot	hood	
doom	shoot	hook	
drool	snoop	look	
droop	snooze	nook	
food	soon	shook	
fool	spoon	soot	
groom	stool	stood	
goose	swoon	took	
groove	swoop	wood	
hoop	too	wool	
hoot	tool		

(continued)

Table 11-8 *(continued)*

oo like in boot		oo like in book	oo like in door
loom	toot		
loop	tooth		
loose	troop		
loot			
moo			
moon			

Choosing from Two Good Spellings

When your child spells, she says the word that she's spelling in her mind. She isolates the chunks of sound and then matches letters to the sounds. When I put it that way, spelling sounds easy, doesn't it? Well, some of it is. Words like *impossible* and *dramatic,* for example, look hard but are really quite simple to spell. They have nice regular chunks of sound that belong with nice regular chunks of spelling. Other words provide your child with choices. Should she write *choice* or *choyce*? Both words are made of good spelling chunks, but only one is right. The sound of "*oy*" can be spelled either *oy* or *oi*, and your child needs to recognize which spelling fits neatly in which words. In this section, I lead you through three pairs of spellings: *oy* and *oi*; *ow* and *ou*; and *aw* and *au*. Each member of each pair represents the same sound as the other member of the pair.

Oy and oi

As a general rule, if your child hears "*oy*" on the end of a word (or root word), it's spelled *oy*. If he hears "*oy*" in the middle of a word, he spells it *oi*.

A *root word* is a word that your child can add bits and pieces onto. *Employ* is a root word. Your child can simply write *employ,* or he can add to it to make *employment, employing,* or *employed.*

When your child puts a spelling chunk like *un* at the beginning of a root word; for example, *unemployed,* she's added a prefix. Endings like *ed, ing,* and *er* are suffixes. I talk more about prefixes and suffixes in Chapters 15 and 16.

Give your child a good look at Table 11-9, tell him that he generally writes *oy* at the end of a word and *oi* in the middle, and then let him loose with this quiz.

Activity: *oy-oi* quiz

Preparation: Make a copy of the quiz that follows, and have your regular pens standing by.

Follow this step: Have your child circle the right spellings.

1. The boi/boy flipped the coyn/coin.

2. The spoiled/spoyled girl was annoied/annoyed.

3. Roy/Roi heard a noise/noyse.

4. The kids said they'd boil/boyl the oister/oyster in oil/oyl.

5. The boss said she can joyn/join his employ/emploi.

6. He made his joynts/joints click.

7. The man gave the royal/roial princess a toi/toy.

8. She had a loud voyce/voice.

9. She said that he spoiled/spoyled her painting.

10. Ann asked the coy/coi girl to join/joyn her.

When your child's presented you with his answers, have an "I bet you can't do this" finale. Dictate the ten words for him to write (accompanied by your appreciative or stricken ooh's).

Table 11-9	oy and oi
oy	*oi*
annoy	boil
boy	broil
coy	choice
decoy	coil
employ	coin
joy	foil
oyster	join
ploy	joint
Roy	loin
royal	moist

(continued)

Table 11-9 *(continued)*

oy	oi
toy	noise
	oil
	point
	soil
	spoil
	toil
	voice

Ow and ou

Any time your child hears the "*ow*" sound, like he'd say if someone pinched him, he has two choices of spellings. He can write "*ow*" or "*ou,*" and the only way he'll get good at deciding between the two is to get plenty of practice with them. Table 11-10 shows a hefty collection of words for your child to get a good start on. Have him go through the "Colors and chunks" routine (from earlier in this chapter) with this table, because it's a solid, reliable drill that feels more like an okay or even fun practice than the usual dull old drill (the kind you'd find in *other* spelling books!).

Table 11-10	ow and ou	
ow words	*ou words*	
bow	about	mouse
brow	around	noun
brown	bound	ouch
cow	blouse	out
crowd	cloud	pound
crown	count	proud
down	flour	round
drown	flout	scout
frown	found	shroud
gown	ground	slouch

ow words	ou words	
growl	grout	sound
how	hound	spout
now	house	sprout
owl	loud	trout
scowl	lout	
sow	mound	
town	mount	

Every now and then I squeeze an extra word table in these pages. It happens when I think of words that don't exactly fit in with the theme I'm talking about but are so irritatingly similar that I can't leave them out. In this section that irritant is words like *snow* and *throw*. Your child must put the *ow* spelling in these words, but it represents a long-*o* ("oh") sound. This spelling has nothing to do with the "Ow, you pinched me" sound that I was talking about, but you can see why I have to mention it, can't you? Make sure that your child is comfortable with the being-pinched sound, spelled *ow* or *ou;* then show him the words in Table 11-11. Have him whiz through the "Colors and chunks" activity, because, well, you know why.

Watch out for the words *bow* and *sow*. They're homographs — words that have two different meanings for the very same spelling ("I bow to the queen and tie her bow." "I sow the seed and hope the sow doesn't dig it up.")

Table 11-11	Spelling *ow*, for "oh"	
ow for "oh" Words		
arrow	barrow	bellow
blow	blown	bow
bowl	crow	flow
glow	grow	grown
low	mellow	mow
narrow	owe	own
show	slow	snow
sow	sparrow	row
throw	thrown	tow
yellow		

Reporting for cleanup duty

Today my kids raced breathlessly into the house from the school bus. "Did the school phone you?" they yelled. Hmm!?!? The school hadn't phoned me, but obviously things — probably bad things — had been going on. It took less than two seconds for the non-offending child to tell me what my other child had done.

"She buried herself in the sandbox, Mom. She and Erika got the other kids to cover them up and then they stayed there. The teachers had to get them out after all the other kids had gone to class," the tattler said.

And so little Miss Daredevil and I had a talk. Sand is fun. Sand is good. Getting yourself buried in the schoolyard isn't good; it's potentially dangerous. And making your teacher trek out to get you is just asking for cleanup duty. What does this vignette have to do with spelling? Some spellings test your child's judgment. She won't get cleanup duty if she makes the wrong decision, but she'll see as soon as she writes a word like "*boyl*" that, like being in the sandbox after hours, it isn't the smart choice. The more she views different options like choice or choyce, coin or coyn, sandbox or classroom, the better she gets at plumbing for the right one.

Aw and au

Table 11-12 contains a collection of *aw* and *au* words, and these words can certainly send your child's head spinning. Following is a silly activity to make good use of those weird feelings that all those spins might stir up.

Activity: Extravagant excuses

Preparation: Open this book to the five exercises listed in this activity and grab some paper and a pen.

Follow this step: Have your child write short excuses for the situations I provide. His answer can be as silly or sensational as he wants but he must include the word or words that I give in parentheses.

1. You didn't hand in your homework. Why? (Word: sauce)

2. You're late for class. Why? (Words: crawl, dawn)

3. Your clothes are filthy. Why? (Words: claw, laundry)

4. You haven't brushed your teeth or hair. Why? (Words: paw, hawk)

5. You left your lunch at home. Why? (Words: lawn, raw, pause)

Table 11-12	aw *and* au	
aw words	*au words*	
brawl	lawn	auto
brawn	paw	author
caw	pawn	cause
claw	prawn	clause
crawl	raw	haul
dawn	saw	laundry
draw	sawn	maul
drawn	shawl	pause
fawn	squawk	sauce
flaw	straw	
jaw	thaw	
hawk	yawn	
law		

Signing off

I spend quite a bit of time saying things like this to my kids:

"You need to sort this out with words."

"No hitting or throwing."

"If I hear one more put-down from either of you I turn this car around and we go home."

All that talk (especially when I'm itching to yell and do other bad stuff) can leave me quite drained, and it isn't unusual for me to hit the sack at about the time that groovier people are heading out for things like meals without ketchup and drinks from real glass. Not much fun, huh? Except that sometimes my kids leave me notes like this:

"I love u, sorry 4 the trouble caused. You're a great mom." — signed Your loving daughter

You'd have to be pretty callous not to go all I-have-nice-kids-after-all with a note like that. It looks like she actually hears the stuff that I say about apologizing. And check out those words. This child, known for breaking into song or walking off when I'm right in the middle of explaining stuff like the "*au*" spelling, may, incredibly, be absorbing some of it after all.

Taking Care with are, ear, and air

Remember when your child read about the Care Bears? And you wondered how on earth you'd help him with all those different spellings of the same sound? Ah, but somehow he managed to get things right. He read the stories and cruised through the spellings. But that was reading (and reading comes easier to kids than spelling). Now it's time to revisit those Care Bears for the sake of your child's spelling. He needs to sort out *ares*, *ears*, and *airs* so he can strut his stuff on paper. You and Table 11-13 are his allies. Help him check out all the words and have fun with the two activities.

Table 11-13		Learning Ways to Spell "air"		
are		*ear*	*air*	
bare	mare	bear	air	pair
blare	rare	pear	airplane	stair
care	share	tear	airport	
dare	snare	wear	chair	
fare	spare		fair	
flare	square		flair	
glare	stare		hair	
hare	ware		lair	

Activity: Which word?

Preparation: Open this book to Table 11-13 and have pen and paper at the ready.

Follow this step: Have your child look at Table 11-13 and write down the answers to these questions:

1. Which word comes after share?

2. Which word comes before chair?

3. Which word is longest?

4. Which word is shortest?

5. Which four words start with f?

6. What are the seven pairs of sound-alike words?

7. Which word names a math shape?

8. Which three words name animals?

9. Which word starts with *gl*?

10. What is the money that you need to catch a bus?

Sound-alike words like *hair* and *hare* are called homonyms or homophones.

Activity: Changing the last letter

Preparation: Open this book to the ten exercises in this activity and grab pen and paper.

Follow this step: Have your child write down the answers to the following statements.

1. Bear: Change the last letter so you have something to eat or have a plant.

2. Stare: Change the last letter so that it means the same as begin.

3. Bare: Change the last letter so you have a place to keep hay.

4. Share: Change the last letter so that it means the opposite of blunt.

5. Pair: Change the last letter so that it means what you'd feel if you were kicked.

6. Dare: Change the last letter so you'd throw this at a dartboard.

7. Chair: Change the last letter so you have something made of links.

8. Mare: Change the last letter so you have a planet.

9. Fare: Change the last letter so you have a place to raise animals.

10. Care: Change the last letter so you have something you push in the store.

Chapter 12

Spelling Sight Words: A Different Family

In This Chapter

▶ Appreciating the importance of sight words

▶ Developing strategies for spelling sight words

▶ Taking care with tricky sight words

▶ Speeding up and having fun

I'm old enough to remember when average people didn't own computers. I learned, fairly begrudgingly, about computers, in adulthood. Now, I can scarcely believe life went on smoothly before. If your child can handle a computer, she's better equipped for writing school reports. But she needs another skill for every written task she does, in or out of school, with or without a computer. That skill is being able to spell common words quickly. This chapter tells you how to help your child with "sight" words.

Introducing Sight Words

Some words like *they* and *were,* crop up time and time again. Your child needs to immediately recognize them and be able to spell them as an automatic reflex. These words are known as sight words. Table 12-1 is a list of the 221 most frequently used sight words. Take a quick look at them and then lead your child through the activity that follows.

Table 12-1				220 Sight Words		
Sight Words						
a	by	full	jump	one	sleep	us
about	call	funny	just	only	small	use
after	came	gave	keep	open	so	very
again	can	get	kind	or	some	walk
all	carry	give	know	our	soon	want
as	clean	go	laugh	out	start	warm
always	cold	goes	let	over	stop	was
am	come	going	light	own	take	wash
an	could	good	like	pick	tell	we
and	cut	got	little	play	ten	well
any	did	green	live	please	thank	went
are	do	grow	long	pretty	that	were
around	does	had	look	pull	the	what
as	done	has	made	put	their	when
ask	don't	have	make	ran	them	where
at	down	he	many	read	then	which
ate	draw	help	may	red	there	white
away	drink	her	me	ride	these	who
be	eat	here	much	right	they	why
because	eight	him	must	round	think	will
been	every	his	my	run	this	wish
before	fall	hold	myself	said	those	with
best	far	hot	never	saw	three	work
better	fast	how	new	say	to	would
big	find	hurt	no	see	today	write
black	first	I	not	seven	together	yellow

Sight Words						
blue	five	if	now	shall	too	yes
both	fly	in	of	she	try	your
bring	for	into	off	show	two	
brown	found	is	old	sing	under	
but	four	it	on	sit	up	
buy	from	its	once	six	upon	

This first activity is your warm-up. Have your child grab some highlighters and run through the simple coloring task so he gets a good first look at all the words.

Activity: Color-coding sight words

Preparation: Make a copy of Table 12-1 and grab some highlighter pens.

Follow this step: Among the words in Table 12-1 are 26 that have only one or two letters in them. Have your child find and color in all 26.

Skipping through the Families

Many of the 220 words in Table 12-1 belong to word families, groups of words that partly spell and sound the same. If your child can spell one family member, she can probably spell the entire family. Table 12-2 shows word families from the 220 sight words with extra words added to some families so you can clearly see the spelling (and sound) pattern. The "Ten neat word families" and "Building word families," activities later in this section can help your child get into family mode.

When teachers show your child word families they start with families that have the identical spelling at the end of the words, like in all, call and ball. In this table I go a step further. I include the identical spelling, the ones teachers typically use, but I give more advanced ones too where the identical spelling is between other letters, like in *about* and *found* in which the identical spelling pattern is *ou*. Show your child the easier families before delving into the advanced families.

If your pronunciation of words in this table is different from the examples I give, you can simply exclude the words that don't seem to fit in with the rest of the word family.

Table 12-2	Families Among the 220 Sight Words		
all	*Two Vowels*	*ou Says "ow" like in "cow"*	
all	been	about	
call	clean	around	
fall	keep	found	
small	please	our	
	read	out	
	sleep	round	
ould Says "ood" like in "hood"	*wh*	*wa Says "wo" like in "was"*	
could	what	was	
would	when	want	
should	where	wash	
	which	wallet	
	why	wasp	
	white	watch	
		swab	
		swamp	
		swallow	
war Says "wore"	*wor Says "were"*	*o Says Short "u" like in "sun"*	
war	worm	some	cover
warm	world	done	shovel
warden	worldly	does	stomach
swarm	work	come	none
dwarf	worth	mother	among
warn	worthy	brother	honey
reward	sword	other	tongue

war Says "wore"	wor Says "were"	o Says Short "u" like in "sun"	
toward	worse	smother	nothing
swarthy	worship	love	money
		dove	front
		glove	Monday
		oven	discover
		above	wonder

The question-forming *who* starts with *wh* too, but it doesn't belong in this *wh* word family because its wh spelling is pronounced as "h." *Who* is a distinctive, class-of-its-own sort of word.

I'm about to squeeze one more table into this section. I'm not trying to over-whelm you, but the next bunch of words is one that your child really needs to have under her belt. This formidable-looking group of words won't faze your child after you present them to her in the short-*u* grouping in Table 12-3, which has the short-*u* sound spelled "ou." When your child gets used to this spelling version of short *u,* she'll find that the words aren't half as tricky as they seemed at first.

Take your time with this chapter. Focus on one or two word families for a week so that your child really masters them and feels confident. A system-atic, one-step-at-a-time approach brings out the great speller in your child.

Table 12-3	*ou* Say Short "*u*" like in "*sun*"	
courage	enough	cousin
touch	country	trouble
young	couple	nourish
tough	double	flourish
rough	thorough	encourage

If your child pronounces a different sound in some words, like *"er"* in *courage,* and long *"o"* in *thorough* (rather than short *"u"*) have him highlight these words. They're ones to watch out for.

The spelling chunk *gh* says *"f"* in six common words (you may think of more): cough, laugh, trough, rough, tough, and enough.

The "Ten neat word families" activity helps you take your child through the word families in Tables 12-2 and 12-3. Some tough words are included here, so encourage your child to use highlighters and scrap paper to mark and jot down unusual spelling chunks.

Activity: Ten neat word families

Preparation: Equip you and your speller with paper and pens or whiteboard and markers.

Follow these steps:

1. **With your child, look at the word families in Tables 12-2 and 12-3.**

2. **Have your child sound out the words.**

3. **Have her highlight the sound (*all, ee* and *ea, ou, ould, wh, wa, war, wor, o,* and *ou*) that makes each grouping a word family.**

4. **Say the following things and ask her to her write down the answers:**

    1. "Which word in the *all* family is hardest?"

    2. "Which word in the *all* family is easiest?"

    3. "Number the words in the *all* family."

    4. "Choose a number and I'll read out that word for you to spell."

5. **Use this drill with the remaining nine families.**

You can find more single words among the 220 sight words in Table 12-1 to which you can add more words to make more families. Your child can make easy families, such as *and, hand, stand, band, grand,* and *brand,* or harder families, such as *saw, paw, law, lawn, fawn, dawn,* and *awful.* In case you don't want to find your own words from which to build new families (you want the full-service option rather than self-serve), I've chosen some families for you in the next activity.

Activity: Building word families

Preparation: Get that paper and those pens or the whiteboard and markers ready again.

Follow these steps:

1. **Tell your child that together you're going to think up some word families.**

2. **Have your child write the first word from the next list and then ask him to think of family members to go with it (without showing him the examples I'm giving you in parentheses — they're the ones he can think up).**

1. big (Examples: pig, wig, dig, and jig)

2. best (Examples: pest, test, and west)

3. bring (Examples: sing, thing, ring, and wing)

4. be (Examples: he, me, and she)

5. by (Examples: my, fry, cry, and shy)

6. fast (Examples: last, past, and blast)

7. far (Examples: star, start, and smart)

8. away (Examples: may, day, say, pay, stay, play, and delay)

9. or (Examples: for, store, and more)

10. find (Examples: mind, kind, and pine)

11. light (Examples: tight, sight, fight, fright, and slight)

12. soon (Examples: moon, spoon, and booth)

13. down (Examples: drown, frown, clown, brown, bow, and now)

14. walk (Examples: talk, chalk, and stalk)

15. would (Examples: could and should)

If you're building a family like *and, hand, stand, band, grand,* and *brand,* and your child suggests *planned,* explain that although this word sounds right, it has a different spelling. That's why writing a few spelling possibilities down (*planed, planned, pland*) and getting good at spotting the right one is best.

Taking Time with the Individuals

A few paragraphs back, I describe the word *who* as a "distinctive, class-of-its-own sort of word." Because *who* has such an unexpected spelling, it's pretty clear that it doesn't belong in a family. No other words are like *who,* so how, you ask, will your child remember how to spell *who* and other singular, renegade words?

Table 12-4 gives you the eccentric individuals that I weeded out of the 220 sight words. These words are here because they don't usually belong to a word family and don't sound out easily. Have your child cast his eye over them and then move on to the "Finding your spelling strategies" activity. These strategies tell you and your child how to start remembering the words.

Table 12-4	Words That Kids Have Trouble With	
Twenty-one Troublesome Words		
any	as	because
buy	give	have
here	laugh	live
many	once	one
pretty	said	their
there	use	were
where	who	your

Some of the words in Table 12-4 belong to teensy-weensy word families. Word families, regardless of how small, help your child remember spellings. Acronyms and rhymes are helpful, too. The next activity takes a look at mini families and cute anagrams.

Acronyms are letters like P.T.O (please turn over) that are short for a whole bunch of words. They help you keep things short but can also be your memory joggers.

Activity: Finding your spelling strategies

Preparation: Grab your paper, pens, scissors, and an envelope, and make a copy of Table 12-4.

Follow these steps:

1. **Tell your child that together (but mostly him), you're going to think up some ways to help him remember the tricky spellings in Table 12-4.**

2. **Say the following to your child. Some examples are given in parentheses.**

    1. "Write *any,* and cut it out."

    2. "Write *many*, cut it out, and put it with *any.*"

    3. "Write *give,* and cut it out."

    4. "Write which word is almost exactly like *give (live)*, cut it out, and put it next to . . . *give*."

    5. "Which word is almost exactly like *there*? *(where)*"

    6. "Write both words, *(there* and *where)* and cut them out."

7. "Write this silly saying: 'Big elephants can always understand small elephants.'"

8. "Write the first letter of each word so you get a word that a lot of people find hard to spell. *(because)*"

9. "Write this saying: 'Laugh and u get happy,' using the letter *u* as shorthand for the real word *'you.'*"

10. "Write each first letter (using *u* for *'you'*) to make its word *(laugh)*."

11. "Write the word *by* like in 'I stand by you.' Cut it out."

12. "When you *buy* something you get more. Write *by* with a *u* in the middle. (See how *u* gets more; it's a bigger word). Cut out *buy*."

3. By now, your child has ten words in front of him. Have him turn them face down, mix them up, and give them to you. Dictate them for him to spell.

Keep the ten words in the envelope and do this practice every night for a week. If your child isn't sure about a word by the end of a week, keep that word (or words) for practicing through another week.

Having your child do the cutting, holding, and passing of these words puts her in control. When she thinks she's learning for herself, and not doing stuff just because you say so, you and she are experiencing active and child-centered learning. This kind of learning is what teachers are always aiming for, because it's the best kind!

The next list gives you the words in Table 12-4 that I haven't talked about yet. They're tricky words so I provide you with suggestions for making them memorable for your child. If you think of other memory aids along the way, by all means use them. Any way that helps your child fix those visual images in his mind is a good way.

If you practice ten sight words every week, include only three or four of these tricky words in that ten. They're too hard to master in one go.

Remembering unusual words:

1. any: Write this "*eny*" sound as <u>*a*</u>*ny* (like "Annie").

2. many: Put *m* on the front of *any*.

3. as: Write the "*z*" sound as *s*. (You do the same in words like *has, does, pleasure, measure,* and *treasure,* and plurals like *stoves, dogs,* and *sands.*)

4. here: *Here* is a Bossy *e* word. I explain Bossy *e* a few lines down.

5. once: Break *once* into *on-ce* (what a word!).

6. pretty: Spell the short-*i* sound with an *e*.

7. said: Spelled *s + aid* (like *first aid*).

8. their: Write *the* at the start of both *there* and *their*. Both have *the* in them, but only *there* has *here* inside it, too (*there* and *here* are directional words).

9. use: *Use* is a Bossy *e* word. I explain Bossy *e* a few lines down.

10. were: Break *were* into *w*+ *er* + silent *e*.

11. who: You'd expect to write *hoo* but have to start with silent *w* instead, and then get even weirder by adding *ho*!

12. one: Spell *on,* and then add *e*.

13. have: Write "*hav*" just like it sounds, and then put silent *e* on the end.

14. your: Write *you* then add *r*.

Looking for Spelling Rules

Spelling rules are truly helpful. But some books rely too heavily on them, giving you dozens of rules and then bombarding you with exceptions to the rules. In this book I keep things simple. I focus on these three main rules that apply to heaps of words:

- ✔ Bossy *e* at the end of a word makes the vowel long (*mat* turns into *mate*).
- ✔ When two vowels go walking, the first one does the talking (like in *boat*).
- ✔ Y makes long-*e* or long-*i* sounds at the end of words (like in *happy* and *cry*).

The sections that follow explain how to make your child comfortable with these three rules.

Bossy e

The rule you'll see at work in words like *came* and *ride* is the Bossy *e* rule.

The Bossy e rule is where *e* added on to the end of a one-vowel word makes the vowel have a long sound. A good way to describe this rule to your child is to say that Bossy *e* sits at the end of the word and bosses the earlier vowel into saying its name.

The sight words in which Bossy *e* is at work are in the minitable that follows.

Bossy e at work

ate	like	these (*z* sound written as *s*)
came	live	those (*z* sound written as *s*)
gave	made	white
here	make	use (*z* sound written as *s*)
live (like in alive)	ride	

Tell your child to spell the *z* sound in *these, those,* and *use* with *s,* and then dictate the words for him to write. Give him as much help as he needs. You may want to do two dictations, the first for figuring it all out; the second to get a clean, error-free sweep at the words.

When two vowels go walking

In words like *clean* and *sweep* the "When-two-vowels-go-walking-the-first-one-does-the-talking (and shouts it name)" rule is at work.

This rule means that when two vowels appear next to each other in a word, the second vowel stays silent and the first vowel takes on a long sound, or says it's own name. The sight words in which you see this rule doing its thing are in the minitable that follows.

Two vowels walking

again	eat	see
been	green	sleep
clean	read	three

In normal speech, you usually pronounce *again* "uh-gen." However, it's easier to spell when pronounced *ag-ain* (like in *pain*). The same pronunciation thing happens in words like *the* and *a.* Your child will remember their spellings more easily when he starts off pronouncing them as "th-ee," and not "thuh," and "ay," and not "uh."

The pairs of vowels that you see most in these sight words are *ee* and *ea.* These pairs are common, and the other two pairs that your child will see in many words are *ai* (*pain, rain, and train*) and *oa* (*boat, soak, and throat*).

Point out the "*ag-ain*" pronunciation of *again* to your child, and then dictate the words for him to write.

Y making long-e or long-i sounds

Y is a letter your child will use quite often. When he's spelling a word that ends with the sound of long *e* or long *i*, he needs to try out a *y* for fit. *Y* makes the long-*e* sound on the end of longer words (*happy, silly, sunny*) and the long *i* sound on the end of short words (*my, by,* and *shy*). *Y* is featured on the end of the sight words in the minitable that follows.

Longing for y

any	carry	very
every	many	why
funny	only	

Before your child ever tries to spell a list of words, take a look at them with him. Look for unusual and similar spelling features. If your child is fore-warned of potential spelling hazards, he won't get caught by them. In the list that follows, I give quite a few things for you to point out:

✔ any and many: "*en*" is written *an*

✔ every: *every* and not *evry* like it sounds

✔ funny and carry: have double letters

✔ why: is one of the six "*wh*" question-forming words (*why, when, where, which, what,* and *who*)

When your child has highlighted the tricky words, circled tricky letters, and scribbled tricky words out a couple of times, you can dictate all the words for her to spell.

Getting Faster at Spelling Sight Words

Your child has to spell sight words quickly. That's because sight words crop up so often that if your child is slow to spell them he'll be a slow writer. If he's fluent and accurate at spelling sight words, he has brainpower in reserve for thinking of other things, like the flow and sense of his writing, whether he's giving the right answer, and how to spell less common words like *infrequent*. Help your child cruise through sight words by focusing on up to ten words at a time. Point out spelling features in those words, like silent or double letters. Establish a regular routine of spelling the ten words every night for a week (it takes only ten minutes a night). After a week, get ten new words. Keep going until your child can spell all 220 sight words quickly and accurately. If he can write a word already, you don't have to add it to your ten words to learn. If after a week he still can't spell one or two words, put them into the next batch of ten to run through again.

When your child writes regular text he doesn't need to worry about getting every spelling right first time. It's better that he gets all his thoughts down. He can underline spellings he's not sure of and come back to them later. When children are overly worried about perfect spelling they don't write as much and use a limited vocabulary. They don't reach beyond what they can already do, so they can't make much progress.

Having Fun With Sight Words

You and your child can have fun spelling sight words. Write them onto slips of paper or use commercial flashcards and then use them in "Seeing and writing" spelling activities. Here are some easy ones to try out:

Seeing and writing

The simplest way for your child to learn to spell is for him to look at a word and then write it plenty of times. Have him do this by using ten of the sight words at a time and playing these "See and write" games with them:

- Have ten sight words on ten pieces of paper. Have your child spread them out facedown and then ask him to turn each word over, take a quick peek at it, and then write it on his paper.

- Have your child put the ten words into a stack and ask him to turn each one over, quickly look at it, and then and write it down.

- Holding the words in a fan facing you, ask your child to pick a word, peek at it, and write it down.

- Holding the ten words in a fan facing you, ask him to select but not look at, a word and then take three guesses at which word he's selected. If he guesses correctly, he takes a peek at it and writes it down. Keep going until he's done all ten words.

Hiding and seeking

Most kids like hide and seek, but younger kids, in particular, like to find their words. Hide the ten words around the house and direct your child to them with hot and cold instructions. You know, when she's getting closer to a word, tell her she's getting hotter, and when she's moving away from a word, say she's getting colder. When she's found all the words, dictate them for her to write.

Racing the clock

If your child wants a challenge, get out your watch or stopwatch. You can blow a whistle to start him off, too. Setting a time for him to beat, dictate the ten words for him to write. Or you can time him writing the words on the first dictation and then have him try to beat his own time with each successive dictation. You can play any of the "Seeing and writing" or "Hiding and seeking" games against a clock.

Keeping track

Your child wants to know that he's doing well, wants to feel proud of himself, and needs you to show that you're proud of him, too. The best way to track and acknowledge his progress is with a visual reminder. In other words, you need a progress chart. You can make a pie chart or line graph, if you're handy on the keyboard, or a simple chart onto which your child sticks stickers is just as good. You can even make copies of the tables in this book and put gold stars over the words he's already learned to spell, if you'd like.

A good way to start keeping a track of progress is to have a ten-week plan, which simply means that you plan to guide your child through ten new words each week for ten weeks, and then plot those weeks on poster paper. You can draw ten circles to be filled with ten stickers or stars each week or a bar graph to be made into ten bars each of ten units. Better yet, try drawing a line reaching to the moon for your child to color or stick stickers onto to see if he can spell into space. You can even make a picture with 100 segments that need to be colored in, or have a marble jar to be filled with 100 marbles or get 100 stick-it labels to be stuck onto a door. I'm sure you get the idea that you can show off your child's progress in a lot of different ways.

Making the most of mediums

By making the most of mediums, I'm not talking about the kind who sit in darkened rooms, see the future, and venture into other dimensions. I don't know a thing about those mediums, but I do know that everyone knows something about mediums like paint, wax crayons, and shaving foam. They're different substances that you can write words with so that spelling is more fun. Jazzing up spelling activities by using different mediums is easy and fun. Get a large tray and reach for some sand, sugar, cream, shaving foam, pudding, mud, or rice. Have your child write his letters in whichever delicious or dirty medium you choose or have him create the letters to the words from modeling compound or pastry mix. Last, but not least, I need to mention the common stuff like pens and markers. Have a selection of colors and types and branch out into making bubble, rainbow, or shadow letters for effect. Bubble letters are the fat kind that kids love to doodle, rainbow letters are letters written in different colors, usually one color after another, and shadow letters appear three dimensional.

Games to go

The easy activities and games that I give next lend themselves perfectly to those times when you're waiting at soccer practice or Brownies. You may remember some of them from your own childhood. If you want even more ideas, flip over to Chapter 21.

Straightforward oral spellings

Although not actually a game, you may be surprised to find how much your child likes straightforward spelling, especially if he's already practiced the words and is pretty sure to get them all right. He actually likes you to ask him to spell them out loud. In the car, at the supermarket, or in the elevator, ask him to spell a few words for you. Younger, energetic kids will want to get right into the act, too.

Oral spellings with a theme

Think of a theme like words that end in *tion* or have more than three syllables, and take turns saying and spelling them. This activity works well with two or more children, and you can make the themes easier for the younger kids.

Boxes

I like this game. Boxes is more interactive than some games and the more your child plays, the better game he can give you. Start by drawing a square grid of dots, 4 dots by 4 dots (16 dots in all). Take turns drawing individual lines between two side-by-side dots. You can draw vertically or horizontally but not diagonally. Your goal is to complete more boxes than your opponent. Whenever you complete a box by adding the fourth side to a three-sided box, you put your mark inside your box (usually your initial) and get another turn. "So," you're asking, "where does the spelling fit in?" Give your child five free turns to start the game off, if he first spells five words correctly.

Words on your back

Have you a child with a vacant back? Write a word onto it with your finger. Write the first letter a few times until he figures out what it is, and then do the same with the remaining letters. When your child figures out the entire word, turn around and offer up your back for reciprocation.

One bite at a time

This week I've been consulting my I-will-not-shout-at-my-kids reminder note. It's summer vacation. My kids spend a lot of time trashing their rooms and thinking up new things to fight over. Sometimes, though, they want me to take them shopping, which I dislike, so they offer to do chores. When they first used this soft-soap approach, I handled it badly. I said things like, "Clean your room." My kids then went about stuffing their clothes, clean or dirty, into drawers, pushing their toys under their bed and, as such, pronouncing their room clean. I learned quickly, and now tell them to do specific things, such as put their clean clothes in their drawers or sweep the floor . . . and they do. A job that looks big, even conceptually, can be off-putting. That same job, broken into single tasks, looks doable. When you help your child with sight words, have him take bite-sized pieces of the whole job. Have him spell no more than ten new words at a time. Stick with the same ten words each night for a week so your child digests the new information and thus has an appetite for more, especially if you make spelling tasks fun.

In Chapter 20, I describe how to play "Boxes" and "Words on your back" with groups.

Picture words

Words like *jump, walk,* and *eat* are good for doodling with. Ask your child to draw in and around the words to make them look like what they're saying. Some letters can jump out of *jump, walk* can have a pair of feet added to the bottom of the *k*; and *eat* can be put on a plate. Let your child come up with good ideas for *again, around, down, drink, grow, light, little, tent,* and *two.*

Chapter 13

Being Vocal about Silent Letters

In This Chapter

▶ Recognizing silent letters

▶ Understanding when to use silent letters

▶ Practicing and playing with silent letters

Silent letters are like the extra gizmos and whatnots I see on my computer. Although there are a lot of them, I'm just not sure what they do yet. I know for sure that even though they puzzle me, they belong there.

Knocking with your Knuckles

Knees, knock, and *knew* all start with silent *k*. The silent-*k* family has many common words in it, and it's an easy one for your child to get familiar with, because that *k* is so darned odd. Goodness knows why it's there, but your child can have fun pronouncing it to remember the spelling. Table 13-1 has a dozen silent *k* words for you and your child to pronounce and marvel at. After your child notices that *kn* always says *n,* have her look for any other spelling features in the words (like *oe, ew, edge*), and then move straight into dictating a few of those words for her to spell. If she spells every word right, rejoice and head to the next table and the "Clever cards" game. If your child spells some words incorrectly, have her jot those words down a couple more times to jog her memory.

When your child struggles with a word, write it on a piece of paper and place it in an envelope. (Younger kids like to decorate their envelopes.) Have him spell that word every night for a week, but use no more than 10 words each week. If you include words from the same word family, like *knee, knock* and *knew,* the common feature (silent *k*) makes them easier for your child to remember.

Table 13-1		*kn* Words		
knife		knee		knock
know		knew		knob
kneel		knelt		knot
knuckle		knit		knowledge

Plunging into a Sea of Silent Letters

If I asked you to write words like *knee* and *comb*, you'd probably write them quickly. But to your child, they're not so familiar and most likely perplexing. In this chapter, I give you a dozen silent-letter families you can lead your child carefully through.

A word family is a group of words that have a spelling and sound pattern in common. Every word in the family has an identical part in it, like in *sing, sting, ring,* and *thing* and *knee, knot, knew,* and *knit.*

Delighting over your Daughter

The silent part of *delight* and *daughter* is *gh*. Silent *gh* turns up in a lot of words. Some of those words are tricky (*taught, through, bought*), so taking your time with them is well worth the effort. Scan over Table 13-2, and then try the five spelling strategies that follow. When you're ready for something lighter, have fun with the "Clever cards" activity.

igh always makes the long "eye" sound.

Table 13-2			Silent *gh* Words		
ight		*igh*	*aught, ought*		*A Mixed Hard Bunch*
light	bright	thigh	caught	ought	though
might	tight	high	taught	bought	through
fight	tonight	sigh	naughty	sought	thorough

ight		aught, ought		A Mixed Hard Bunch
fright	night	daughter	brought	bough
delight	flight	thought		

The words in Table 13-2 are tricky. Give your child a few helpful strategies for remembering how to spell them.

The five best spelling strategies your child can use with hard spellings are

- ✔ Spelling words in family groups (*tight, fright, light*) rather than as individuals.
- ✔ Highlighting the tricky part within a word to remember the sound and look of it better.
- ✔ Writing out a word five times.
- ✔ Spelling the same ten words every night for a week.
- ✔ Taping words onto often-seen walls (like bathroom walls).

Your child will come upon the silent *gn* family at some point. Its words are *resign design, gnaw, gnat, campaign, foreign, and reign*. You may not want to spell these words right now, but I give them to you now so you can refer to them when you need to.

Activity: Clever cards (two players)

Preparation: Onto each of 26 index cards copy one of the 26 words from the *kn, ight,* and *aught* families in Tables 13-1 and 13-2. Remember only one word on each separate card. Onto six more index cards write the word "Spell."

Follow these steps:

1. **Player 1 shuffles all 32 cards together and deals 7 cards each, and then places the remaining cards in the deck facedown.** He turns up (exposes) the top card on the deck to start a discard stack.

2. **Player 2 starts play by laying one of his cards onto the discard pile.** The card must be either a "spell" card or a card of the same family as the last card on the discard stack. If he lays a "spell" card, he takes a card from his opponent and reads out the word for his opponent to spell.

3. **If the opponent spells correctly the card goes on top of the discard pile and play goes back to Player 2.**

4. **If he spells incorrectly, he keeps the incorrectly spelled word and picks up another card.**

5. **Play then advances to Player 2 who lays any card he wants** (on top of the "spell" card). The object of the game is to be the first person to play all of your cards

If the first card you overturn to start the discard stack is a "spell" card put in on the bottom of the stack and turn up the next card.

You can play this game with any word families, as long as you end up with a deck of about 30 cards.

Wriggling your Wrist

Silent *w* is an important letter. Your child sees it again and again. It's in the word *write* for one thing and in *wh* words like *who* and *whole*. Table 13-3 gives *wr* words and I say more about *wh* words later in this section.

Table 13-3	Silent *w*	
wrist	wrong	wreck
wriggle	wrap	write
wrote	written	wretch
wrinkle	wrestle	wren
wring	wreath	wrench
writhe	wry	

The *"wr"* spelling always says *r*.

Some of the really important silent *w* words are: whole, who, whose, and whom.

One way to sort them is to say that *whole* is easy because it's simply a regular *hole* with a *w* in front, and the rest of the words use a single *o* to make the *oo* sound like in moon.

Squealing and Squirming

Tell your child to always jot down a silent *u* after a *q* like in *quick* and *quiz*. Table 13-4 shows a lot of *qu* words. Look out for spelling features like the *a* in *quad* (it sounds like short *o*) and the *or* in *equator* (it's *or* not *er*). When you and your child have read through the table noting tricky spelling chunks, try your luck in the next activity, Eight-square bingo.

Very occasionally your child comes upon a word that has a *q* in it but no *u*, like in Iraq and Qatar (words of foreign origin).

Table 13-4	*qu*	
quack	quick	quilt
quads	quit	quiz
quadrangle	quarrel	quality
quantity	queen	quail
queasy	equipment	equal
equator	liquid	quote
squirm	squeal	squash
squirrel	squander	adequate
inquire	enquire	quiet
quite	square	squeamish

q never goes anywhere without *u*.

The usual sound of *qu* is "*kw*" like in liquid but sometimes you hear "*k*," like in liquor.

The words *inquire* and *enquire* are interchangeable. But in newspapers an *inquiry* is a formal, official looking-into and an *enquiry* is a more informal question.

Spend extra time on the two look-alikes; *quiet* and *quite*. Have your child pronounce them clearly so he can see that the spelling arrangements make good sense.

Activity: Eight-square bingo

Preparation: Have your child write eight words from Tables 13-3 and 13-4, well spaced on a piece of paper and then cut out each word. Each of you also needs an index card and a pen.

Follow these steps:

1. **Each of you draws eight squares on your card in two rows of four squares and then writes each of the eight words in any order in the individual squares.**

2. **Have your child put the cutout words in a bowl, and without looking, draw out a word.**

3. **Cross off the words as they're drawn.** The first person to cross off a complete row of four words wins.

Disguising as a Guard

In many words, your child writes *gu* but says only *g*. Show your child the words in Table 13-5 so she isn't bewildered by this *gu* spelling. Have her write the words out a few times to help her remember that this *gu* isn't a soft *"gee"* sound like in *gy, gi,* and *ge*. I talk at length about soft sounds in Chapter 14, but right now, I have other *g* spellings to show you. When you and your child have taken a look at Table 13-5, move to the *gue* and *gn* spellings. Between these two groups, you can see what must be some of the most bizarre spellings in use. When you've cast your be*gu*iled, intri*gu*ed or resi*gn*ed eye over Tables 13-5 through 13-7, be sure to check out the "Looney letter" activity.

Table 13-5	*gu* Words	
guess	guest	guilt
guide	guard	guarantee
guitar	disguise	guardian
beguile	guile	guinea

I have a little bunch of words to squeeze in here. It's the family of words in which *ui* is pronounced as short *i*, like in *ink*. From the table, you find out that *guitar, guilt,* and *guinea* belong to this family. Other members are *biscuit, builder, built,* and *build*.

Being Vague about the League

Show your child the *gue* combination that tags onto the ends of words and keeps that hard *"guh"* sound. It makes words look fairly ferocious, so you may want to write them out a few ways in different colors, in bubble letters, or going vertically. By joining in with your child's artistry, this basic spelling practice won't seem arduous.

A happy, creative attitude distinguishes great teachers from merely okay teachers. Keep a can-do and upbeat manner for your child as you do the spellings together. Use different colored pens to write (and compare) words, finger-write (no ink) on each other's backs, and munch on favorite snacks together.

Table 13-6	*gue* Words	
fatigue	morgue	dialogue
monologue	intrigue	rogue
vogue	plague	vague
tongue	league	colleague
catalogue		

An interesting thing about "tongue" is that you pronounce it differently depending on whether you mean the tongue in your mouth or the tongs you serve food with.

Gnawing on a Sign

G has dominated two tables already in this chapter, and in Table 13-7, it partners up with *n*. Show your child that anytime she writes these *n*-sounding words, she, in fact, writes *gn*. That way she's more at home with the "Writing a loony letter" activity that comes next.

Table 13-7	Silent *g*	
gnome	gnash	gnaw
gnarled	gnat	campaign
gnu	foreign	champagne
sign	resign	design
consign	reign	lasagna

The time may come when your child writes words that have to do with bodily stuff, in which she spells silent *g* followed by *m* (and has to feature *ph*, too). Check out *diaphragm* and *phlegm*.

Activity: Writing a loony letter

Preparation: Open this book to Tables 13-5 to 13-7, and grab pen and paper.

Follow this step: With your child, write a short letter. Aim to use at least ten words from the tables. Your letter can be as absurd as you like. Here's an example:

> Today, I lay in foreign champagne and then listened to a dialogue between a gnat and a guard. The gnat gnawed on a catalogue, but I left in disguise to paint my guitar. I didn't design this letter, but I might sign it.
>
> Guess who?

Combing the Lamb

The words in Table 13-8 aren't common, but they're distinctive. There doesn't seem to be a reason in the world for *b* to make an appearance in these words, but it's there anyway. Most children seem to remember these spellings best if they start off by pronouncing that *b* until they remember to include it without the whacky pronunciation. The activity that I give for silent-*b* words gets into the whole pronunciation thing.

Table 13-8	Silent *b*	
lamb	bomb	thumb
comb	subtle	climb
debt	numb	limb
crumb	tomb	womb
doubt	succumb	

Activity: To *b* or not to *b*

Preparation: Open your copy of *Teaching Kids to Spell For Dummies* to Table 13-8 and have pen and paper ready.

Follow this step: Dictate ten words from the table, but do it with either of these two quirks:

- ✔ Pronounce the *b*. Ask your child to write the word and tell you how it should really sound.

✔ Spell out the word for your child (she can write it down) and ask him how it's pronounced.

Walking and Talking

Here's a group of words to take your time with. You can skim over the less common words in Table 13-9, but *walk* and *talk* and *would, could,* and *should* are words that your child definitely needs to get familiar with. You'll probably notice *psalm* in this group. What a word! I've included it for interest, but it isn't included as one of the answers that your child needs to know in the "Which word does this describe?" activity later in this section.

Table 13-9		Silent *l*	
alm and alf Words	*alk Words*	*ould Words*	*olk Words*
calm	chalk	would	folk
palm	talk	could	yolk
psalm	walk	should	
embalm	balk		
half	stalk		
calf			

One odd word in the silent-*l* group is *salmon*. You can't make a family of salmon-like words because no other word is very like salmon.

Activity: Which word does this describe?

Preparation: Make a copy of Table 13-9 and give it to your child, and then ask her the ten questions.

Follow this step: Have your child write the answers to these questions:

1. What's an eggy word?

2. Which three words rhyme with *pud* (like in *pudding*)?

3. What grows on a plant?

4. When you share a pie equally with one friend, how much of the pie do you get?

5. What's another word for people?

6. What can you write with?

7. Which word has a pal in it (clue: pal)?

8. Which word is a homonym (sounds the same) for "wood?"

9. Which word is Something that can happen to a dead body?

10. Which word means too slow to be a jog?

Answers (in order): yolk; would, could, and should; stalk; half; folk; chalk; palm; would; embalm; and walk.

Being Honest at the Exhibition

In the silent-*h* group you find interesting, not to mention hard, words. Ask your child which ones he likes the look of or doesn't, and which is the easiest, hardest, or most common word. When you and your child have scanned through the words in Table 13-10, do the "Pictures and mnemonics" activity at the end of this section and watch as your child's artistic and cerebral sides get cozy with one another.

Mnemonics are triggers (usually rhymes and codes) that people use to help them remember stuff. The saying, "Spring forward, fall back" is a mnemonic that helps you remember which way to change the setting of your clock in spring and fall, and if you're anything like me, you rely pretty heavily on mnemonics to pass yourself off as someone who knows what he's doing. Your child, pristine as his memory is, can use mnemonics, too. Two of the words in Table 13-10 have their own mnemonics.

To help your child remember the difference between *our* and *hour* tell him this:

There's a **h**and in ***hour***, like the hand on a clock.

This mnemonic is good for teaching your child to tell the time on an analog clock, but the digital era may soon make it defunct.

To help your child remember how to spell rhythm, tell him this:

Rhythm **h**elps **y**our **t**wo **h**ips **m**ove.

If your child decides that these mnemonics aren't for him, that's okay. In the "Pictures and mnemonics" activity that follows, he can make up his own.

Activity: Pictures and mnemonics

Preparation: Turn in your book to Table 13-10 and have paper and pencil ready.

Follow this step: Tell your child about the hour and rhythm mnemonics earlier in this section, and then ask him to think up some memory joggers for words in the table. Can he draw word pictures (like *l☺☺k!*) or think of word-play to help him remember the spellings of *ghost, school,* and *exhibit*?

Table 13-10	Silent *h*	
hour	honest	rhyme
rhythm	exhibit	exhaust
vehicle	ghastly	heir
rhubarb	ghost	school
rhinoceros	psychic	psychotic
psychology	psychiatry	

Listening to Whistles

T is another silent letter that kids like to pronounce at first. You probably did the same thing when you were a kid and may still say that silent sound in your head when you're writing it. Read through Table 13-11 with your child then adapt the "To *b* or not to *b*" activity from earlier in this chapter into a "To *t* or not to *t*" activity.

Table 13-11	Silent *t*	
whistle	thistle	bristle
mistletoe	gristle	hustle
rustle	bustle	castle
fasten	glisten	soften
moisten	often	

Going Psycho!

What should your child do to remember the spelling of the silent-*p* words? Ask her. Have her tell you what her strategy is. Will she break the words up? Will she highlight the tricky parts? Will exaggerated pronunciation help? Have her write the words a few times until she thinks she can remember them, and then offer to test her in a few hours time to see if she still remembers. Run through a game of "Eight-square bingo" (explained earlier in this chapter) and make a bet with her. (You win; you get ice cream. I win; you get ice cream!) Table 13-12 provides a collection of silent *p* words.

Table 13-12		Silent *p*
psalm	psychology	psychiatry
receipt	pneumatic	cupboard
pneumonia	psychic	pseudonym
raspberry		

Feeling Solemn about the Column

This group of words is such a little one that it doesn't even warrant a table. But don't be lulled into a false sense of security. The *mn* group of words is definitely no less strange than the bigger groups. Your child won't use these words often but she'll notice them when she does. The *mn* group is: h*ymn*, *autumn*, *solemn*, *condemn*, and *column*.

My guess is that *column* is the word she'll have most need of — in math when she plots graphs, puts numbers in tables, and does all manner of other impressive math stuff. How will she remember the spellings? Ask *her!*

How many psychiatrists does it take . . .

Ending this chapter with my "Feeling solemn" heading would be bleak of me, so I'm signing off on a high note. Here, for your absolute enjoyment, are two of my hugely funny jokes:

✔ How many psychiatrists does it take to change a light bulb? Only one. But the bulb has to want to change.

✔ **Man to his psychiatrist:** I keep thinking I'm a dog.

✔ **Psychiatrist:** Lie down on the couch and I'll examine you.

✔ **Man:** I can't. I'm not allowed on the furniture.

Chapter 14

Spelling Some Letters "Softly"

In This Chapter

▶ Recognizing soft sounds

▶ Understanding when to use soft spellings

▶ Distinguishing between soft and hard spellings

Question: Why shouldn't you tell a pig a secret?

Answer: Because pigs are squealers!

I'm sure *you* only entrust your secrets to trustworthy pigs, but have you shared the soft-letter secret with your child? The secret is this: Only two letters make a soft sound, and they do it only on occasion. I'm convinced that this information is kept a secret from a lot of kids, because I see so many of them writing soft letters all over the place. This chapter shows you how to help your child ace it with the softies.

Hearing Hard and Soft Sounds

The two letters in the alphabet that make sounds called hard and soft sounds are *c* and *g*. Your child already knows the hard sounds well. He learned them when he learned his alphabet: *"cuh"* for the letter *c* and *"guh"* for the letter *g*.

Soft sounds are soft because they have a softer pronunciation than hard sounds. The soft sound of *c*, is *"ss,"* and the soft sound of *g* is *"juh."*

Relaxing with Identical Sounds

Here's the rub with soft sounds: The sound *"ss"* is made by either *s* or *c*, and *"juh"* is made by either *j* or *g*. So when does your child use *c* and not *s*? And when does he use *g* and not *j*? Just how does it all work?

Ta-da. I come bearing rules! No need to call out the spelling squad or resort to searching through the dreary dictionary; the next few pages help you tread lightly, with your child, through soft and simple rules.

Scanning the Soft-c Rule

Words like *cot, crate,* and *actor* use hard (or regular) *c*. Words like *receive, race,* and *cylinder* use soft *c* (which sounds like *"ss"*). Tell your child that when he reads new words, he can tell when a letter is a softy by looking at the letter right after it. The pattern or rule is:

When *c* is followed by *e, i,* or *y,* it usually says its soft sound.

Recognizing Soft-c Words

Isolated rules are hard to remember, and for that reason, you need to spend plenty of time practicing these rules with your child. With that in mind, read through all the words in Table 14-1 with your child and have her highlight the *ce, ci,* or *cy* parts of all of them. When you're done, zip to the "Spot the right spelling" activity.

Table 14-1		Soft *c* Words	
ce Words		*ci Words*	*cy Words*
ace	peace	city	fancy
pace	glance	circle	cylinder
face	slice	circus	cyst
race	dance	cigar	spicy
space	brace	civil	Nancy
ice	receive	cistern	Quincy
lice	perceive	cinch	Tracy
rice	niece	Cindy	Stacy
nice	center	cinder	cymbal
mice	twice		cynic
prince	since		
price	chance		

The words receive, perceive, and niece follow the *i*-before-*e*-except-after-*c* rule.

The "Spot the right spelling" activity (coming up next) is quick and easy. Your child must sort through words that all are phonetically fine (they sound-out fine), but aren't always spelled correctly.

Children's spelling errors usually are phonetically accurate. Think about it; they write words like *thay* and *wur,* which sound-out fine, but nevertheless are spelled incorrectly. To be a good speller, your child needs to spot the right spelling by writing out different possibilities. Seeing the differences in written words is called *visual discrimination,* and matching the right sound with a bunch of letters is called *phonographics* (or sometimes *graphophonics*).

Activity: Spotting soft *c* spellings

Preparation: Make a copy of the list of questions that follows and have a pen or pencil ready for your child.

Follow this step: Ask your child to circle the right spelling. Give him "you're getting warmer (or colder)" hints whenever he needs them.

- ✔ fase — faice — face
- ✔ prince — prinse — prinss
- ✔ fence — fens — fense
- ✔ mice — mise — miyse
- ✔ surcus — curcus — circus
- ✔ spisee — spicy — spisey
- ✔ twise — twice — twyce
- ✔ circel — circle — sircle
- ✔ fansy — fansey — fancy
- ✔ spayce — spase — space
- ✔ reseve — receve — receive
- ✔ chanse — chanes — chance
- ✔ niece — neice — neece
- ✔ dance — danse — daence
- ✔ slise — slyce — slice

If your child wants a challenge, try dictating the correct words for him to write out.

Writing Soft c Words

The two activities that I offer up next enable your child to practice writing soft-c words from scratch. They're basic dictation (reading out words for your child to write) and proofreading (reading to spot errors) tasks, tweaked here and there for more interest.

Dictation and proofreading are the mainstays of any spelling program. The more of them your child does, the better she gets at spelling.

Activity: Dictated spellings

Preparation: Turn in this book to Table 14-1 and have a piece of paper and a pen or pencil ready for your child to use.

Follow this step: Dictate words from Table 14-1 for your child to write but vary the way you dictate by:

1. Reading words together in families (*ice, mice, and nice*).

2. Giving clues rather than words, like, "You put this into your drink to make it cold."

3. Acting out or miming some words (*dance, face, lice, race, circle,* or *circus*).

Activity: Silly sentences

Preparation: Make a copy of the list of questions that follow, and have some highlighters on hand for your child to use.

Follow these steps:

1. **Have your child read the sentences and highlight the right answer from the two possibilities.**

2. **Have him finger-write five answers on your back for you to figure out.** (Unlike finger painting, finger writing is impressing letters with your finger, no ink!)

   • Give me a second *chance — hopping.*

   • We ate chicken with *rice — trees.*

   • I've been to Disneyland *cookies — twice.*

   • The rocket flew into *buckets — space.*

   • The plumber had to fix the *cistern — donkey.*

- The runner set a fast *pace — pumpkin.*
- In math, I drew a *circle — talking.*
- The skater stepped onto the *lemon — ice.*
- Her birthday cake was *fancy — grass.*
- I live in the *telephone — city.*
- Her name was *Stacy — book.*
- She had pet *mice — wheels.*

Deciding Whether to Write c or s

The next activity is a fun story for your child to correct. I've left *s* and (soft) *c* out all over the place, so your child has to put on his thinking cap and really get out there!

Activity: Tackling a tampered-with story

Preparation: Make a copy of "Prince Stan and Cindy The Soccer Ace."

Follow this step: Ask your child to read the story and change every * (asterisk) to an *s* or *c* to make the missing *ss* sound. Advise him to use scrap paper to scribble down the two possible answers when he isn't sure which one's right.

Prince Stan and Cindy The Soccer Ace

Prin*e *tan's father, King Lee, wanted hi* *on to play *occer *o the people in his kingdom could *ee him beat other *occer teams and do *ome fan*y footwork. *o the King *ent Prin*e *tan off to *occer *chool. But Prin*e *tan was awful at *occer. He lost all the training ra*es and couldn't keep up the pa*e. In fact he would much rather have been cooking. Prin*e *tan was a great cook. He cooked ri*e with a lot of ta*ty spi*es and baked a ni*e cu*tard sli*e too. Cooking was a *inch for the prin*e but at *occer *chool he was miserable. Then the prin*e met *indy. *indy loved *occer. She could dan*e the ball around all the other players' feet and could run twi*e as fast as any of them. Because *indy was always playing *occer she was always *tarving. So Prin*e *tan (who thought *indy was cute) cooked her his famou* cu*tard *li*e. In*tantly she fell in love with him. You know what happens next don't you. They got married and *indy played *occer for all the kingdom to *ee. King Lee was delighted. Prin*e *tan cooked mountains of cu*tard *li*e for the hungry *indy and everybody el*e in the kingdom. And they all lived happily ever after, of cour*e!

Cinders in the city

This sidebar is a teensy-weensy bit of extraneous information, but I just can't resist it!

What did Cinderella say when she left the photo shop?

"Some day my prints will come!"

(See! How funny was that?)

Scanning the Soft g Rule

Words like *gum, grate,* and *aggressive* use hard (or regular) g. Words like *gem, giant,* and *gym* use soft g (which sounds like *"juh"*). The pattern or rule is:

If g says its soft sound, it's usually followed by *e, i,* or *y*. (The same goes for *c*.)

Recognizing Soft g Words

Read through all the words in Table 14-2 with your child and have him highlight the *ge, gi,* or *gy* parts of each one. When your child's pretty comfortable with how that g makes its appearance, speed forward to the "Spotting the right spelling" activity.

Your child needs to jot down any words he thinks are particularly sneaky (I'd opt for *giraffe* and *general*). Whenever he writes them out a few times, he's more likely to keep them in his mind for future reference.

Table 14-2		Soft g Words	
ge Words	*gi Words*	*gy Words*	
gentleman	plunge	giant	gym
gentle	bulge	giraffe	gyrate
gem	huge	ginger	gypsy
general	page	fragile	Egypt
gender	rage	agile	
generous	bridge	magic	
gesture	strange	tragic	
genuine	legend	logic	

ge Words	gi Words	gy Words
stage	dungeon	region
age		imagine
wage		engine

Is it *ge* or *dge?* Short vowel sounds are nearly always followed by *dge* (*edge, ledge,* and *badge*).

The activity I provide for you here is another proofreading activity. I include proofreading all through this book because there's no better way to help your child get into the habit of checking his own spelling. Developing a good eye is a big part of being a good speller, so have your child get down and get focused!

Activity: Spotting soft *g* spellings

Preparation: Make a copy of the list of questions that follow, and have a pen or pencil ready for your child to use.

Follow this step: Ask your child to circle the right spellings.

- page — paje — paydge
- bulge — bulje — buldge
- lejund — ledgend — legend
- brige — bridge — brydge
- jiant — gyant — giant
- gentel — gental — gentle
- emagine — imajine — imagine
- plunge — plunje — plundje
- rayge — rage — raje
- stranje — strandge — strange
- fradgile — frajile — fragile
- engyn — engin — engine
- Egipt — Ejypt — Egypt
- genral — general — jeneral
- tragic — trajic — tradgic

If your child has untapped mental stamina, dictate the correct words for him to write out.

Writing Soft g Words

The "3 by 3 by 3" activity is a short thinker of an exercise. Although your child has only a little writing to do, she must get it right.

Activity: 3 by 3 by 3

Preparation: Open your copy of *Teaching Kids to Spell For Dummies* to this activity and have paper and pen ready.

Follow these steps:

1. **Show your child the three word endings that follow.**

2. **Have him write three words in each group in less than three minutes.**

   1. _age

   2. _edge

   3. gen_

The "Imagining sentences" activity up next fires up your child's imagination. She has to put some soft *g* words together to make sentences. The sillier or more impossible the sentence, the better.

Activity: Imagining sentences

Preparation: Have your book open to this page and paper and pen in hand

Follow this step: Ask your child to look at Table 14-2 and make up five "Imagine . . . " sentences from the words. For example, you can write:

- Imagine a huge, million-dollar gem.
- Imagine two fragile giraffes.
- Imagine a bag bulging with magic.

If your child groans at the prospect of writing the sentences, offer to be her secretary. Write the sentences for her, asking her to spell out the soft-*g* words.

Deciding Whether to Write g or j

The "Fixing a muddle" activity asks your child to quickly sort through and write a few words that feature *g*'s and *j*'s. The more practice your child gets at writing *g* or *j*, the better he gets.

Activity: Fixing a muddle

Preparation: Make a copy of the sentences that follow and have paper and pencil ready for your child to use.

Follow this step: Give your child the list of sentences and have him write the right answers from the muddle of answers that I put willy-nilly on the ends.

This boy climbed a beanstalk *page*

Makes you laugh *general*

A slow run *Jasmine*

A famous old story *bridge*

In a zoo *wage*

In a book *giraffe*

A road over a river *stage*

Pay for a job *Jack*

Shows happen on this *rage*

Fury *joke*

An important person in the army *legend*

A plant that is also a girl's name *jog*

Sorting your cs and juggling your gs

I'm not totally heartless. I know that the activities in this chapter have leaned more toward the sit-down-and-write side, so I'm lightening up here. Here's a fun game that you and your child can play with soft-*c* words, soft-*g* words, or a mixed bunch of both.

Activity: Chutes and ladders with chances

Preparation: You can use a commercial Chutes and Ladders board or make your own, along with a cup and a dice.

1. **Write instructions on 20 index cards.**

2. **Write five sets of four identical cards with the following instructions on them:** "Miss a turn," "Move forward five squares," "Move back five squares," "Spell three soft-*c* words," and "Spell three soft-*g* words."

3. **Shuffle this pack of "Chance" cards at the start of the game.**

Follow these steps:

1. **Play Chutes and Ladders in the normal way, but mark ten of the squares on your board as "Chance" squares.** Mark random squares with a sticker, or nominate every tenth square; either way works.

2. **When players land on a chance square, they pick up a chance card and do what it says.** No player can spell the same word twice, and if a player can't answer his card, he stays on the chance square and answers a new card when it's his turn again.

You can find another version of "Chutes and ladders" in Chapter 20.

Part V
Spelling Words in Chunks

The 5th Wave   By Rich Tennant

"I always speak to the kids in a quiet and respectful way, but occasionally I wear this to add a little punctuation."

In this part . . .

Good spellers spell words chunk by chunk. But where are the best places to break words up? That's the question. The chapters in this part show you not only where to put those breaks but also how to avoid doing bad things to nice suffixes and how to handle your contractions, too.

Chapter 15

Cheerfully Chunking Sounds

In This Chapter

▶ Developing an ear for chunks of sound or syllables

▶ Discovering the do's and don'ts of syllables

▶ Making friends with popular syllables

Children who struggle with spelling often jumble up their syllables. They hear *sledding* and write *selding,* or *soling.* It isn't a big deal if your child sometimes makes mistakes through rushing (I do it all hte tiem), but it is a big deal if she can't hear the sounds in a word and then write them down in order.

In this chapter, I show you how to help your child hear, arrange, and write down the chunks of sound inside of words. I walk you through the rules of how to break words up into nice little chunks of sound and let you decide whether you can use those rules a lot or a little. The rules may make perfect sense to you, or you may decide to ad lib now and then.

Syllables or Chunks of Sound

Words are made up of chunks of sound called *syllables*. You and your child need to spend plenty of time among these chunks, because good spellers spell in chunks. If you're not sure which piece of a word is a syllable, remember that a syllable has to have a vowel in it. That's all you really need to know to start with.

The letter *y* is a special one. When it sounds like a vowel, you count it as a vowel. Words like *myself* (*my-self*) and *Sally* (*Sal-ly*) use *y* as a vowel in one of their syllables.

Hearing Syllables in Words

The best place for your child to start exploring syllables is in his ears. Your child must first hear the chunks of sound inside words before he can write them. Where long words are concerned, he needs to be extra tuned in, because he needs to hear and correctly write down three or more syllables. The next activity is every teacher's warm-up game for syllables — the clapping game. All your child has to do is clap out the number of syllables he hears in a word.

Activity: Clapping out syllables

Preparation: Open your copy of *Teaching Kids to Spell For Dummies* to this activity.

Follow these steps:

1. **Describe the following name steps to your child (recommended dialog is in quotations).** When you're done with the names I give you, use other names you know.

    1. "Listen to this: **Ken** (Clap once). **John** (Clap once). **Kate** (Clap once). **Lynn** (Clap once). **Ja-son** (Clap twice). **Sal-ly** (Clap twice). **Ash-ley** (Clap twice)."

    2. Clap your first name, then have your child clap out her own name.

    3. Clap three other names that you know, and have your child clap out names she knows.

2. **Take turns clapping out names.** Have fun with names like Elizabeth ("Ee-liz-uh-beth") and try big words like Mis-sis-sip-pi and tar-ran-tu-la.

Soup up this game by including middle and last names.

Keeping Letter Friends Together

Help your child write down the syllables he hears by pointing out a few special characteristics about syllables. First, tell him about the vowel thing: All syllables have a vowel in them. Next, show your child that when he's writing down syllables, some letters are never parted. Buddies like *ck* and *ch* are never apart from each other. They belong together always like milk and cookies, and they count as one letter. The letter friends in this category are:

- *ck* (*tick-et, pock-et, sick-en*)
- *ex* (*ex-it, ex-act, ex-am*)
- Consonant digraphs (*ch, sh, th, wh,* and *ph*)
- Vowel digraphs (like *au, ar,* and *oi*)

- ✔ Consonant blends (like *bl, pr,* and *st*)
- ✔ Whole words inside compound words (like *camp-fire, sea-shore,* and *pan-cake*)
- ✔ Prefixes (like *dis, re,* and *un* — to name a few)
- ✔ Suffixes (like *ing, er,* and *est*)

A *digraph* is simply two letters together making one new sound. All the scary-sounding terms like *prefix, suffix,* and *diphthong* simply describe little chunks of sound that are common and therefore good to know about. Helping your child write bunches of *ai, au,* and *oi* words and chop words into chunks is perfectly okay, and probably best, without ever uttering the words "digraph" or "syllable."

This keeping-friends-together rule actually looks harder than it really is. When you start breaking words up, you hear and see that most breaks occur in pretty obvious spots. If you're not sure, put the break wherever it makes sense to you.

I provide you with examples of keeping letter-friends together in two-syllable words that I examine in the next paragraphs. Before that, though, I talk a bit about one-syllable words. When your child spells a word comprised of one syllable, she won't need to remember much. She doesn't need to put any breaks at all in one-syllable words.

One Syllable Is a Cinch

One-syllable words look like this: *Sam. Pete, and Tris; green, blue,* and *pink; milk, cream,* and *egg; bat, ball,* and *net;* and *crunch, shout,* and *spin.* These words are made of one straight, unsplit sound. Your child simply says the whole word and writes it down. What could be easier? Run through one-syllable words with your child, and if a word has a blend (*str, dr*) or digraph (*ch, sh, ai, au*) in it, point this out to her. You don't have to say, "Here's a digraph," but just show her that you can see a tricky little part of the word (that's really what a digraph is) and what it is. Have your child spot and high-light that tricky part. To help her remember the digraph better, take time out and make word families. If your child is writing *dream* have her highlight the *ea* part and take a quick run through the *ea* word family (*mean, cream, clean*). With *night* have her highlight *ight* and take a foray into *sight, fight,* and *might.* (You can find the *ea* word family in Chapter 8 and in Chapter 11 I tackle the *ight* family)

Two Syllables Are a Pic-nic

Two-syllable words (or words you break into two chunks) are pretty easy, but several kinds of them are out there. Take a look at the next bulleted list to get the general idea, and then move to the explanations in the sections that follow. You can store this information in your mind for the next time your child needs to spell a word like *account* (*ac-count*) or lead her through the exercises that I give you so she's forearmed. Here they are then, categories of two-syllable words that you'll come across:

- Compound words (*nowhere: no-where*)
- Words with a double letter in the middle (*letter: let-ter*)
- Words with two consonants in the middle (*picnic: pic-nic*)
- Words with first syllables that have open vowels (*remind: re-mind*)
- Words starting with a prefix (*invest: in-vest*)
- Words ending with a suffix (*spying: spy-ing*)

Cruising through compound words

The easiest two-syllable word of all is a compound word. A compound word is a big word made of two smaller single-syllable words joined together. When you help your child spell a compound word, all she has to do is write the two distinct words it's made of. The two separate words will be obvious to your child but he may be uncertain of the spelling for each one. Have him cast his eye over each word's features. Are any digraphs lurking in there (*ch, sh, ea, ai, aw,* or *ar*)? What about double letters (*egg-shell*)? Is a *y* making a vowel sound (*my-self*)? Table 15-1 shows the easy breaks in compound words and the spelling features on which your child can focus. After the table, I give you a nice quiet activity and then a runaround one.

Table 15-1	Looking at Compound Words	
Compound Word	*Breaking Up the Word*	*Spelling Features*
bookshelf	book-shelf	*oo*
raincoat	rain-coat	*ai, oa*
teaspoon	tea-spoon	*ea, oo*
moonlight	moon-light	*oo, ight*
wheelchair	wheel-chair	*wh, ee, ch, air*
downhill	down-hill	*ow*

Compound Word	Breaking Up the Word	Spelling Features
myself	my-self	*y (y in the middle of a word sounds like short or long i)*
quicksand	quick-sand	*qu, ck*

In the "Spelling compound words" activity your child takes a close look at the words in Table 15-1 and then breaks them up and spells them for herself.

Always give your child instruction and practice with words before asking him to spell them for himself

Activity: Spelling compound words

Preparation: Open this book to Table 15-1 and have paper and pen for each of you (or a whiteboard) and a color highlighter. You're going to look at the tricky parts (like *ai* and *ow)* in these compound words. If you want to recap on the when-two-vowels-go-walking rule, flip to Chapter 8. To find out more about word families, scan Chapter 10.

Follow these steps (recommended dialog is in quotations):

1. **On your paper, write the word "bookshelf" for your child to see.**

2, **Explain that, "*Bookshelf* is made of two small words."**

3. **Tell your child to "draw a line to break *bookshelf* into two small words."**

4. **Repeat this routine with the remaining seven words (*raincoat, teaspoon, moonlight, wheelchair, downhill, myself, quicksand*).**

5. **Be sure your child knows to "mark any special letters you see in each word." Help your child find the spelling features. (I show them to you in the third column of Table 15-1.) Talk about why they're special.**

6. **Say, "Now I'll read each word out, and you write it down." Dictate each word for your child to write.** If he struggles, let him look at the word before trying again.

Every spelling feature in Table 15-1 belongs in a word family. If your child can't spell the hard part (the spelling feature) of a word, have him practice writing word families. If he writes *whealchair,* practice a bunch of *ee* and *ea* words so he develops a better eye for picking *ee* or *ea.* If he writes *moonlite,* write some *ight* words. And if he's weak with *c*'s, *k*'s, and *ck*'s, write words with the *"cuh"* sound in them and spot any patterns. (When words with one syllable end with the *cuh* sound, they're nearly always spelled *ck* (*brick, sock, duck,* and *neck*).

Activity: Making sense

Preparation: Print each of the six words from Table 15-1 (in large letters) on one piece of paper. Cut each word into its two component words. In six different places around the room or house, put a mismatched beginning and end, like *rain-self.* Make sure that you have a watch or timer.

Follow this step: Ask your child to find the mismatched word parts and rearrange them into the six real words, all within a time limit perhaps three minutes.

Dealing with double letters

When you spell a two-syllable word that has a double consonant (*ll, tt, or, pp*) in the middle, break the word between those consonants. Table 15-2 gives you plenty of double-consonant words to read through with your child. When you've had a good look at all the double-letter words, move on to the "Twins (spelling double-consonant words)" activity.

Table 15-2	Breaking Up Double Consonants	
ap-pear	bal-loon	bot-tle
but-ter	din-ner	con-nect
fol-low	ham-mer	hap-pen
hid-den	hol-low	kit-ten
les-son	let-ter	mit-ten
pil-low	pol-len	rab-bit
rob-ber	rub-bish	sun-ny
sup-per	writ-ten	yel-low

The "Twins" activity asks your child to find things, and as you know, finding things is fun, so any time your child dozes while working on a spelling list (not mine of course!), chop out the words, hide them, and have her run around finding them so she's reinvigorated to tackle them again.

Activity: Twins (Spelling double-consonant words)

Do every practical step in this activity with your child, but make sure each of you is using your own paper so you're working on "twins."

Preparation: Each of you needs paper and pen (or a whiteboard) and a colored highlighter. Neatly print the whole words (not the split-up versions) from Table 15-2 onto your paper and have your child do the same.

Follow these steps (recommended dialog is in quotations):

1. **Ask your child, "What's the same about every word?"**

2. **Tell him to: "Break each word between the double letters."**

3. **As you do the same, have your child: "Draw a line between the middle letters."**

4. **Next both of you need to: "Look at the word *hollow*. Highlight the *ow* part."**

5. **Say, "Highlight two other words that end with the same *ow* ending."** Both of you need to highlight *pillow* and *yellow*.

6. **Say, "Find *happen*. Highlight *en*. Find five other words in Table 15-2 that end with *en*."** Both of you find *hidden, kitten, mitten, pollen,* and *written*.

When your child groups like words together (*bitten, kitten, mitten, and written,* for example), he makes a word family. If you buy him several different-colored highlighters, he can highlight each word family in its own color.

7. **Say, "Now we can spell the words for ourselves."**

8. **Say, "I'll read a word out and you write it down. Then you read me a word and I'll write it down."**

Read the words with normal pronunciation first, and then as two distinct syllables if your child needs you to.

If your child doesn't quickly grasp these spellings, repeat the words with her one or two more times so she gains more confident and fluency. As a rule of thumb with any teaching, instruct your child, and make sure you give her plenty of practice, before testing her.

The "High five" activity that I give next is a quick, fun way to consolidate what your child has just experienced in the "Twins" activity. It's a spelling test turned into a quiz.

"High five" has your child drop coins into a mug whenever he gives correct answers. If you'd prefer not to use rewards, privileges, and that kind of stuff, you'll want to make modifications to this activity. Maybe a star chart suits you better? Or maybe you plan to do a shared thing like playing ball when your child does a good job? The key is doing something, anything, to show your child you're proud of him (and that spelling can be fun).

Activity: High five

Preparation: Open your book to the list of questions for this activity and have paper and pen (or a whiteboard) handy for each of you, and a mug or bowl and some pennies (or marbles).

Follow these steps (recommended dialogue is in quotations):

1. **Say to your child: "I'm going to ask you five questions. If you write the right answer, I'll tell you, and you get to drop a penny into the mug. After five correct answers, you choose whether to stop or take three bonus questions."**

   If your child stops after five questions she keeps the coins she's collected. If she goes on to the bonus questions she gets extra pennies. If she gives an incorrect answer she simply loses out on that penny.

2. **Write down the answer, too, so you can show your child the answer after each question.**

Little kids may simply want to keep the coins at the end of this game. Give them a piggy bank and start a penny collection. Older kids can trade in their coins for privileges. Have privileges worked out in advance so you don't, in an absent-minded moment, get conned into doling out 3 a.m. bedtimes or 60 bags of candy.

1. This tool is used with nails (hammer).
2. Put this object under your head when you go to bed (pillow).
3. A baby cat (kitten).
4. A color beginning with *y* (yellow).
5. Wear these to keep your hands warm (mittens).
6. Bees gather this from flowers (pollen).
7. You buy water in this (bottle).
8. The real name for a bunny (rabbit).

Finish this section with the "Right or wrong?" activity, which asks your child to spot spelling errors. Proofreading is *such* a great way to improve spelling.

Activity: Right or wrong?

Preparation: Turn your book in to your child for this activity but cover over the answers at the end of the word list, and give your child a pencil and paper.

Follow these steps:

1. **Keeping the answers (written at the end of the word list) to this quiz covered with a sheet of paper, tell your child to find the five errors in the word list and write the correct words on his paper.**

2. **When he's done, have him move the paper to check his answers.**

   Word List:
   - patern
   - bottle
   - runner
   - willing
   - yelow
   - cabbage
   - errand
   - shellter
   - pillo
   - surffer

Answers: These five spellings are wrong: patern, yelow, pillo, shellter, and surffer

Taking on two consonants

When your child spells out a word with two consonants, side by side in the middle, she breaks the word into syllables between those consonants (just like she did with two identical consonants).

The rule about breaking a word into syllables between two consonants is known as the VCCV rule (*V* stands for vowel, *C* stands for consonant). When you spell a word that has the VCCV pattern in it (starting at the first vowel), you break it into syllables between the two consonants (VC — CV). Table 15-2 shows you how it works. Don't stress too much over the VCCV formula, though, because although it's important for your child to break words up, it isn't important that he always puts the break in the right place.

The VCCV pattern begins with the first vowel in the word.

Table 15-3 gives you a whole bunch of words to look at with your child before tackling the activities that use them.

Table 15-3	Breaking Words Up between Two Consonants	
ac-tive	ad-mire	ad-mit
blan-ket	car-pet	car-toon
chap-ter	clum-sy	cur-tain
doc-tor	en-joy	fif-teen
ig-nite	in-sult	in-vite
moun-tain	nap-kin	pen-cil
per-fect	per-mit	sel-fish
ser-pent	sis-ter	un-der

Breaking words into syllables is a strategy that helps your child spell. If your child decides that *carp-et* works fine for him, don't insist that he use the strictly correct break of *car-pet*. Instead have him practice breaking words up in ways he chooses for himself and feels comfortable with.

The "Choosing your spelling list" activity is a quiet, straightforward one, but your child gets to choose her own spelling list and can reduce the number of words she must spell.

Beware of taking over this activity. Watch out that you don't slip into the habit of holding onto lists, books, and pens when you can let your child do so for himself. Such small acts of ownership are important. Your child needs to own his learning — so back off!

Activity: Choosing your spelling list

Preparation: Open your book to Table 15-3 and look at it with your child.

Follow these steps (recommended dialog is in quotations):

1. Say to your child: "Choose two columns for a spelling list. You'll write those words but you can cut down the total number you have to write to only one column."

2. Next tell your child: "If you get all the words in the first column right, you're done!"

3. **Take away the book and dictate his chosen words to him.** Finish up when he gets the entire first column right, or proceed on to the second column if he doesn't.

Kids, especially younger ones, get upset when they make spelling mistakes. If you see your child writing the wrong spelling, pronounce the word in an exaggerated way that helps him spell it right; write down any distinct sound (like *ou*) so he can put it into his word (*mountain,* for example); focus on success, and be generous with your help. Oh, and be sensitive. Don't say things like "Of course it isn't spelled like *that!* Here let me (Ms. I-Know-It-All-And-You-*Don't*).

Hearing open vowels

Consider the words *direct, reply,* and *over.* They all have an open vowel. An *open vowel* is a vowel that stands alone, without a letter following it, after you've put in a syllable break *(di-rect, re-ply,* and *o-ver).* You put the syllable break right after an open vowel and pronounce the vowel in its long form. Many words have open vowels. Table 15-4 gives you some of them and the "Easy, medium, and hard" activity that follows goes with it.

The formula for this kind of word is the "VCV" rule. When you see the VCV combo, starting with the first vowel in the word, break it into V-CV. In words like apron and maple the consonant blends (in this case *pr* and *pl*) are treated as *one* consonant.

Table 15-4	Breaking Up Open Vowel Words	
e-ject	o-pen	de-lay
A-pril	o-ver	pa-per
na-vy	a-corn	he-ro
re-ply	ma-ple	fi-nal
re-pair	di-rect	no-tice
fro-zen	sto-ny	ba-ker
to-ken	ta-ble	re-spect
a-pron	de-cide	re-place

Read through Table 15-4 with your child. Point out to her that *notice, decide,* and *replace* all use soft *c. Notice* is tricky, too, because you'd expect the *ice* part to sound like the cold stuff, but it isn't! Next up, the "Easy, medium, and hard" activity asks your child to look carefully at Table 15-4 and decide for herself what is tricky and what isn't.

Activity: Easy, medium, and hard

Preparation: Make a copy of Table 15-4 and place it in front of you with some highlighters. (You can quickly write a neat copy; you don't have to wear a path to the copy machine at the library.)

Follow these steps:

1. **Give Table 15-4 and three highlighters to your child.** Her task is to color the easiest words in one color, medium difficulty words in another, and the hardest words in the third color.

2. **When your child has chosen and colored her three groups, tell her,** "Now I'll read the words for you to write, but you get to choose which group (easy, middle or hard) you want to write first."

3. **Have your child write all the words. Give her tips whenever she needs them. Say things like,** "Watch out for the *s* sound, it can be made by *s* or *c*," or "Watch out for *ee* on the end of a word; which letter makes that sound on the end of words?" or "Take care with *pair*, that "*air*" sound can be spelled *ear*, *are*, or *air*."

Some word beginnings and endings have vowels in them that are barely pronounced at all or are pronounced as *"uh."* The technical word for this pronunciation is the *schwa* sound. Some words with the *"uh"* or schwa sound are: *a*cross, *a*go, *a*gain, *a*way, and c*o*ntrol.

When you see an *a* on the end of a word, it's nearly always pronounced *"uh."* too. Try *gorilla, zebra, Canada, Austria, Australia, Uganda, and Nevada,* as examples.

For some of the words in this chapter, you may want to revise the *y*-behaving-as-a-vowel rule: When your child hears *ee* at the end of a word that's more than one syllable, it's written with a *y (sto-ny, na-vy)*. When she hears the long *i* sound at the end of words, it's made with *y, too (re-ply)*.

Putting prefixes first

By now you've probably noticed that when you split words up, small prefixes like *dis* and *re* are never broken up; they stay whole. You can hear this undivided sound when you say the words, so teaching your child to break a word after the prefix is easy. Table 15-5 gives you some examples and the "Sorting prefixes" activity follows it.

A prefix is a chunk of letters that comes at the front of words. Among the more common ones are *un, dis,* and *re*. A prefix changes the meaning of the word (or word base).

Being a great spelling snoop

Helping your child to spell is all about finding what he's shaky at and making things clearer for him. When you know the rules and tips in this book (Bossy *e;* When two vowels go walking, the first one does the talking; and *y* behaving like a vowel), you can remind your child of them whenever he needs them. You can run through a few word families with him so he can practice applying the rules. You can remind him that when he's in doubt, the best strategy is to write the spelling options he has in mind and try to spot the one that looks right. And that's largely what good spelling is about — trying out the options.

You hear me mention root words now and then. A *root word* is the original word to which beginnings and endings have been attached. In *discontented,* the root word is *content.*

Table 15-5	Breaking Up Words After a Prefix	
un words	*dis words*	*re words*
un-hap-py	dis-ap-prove	re-lo-cate
un-im-por-tant	dis-ap-point	re-gain
un-kind	dis-ag-ree	re-con-si-der
un-like-ly	dis-con-ten-ted	re-mind
un-spo-ken	dis-con-nect	re-ad-mit
un-done	dis-al-low	re-in-vent
un-tied	dis-lo-cate	re-do
un-help-ful	dis-in-her-it	re-e-lect

Straight spelling tests aren't hugely fun for your child, but finding and sorting are fun, and running definitely is fun! The "Sorting prefix" and "Prefix run" activities ask your child to sort a few words before she spells them. As she sorts, she'll look carefully at the words so she's warmed up for the spelling. Then, when she needs to stretch her legs, she gets to do a few sprints.

Activity: Sorting prefixes

Preparation: Make a copy of Table 15-5 and have some highlighters ready. Give the table to your child.

Follow these steps (recommended dialog is in quotations):

1. **Say to your child: "Read the words to me."**

2. **Explain that: "Each word has two, three, or four syllables (or parts)."**

3. **Tell him to: "Choose a color for all the words with two syllables and color them. Use another color for words with three syllables and another color for words with four syllables."**

   Give your child time to finish the 24 words.

4. **Say, "Now I'll read the words for you to write. Which group (two, three, or four syllable) shall I read out first?"**

5. **Dictate the words for your child to write.**

If your child can't easily read the words in Table 15-5, sound out each syllable for and with him and explain and practice any tricky sounds (like the *oi* in disappoint).

If your child's taking these words in stride and you think he'd enjoy a challenge, ask him to try some of these words: *unconstitutional, unconventional, uninspired, unimpressed, unperturbed,* and *unintelligible.*

Activity: Prefix run

Preparation: Copy the words from Table 15-5 and cut each one out. Put the words into a bowl. Make three signs with the numbers 2, 3, and 4 (representing the number of syllables in a word). Make sure you have a watch or timer.

Follow these steps:

1. **Put the bowl at one end of a room and the three signs at another.** The bowl is the starting point, and you'll time your child from the time she leaves the bowl until she returns to it.

2. **Your child takes a word from the bowl and drops it on the right sign.**

3. **If the word has two syllables she runs to the sign marked with a 2, and so on.**

4. **She keeps running back for each word and dropping it onto a number then when all the words are dropped, she runs to the bowl and takes it with her to gather up the groups of words.**

5. **When she reaches the spot where the bowl sat she's done . . . except that you have her take three words, without looking, and spell them to you!** Errors earn her a sprint.

A spoonful of sugar

If your child struggles with spelling, stay calm. Let her know that nearly everybody struggles with spelling at some time. Tell her that spelling is like figuring out a maze. She has to try several routes to find the right one. After she's found her way, though, she can find it easier the next time. If your child is disheartened or resistant, don't battle with her. Keep things sweet; bargain with her; if necessary pay her! Ideals like never bribing your child (remember vowing that before you had real live kids?) can be hard on you. Keeping your child happy and a continued spelling participant, with a judicious carrot-and-stick approach, is easier, especially when you know your carrots.

Running a marathon for serious spellers

Table 15-6 isn't for the fainthearted, but if you want to brush up on prefixes yourself or give your child a *super, hyper,* and *ultra* understanding of prefixes, this table is definitely for you. I haven't included every prefix but pretty nearly every one.

Table 15-6	The Lowdown on Prefixes	
Prefix	*What It Means*	*Examples*
alti	height	altimeter, altitude
ambi	both	ambidextrous, ambiguous
ante	before	anterior, antenatal
anti	against	antiwar, antifreeze
auto	self, same one	autograph, autobiography
bene	good	benefactor, benefit
bi	two	bicycle, biweekly, bifocals
bio	life	biology, biography
centi	a hundredth of	centimeter
circum	around	circumnavigate
co	together	coauthor, coexist, cooperate
contra	against, contrary	contradict, controversy
demi	half	demigod

(continued)

Table 15-6 *(continued)*

Prefix	What It Means	Examples
dis	opposite	disabled, disappear
dys	difficulty with	dysfunction, dyslexia
equi	equal	equidistant, equivalent
ex	former	expatriate
extra	beyond	extracurricular extraordinary
fore	first, previous	foreground, forecast
geo	earth	geography
hemi	half	hemisphere
hydro	water	hydroplane
hyper	too much	hyperactive, hypersensitive
il, im, in	not, without	illegal, impossible
inter	between	interstate, interlock
intra	inside	intrastate
mal	bad	maladjusted, malfunction
micro	small	microphone microscope
milli	a thousandth of	milligram
mis	bad, wrong	misdemeanor, misbehave
mono	one	monorail, monologue
non	not	nonsense
oct	eight	octopus, octagon
orth	regular, correct	orthodox
over	above, more than necessary	overzealous, overbearing
pan	all	Panorama, pandemic
ped	feet	pedicure
poly	many	polygon, polysyllabic
post	after	postmortem
pre	before	prefix, preschool
pseudo	fake	pseudonym

Prefix	What It Means	Examples
re	again	rebound, retell
retro	backward	retroactive, retrospectively
semi	half	semidetached, semicolon
sub	under	submarine, subordinate
super	more than	superman
tele	far	telescope, telephone
trans	across	transport
tri	three	triathlon
ultra	extreme	ultraviolet
un	not	unfinished
uni	single	unicycle, unilateral
vice	second in rank	vice-principal, vice-president

Quickly peering at suffixes

I talk about suffixes (or word endings) in Chapter 16, but here's a preliminary peek: *Suffixes* are word endings like *ed, ing, ant,* and *ness*. Your child can quickly get used to writing them, because they behave predictably. Your child just has to latch them onto the ends of words, making tweaks now and then, like when a root word ends in *e*. Chapter 16 gives you the details and plenty of activities for your child to run through.

Three or More Syllables Are Pre-dict-a-ble

Little kids love to ask you if you can spell *supercalafragalisticexpialidoceous*. Thankfully, when I've spelled that word for a child, Mary Poppins has been so busy getting children to tidy their closets that she hasn't seen my spelling. But even if that weren't so, I wouldn't be all that worried. Although big words often look imposing, they're really no harder than smaller words. The same breaking-up rules apply, except that you do the breaking-up a few more times. So, now that you know how easy the big words really are, you won't be concerned by the ones in Table 15-7 or the "Demon dozen" activity that follows it.

Table 15-7	Making a Small Thing of Big Words	
com-bi-na-tion	com-for-ta-ble	com-part-ment
com-pe-ti-tion	com-pe-ti-tion	com-ple-ment
con-fid-ent	con-ser-va-tion	con-ta-min-a-tion
de-di-ca-tion	de-part-ment	des-per-a-tion
di-sa-gree-ment	dis-ap-point-ment	dis-in-fect-ant
dis-re-spect-ful	ex-am-ple	ex-cite-ment
ex-haus-tion	ex-plain-ing	in-de-pend-ent
in-flam-ma-ble	in-fla-ta-ble	in-no-cent
in-sig-ni-fi-cant	in-strum-ent	in-tel-lig-ent
in-vi-si-ble	pre-dic-ta-ble	pro-ces-sion
pro-duc-tion	pro-mo-tion	pro-nun-ci-a-tion
re-spect-ful	sig-ni-fi-cant	tre-men-dous

The *le* ending is grouped with the letter in front of it (*ble, dle*).

Pronounce *tion* as *"shun."*

Some long vowel sounds inside words are written with only one vowel: d*i*-rec-tion, con-tam-in-*a*-tion, com-bin-*a*-tion, in-fl*a*-ta-ble.

If you like the VCCV and VCV formulas, here's how they work in big words. (This stuff is deluxe technical so skip past it unless you're keen!) Look at the first vowel in a big word and decide what formula you have (VCCV or VCV). Break the word into VC-CV or V-CV then start over again at the last vowel of the first syllable. This comparison chart shows you the steps in breaking up words, using these two formulas.

Your child doesn't need to wrestle with these syllables. If prom-o-tion and sup-er-vise suit her (rather than the linguistically correct pro-mo-tion and su-per-vise), she need not try to spell according to linguistics books. Whichever way she achieves the right spelling is the right way for her.

The "Demon dozen" activity eases your child into big words, giving her the spellings to view, break up, take a good look at, and then write out for herself.

Activity: Demon dozen

Preparation: Make a copy of Table 15-7, and have some highlighters ready for your child to use.

Follow these steps:

1. **Give Table 15-7 to your child and ask her to read the words from any one column to you.** These words are her "demon dozen."

2. **Listen to your child read the words, and help her sound out any syllables she doesn't know.** Have her highlight any tricky word parts.

3. **After she's had a good look at each word, tell her she can practice the three hardest words with the look, cover, and write routine.** Now, can she spell the demon dozen with a score of at least 10 words spelled correctly out of the 12?

4. **Dictate the words for your child to write, giving her clues and pronouncing the syllables clearly.** You can work on the other two columns of words later.

Look, cover, and write is a simple routine for remembering spellings. Your child looks at a word, covers it, and writes it from memory. The trick with this technique is looking for spelling features, sounding out where you can, and then writing the word several times.

If your child gets flustered when you time him, forget about racing the clock. Instead you may like to add some pep by simply saying things like, "Wow, you're really taking on a challenge here!" or "You're doing so well with these words; even I find them hard."

Quickly Revising Key Spelling Patterns

When your child breaks words up, she gets to know all sorts of sounds and rules and becomes a better speller. You're one step ahead, though. When she's stuck, you give her a quick explanation and maybe a word family. If your child can't spell *explanation,* you say: "*Ex* is easy. *Plan* in easy, too, and *ay* is written with just the letter *a. Shun* is written *tion,* just like in *action*, *fraction*, and *mention*." This one-step-ahead-of-you version may sound optimistic right now, but you'll find on-the-spot instruction easier as time goes by. To inspire (and calm) you right now, Table 15-8 lists bite-sized pieces of good advice to give to your child.

Table 15-8	Quick and Easy Spelling Tips
Rule	*How It Works (In Brief)*
Open vowels: *ex-plan-a-tion, o-pen*	Write the *ay* sound in the middle of words as *a*. Long, open vowels start words like *a*-corn and *o*-pen.
Keeping the vowel short: *hopping, skipping*	In words like *hop*, double the last letter before adding an ending (to get *hopping* not *hoping*).
Making *hoping, latest, and lovable*	To add an ending that starts with a vowel to a word that already ends with *e*, lop off the *e*.
tion	It's sound is *shun*!
"*Uh*" on the end: *Canada, Austria*	"*Uh*" on the end of words (especially country names) is written *a*.
c or *ck*: *brick, clock, picnic*	It's always *ck* on the end of short vowel words of only one syllable.
q: *queen, quick*	*q* never goes anywhere without *u*. Handy words to teach are *quiet* and *quite*.
The sounds of *s*: *boys, brushes*	The *ez* sound in words like *foxes* and *finishes* always is written *es* not *ez*.
The sounds of *ed*: *lasted, napped, jammed*	Always write *ed* as though you hear *ed (lasted)*, *t (napped)*, or *d (jammed)*. The family that breaks this rule is: *crept, wept*, and *slept*.
le an *al*: *little, bottle, principal*	When it sounds like *ul*, its written *le* or *al*.
The sounds of *y*: *cry, happy* (also, short *i*: *mystery, system*)	Write *y* on the end of short words that end in "*eye*" (*cry*) and on the end of longer words that end in "*ee*" (*silly*).
If you don't know; have a go: *boyl, boil, boyal, boyle*	Jot down the ways that a word might be spelled. Choose the version that looks right.

To finish this chapter, I show you a great game for two players — "Mancala Spellorama!" It takes a bit of preparation, but after that's done, you'll love it. If you're a teacher, you can send two kids to a corner with this game and know they'll be gainfully occupied for at least 20 minutes.

Activity: Mancala Spellorama!

If your kids play Mancala, you'll probably recognize this game. It's a spelling version of Mancala, except that you make your own board and the pieces you move around are rolled up words.

Preparation: Onto a piece of cardboard or poster paper, have your players draw 12 rectangles in 2 rows of 6. They can color and decorate them, if they'd like; it's their game board. Now write 24 words on 24 small pieces of paper and roll each one up. Give each player a bowl or lunchbox with some of the rolled up words in it. You're set!

Follow these steps:

1. **Have each player sit at a short end of the board facing each other.** Players put two words in each of the 12 compartments until all 24 words are on the board, 2 in each rectangle. The players' homes are their respective bowls, which are placed directly in front of where they are sitting, in view of the board.

2. **Player one picks up the two words in any compartment.** He moves his hand to the next compartment, going clockwise, and drops one word in it. He keeps doing this, dropping a word in each compartment he passes. When he passes his home spot (after he's gone all around the board), he drops a word into the bowl, too. (He doesn't drop a word into his opponent's home spot, because the point of the game is to get the most words into your own home.)

3. **From the last compartment in which he drops a word, he picks up all the words** (three). He keeps moving and dropping words until the compartment into which he drops his last word has only that one word in it or he's dropped his last word in his home. Play now moves to player two.

4. **Player two starts with any compartment she wants and moves around the board in exactly the same way.**

5. **When all the words are in the two homes, players count their words without opening them, write down their scores, and then pass their pile to their opponent.**

6. **Next, players take turns reading each other's words out loud for their opponents to spell.** Players write down their spellings, and score 1 point for each correct spelling.

7. **Score this game depending on how old your kids are.** Be tough on older kids and don't give them second chances. (They usually prefer it that way.) Have younger kids simply help each other out when they make mistakes. They keep giving clues until the right answer surfaces.

Explain the scoring system to your kids so you can avoid disputes. Be clear that no arguing is allowed (and enforce dire penalties for miscreants!). For more spice, don't put words on all 24 pieces of paper; instead, write your own special instructions, such as "Give yourself two points, or "No spelling = score 0," or "Lose 1 point."

Chapter 16

Finishing Off with Suffixes

In This Chapter

▶ Seeing the big picture of suffixes

▶ Sorting through similar suffixes

▶ Adding on and dropping off the right letters

Adding endings (or *suffixes*) to words is a bit like adding accessories to your outfit. If you add the right hat and shoes, you walk with a spring in your step. If you're not sure whether this goes with that, you're more of a slouch. When you spell, it's the same. If you're not sure whether to finish your word with *able* or *ible,* you're unsettled. Have you chosen your ending wisely? Will an error matter very much? Should you get out of your seat right now and find that dictionary once and for all? This chapter takes you through the suffix spelling rules so you can help your child spell — with perk, not plod — all the right word endings.

An Ending by Any Other Name

I am sitting; I sat; I will sit. Remember dozing off when your teacher went over verb conjugations and tenses in school? You learned plenty of words back then. Some, like *conjunction* and *preposition,* went straight in one ear and straight out the other (at least they did for me). You were able to get the hang of what to write, but it wasn't because of all those terms. In this chapter, I don't get caught up with grammatical terms. Instead, I talk about word endings. Strictly speaking, they're *suffixes,* and they change according to what *tense* you're using and whether you're making *plurals.* Even so, they're still word endings. Relax, put drab classroom memories behind you, and skip among perky little endings like *ed, able,* and *tion.*

 A verb is a doing word like run. When you change the tense of your words, you change whether you're talking about now or sometime in the past or future: I am running, I ran, I will run. A singular thing is one thing, like a cat, the plural version of a thing is when you mean more than one thing: the cats.

Playing with Plurals

When your child writes about *cats* and not *a cat*, she's writing about plurals. Any time she changes the singular form of a thing (*cat, dog,* or *table*) into more than one thing *(cats, dogs,* or *tables)*, she's making plurals. Plurals are easy. Most of the time, your child simply adds an *s.* She can hear that *s,* too. It sounds like *s* or *z* (but not *ez,* which I tell you about in the later "Adding *es*" section).

Just now, in the previous paragraph, I said "the singular form of a thing." That thing, strictly speaking, is a noun. Nouns are the names of things. All through this chapter, when I talk about "things," I'm talking about nouns.

Adding s

Thousands of plurals end with *s.* Single, no-fuss *s.* In Table 16-1, I list some words in singular form for your child to add *s* onto. Skim through the table, and then dive into the "Adding *s*'s quick and easy" activity that follows.

Table 16-1	Adding on *s*	
cat	carpet	book
finger	soap	lamp
car	hand	toy
teacher	boy	girl
dog	meal	shop
stick	flower	bird

When your child says *dogs,* he hears *z,* not *s,* on the end. Tell your child that many words end in *s* but sound like they end in *z* (*stoves, sands,* and *crabs*).

Activity: Adding s's quick and easy

Preparation: Make a copy of Table 16-1, have a watch or timer handy, and grab some highlighters for your child to use.

Follow these steps:

1. **Have your child read the Table 16-1 words to you.** Help her sound out and spot any tricky spelling features (*oa, ow, oo, ir, ea, oy*).

2. **Have her highlight the spelling features while she says the word out loud, and then ask the following questions:**

   1. "How many words end with *er?*"

   2. "Can you find the two words that have *ir* in them (it's the same sound)?"

   3. "When you add s to each word, what's special about the sound it makes?" (*Answer: It sounds like "z."*)

3. **Dictate the words for your child to write.**

4. **Dictate them again with a time limit (maybe three minutes) and record her actual time.**

5. **Dictate them once more so she can better her own time.**

You can do all the spelling activities in this book quickly and easily, but that doesn't mean you can't be creative. Make spelling more fun for your child by having him use different colored pens or a whiteboard. Get a tray of cream or pudding and have him finger write words in it. Between spelling tasks, hula hoop with him (remember that jiggling a hoop around the waist thing?) or race him to the end of the block. The neighbors may peg you as eccentric, but your child will love your version of spelling work.

Adding es

When you don't add *s* onto a word to make it plural, you usually add *es* instead. The three groups of *es* words to show your child are

- ✔ Words that end with *ch, sh, s, x,* or *z,* like *bunch, bush, boss, box,* and *fizz.*
- ✔ Words that ends in a consonant followed by a *y,* like *lady* and *baby.*
- ✔ Words like *tomato* that end with the long-*o* sound.

Adding es to words that end with ch, sh, s, x, or z

When a word ends with *ch, sh, s, x,* or *z,* your child must add *es.* This distinct *es* sound (pronounced *ez*) is easy for your child to hear. It's simple. When he hears *es,* he writes *es.* Table 16-2 makes the *es* ending clear to see and hear. In Chapter 3, I describe how to help your child hear the different chunks of sound inside words.

Table 16-2		Adding *es*		
ch	*sh*	*s*	*x*	*z*
benches	dishes	dresses	boxes	buzzes
punches	wishes	hisses	foxes	whizzes
lunches	thrushes	mosses	fixes	fizzes
inches	dashes	buses	mixes	
bunches	washes	losses	sixes	
clutches	flashes	classes	faxes	
matches	sashes	crosses	axes	
riches	bushes	kisses	waxes	

In the "Taking the word away!" activity, you may recognize a game in which you put ten small objects on a tray. Your child has a good look at them and then closes his eyes while you take one away. He then has to guess which object you've taken away. In this version of the game, you do the same thing with ten words.

Activity: Taking the word away!

Preparation: Turn in your book to Table 16-2 so your child can see it. Have paper or index cards ready.

Follow these steps:

1. **Have your child write any ten words from Table 16-2 onto individual pieces of paper or index cards.**

2. **Tell him to look at all ten words for 30 seconds, because you're going to take one away.**

3. **Have him close his eyes while you take one of the words away.**

4. **He then has to look at the remaining nine words and try to remember which word is missing.**

5. **Try the same thing once more, taking a different word away from the ten.**

6. **Now reverse roles.** Your child takes a word away and you have to remember which word is missing.

You can liven up this activity by adding a quick physical component to it. Have your child run a sprint while you take a card away and then let him set you a breezy 400-meter hurdle or a quick 50 chin-ups! Physical breaks can be things like running around the house or doing push-ups, or jumping rope until one of you hyperventilates (only kidding!).

Adding es to words that end in a consonant and then a y

When a word ends in a consonant followed by a *y*, like *lady* and *baby*, the rule is:

Change the *y* to *i* then add *e-s*.

Put more simply, your child needs to get to know the ending *ies*, because she can turn words like *baby, lady,* and *puppy* into *babies, ladies,* and *puppies.*

Table 16-3 gives you some examples of words that end in a consonant followed by a *y* that can be turned into plurals that end with *ies*. Look through the table with your child, paying attention to those endings and any tricky sound chunks. (*Library* and *secretary* look hard but are easy when you break them up and pronounce each part clearly.) When you're done, surge forward to the "Pointing and spelling" activity that comes next.

Table 16-3	**Changing *Lady* into *Ladies***
Singular Word	*Plural Word*
lady	ladies
baby	babies
city	cities
mommy	mommies
poppy	poppies
puppy	puppies
dolly	dollies
penny	pennies
secretary	secretaries
library	libraries

Activity: Pointing and spelling

Preparation: Have your copy of *Teaching Kids to Spell For Dummies* turned to Table 16-3, ready for your child to see and then grab a large piece of paper and some markers.

This game is a bit like pin the tail on the donkey. You have your child point to a word and then write it in its other form, singular or plural.

Follow these steps (recommended dialogue is in quotations):

1. Say, "Look at this table of words." (Table 16-3.)

2. Say, "Write one word from each pair anywhere on the paper." (Diagonally and bottom to top is fine.)

3. Say, "Close your eyes and point at the paper." Have your child point until he's touching a word.

4. Say, "Open your eyes, read the word you're pointing to, and tell me how to spell the partner to that word." (Singular or plural.)

Have your child spell out the words to you. She can jot them down if she prefers.

Adding es to words that end with long o

Are you someone who isn't sure of your *potato* and *tomato*? When I was a kid, I never could decide between *potato* and *potatoe,* so in this section I go over some tasty words like *potato, tomato,* and *mango,* so you can make them clear for your child. I dig up those potatoes and show you once and for all that it's *potato* in the singular and *potatoes* in the plural. I get to grips with other words that end with *o,* too, like *volcano* and *echo,* and show you that each one turns into an *oes* plural. The rule is:

When a word ends with long *o,* add *es* to make it plural.

Table 16-4 gives a healthy bunch of *o*-ending words so you and your child can see at a glance that I'm telling the truth about *o* turning into *oes.* Take a good look at the words with your child, and then lead him to the easy "Sorting your tomatoes and heroes" activity that comes next.

Table 16-4	Changing *Tomato* into *Tomatoes*
Singular Word Ending with o	*Plural Word Ending with es*
buffalo	buffaloes
tomato	tomatoes
hero	heroes
cargo	cargoes
mosquito	mosquitoes
volcano	volcanoes
echo	echoes
mango	mangoes
potato	potatoes

For a few words that end with *o*, you don't add *es*, just *s*. The ones I can think of are *patios, studios,* and a bunch of musical instruments: *pianos, banjos,* and *cellos.* To help her remember them your child may like to think that pianos, banjos, and cellos can be played in studios or on patios (just a suggestion!).

Activity: Sorting your tomatoes and heroes

Preparation: Make a copy of Table 16-4 for your child.

Follow these steps:

1. **With the plurals column covered by a piece of paper, ask your child to write the right words, in plural form, for the categories you call out (recommended dialog is in quotations):**

   - "Write down three foods." (*Answer: tomato, mango, potato*)

   - "Write down two animals." (*Answer: buffalo, mosquito*)

   - "Write down a cool person." (*Answer: hero*)

   - "Write down the load that's carried in trucks, trains, and boats." (*Answer: cargo*)

   - "Write down a sound you hear when you shout down a big canyon." (*Answer: echo*)

   - "Write down a land form that can erupt." (*Answer: volcano*)

2. **Now your child can take the paper away to check his spelling.** (And after that you can tell him the timeless and incredibly funny tomato joke: Why did the tomato blush? Because it saw the salad dressing.)

Adding to f words

Uh oh, is it time to flip quickly past an unsuitable section? No. Relax those parenting shackles, because this section is about turning nice words that happen to end with *f* into plurals.

In short, when your child hears the *f* sound at the end of a word, he has two ways to make that word into a plural. He can simply add *s,* like in *beliefs* or *chiefs,* or he can make a *ves* ending, like in *loaves* and *knives.* To make the *ves* ending, he lops off the *f* (like in *loaf)* or *fe* (like in *knife)* and then adds *ves.*

If this rule sounds complicated, don't worry. When you and your child start writing down those plurals, you can see how they work. Table 16-5 lists a lot of words for you and your child to check out so he gets smart at choosing the right ending for his *f* words. The "Finding the word" and "Finding, running, and writing" activities after Table 16-5 show you a couple of different ways to give your child some practice.

Table 16-5	Adding onto *f* Words
f Changing to fs	*f Changing to ves*
belief/beliefs	calf/calves
chief/chiefs	elf/elves
woof/woofs	knife/knives
roof/roofs	leaf/leaves
dwarf/dwarfs (or dwarves)	life/lives
turf/turfs	loaf/loaves
puff/puffs	thief/thieves
cuff/cuffs	wife/wives
hoof/hoofs (or hooves)	scarf/scarves
wharf/wharfs (or wharves)	wolf/wolves

Table 16-5 includes three *ie* words. Tell your child that some words make the *ee* sound with *ie* or *ei*. The *ie* spelling is more common than the *ei* spelling. The rule to remember is:

i before *e* except after *c*.

The full version of the *i*-before-*e*-except-after-*c* rule is this:

i before *e* except after *c*, unless you're making the "ay" sound as in *neighbor*.

The last bit of the rule helps you with words like *neighbor*, *eight*, and *reins*, where you hear the *ay* sound. If in doubt, opt for *ie*; it's more common.

Activity: Finding the word

Preparation: Have this book opened to Table 16-5.

Follow this step: Ask your child to look at Table 16-5 and write the word that corresponds with the following comments:

- ✔ "Use these to cut with." (*Answer: knives*)

- ✔ "Two animals." (*Answer: calf, wolf*)

- ✔ "Something you eat." (*Answer: loaf*)

- ✔ "Three words that have *i* before *e* except after *c*." (*Answer: belief, chief, thief*)

Activity: Finding, running, and writing

Preparation: You need Table 16-5, ten index cards or slips of paper and a watch or timer.

Follow these steps:

1. **Write ten singular-form words from Table 16-5 onto ten separate index cards or slips of paper.**

2. **Ask your child to look at Table 16-5 and then do the following:**

    1. With the words facing away from him, show your child the ten cards.

    2. Tell your child: "These ten words are from the list."

    3. Say, "Close your eyes and count to 100 while I hide them." (Around the room, in the garden, in the basement.)

    4. Say, "When I come back, you have to find the words then race back here with them and write down their (plural) partners." (If the word is *knife,* you write *knives,* if it's *chief,* you write *chiefs*.)

    5. Say, "I'll time you, and then you can pick ten new words for me so I can to do this activity. I'll try to beat your time!"

(Did I mention that you may need to work out for a few months before doing this activity?)

Be enthusiastic in this activity and ham up your performance. And, of course, let your child beat your time . . . fractionally.

Staying Calm with Tenses

I promised not to bog you down in terminology, and I won't. Suffice to say, words change when you shift from talking in the now (I sit; I am sitting) to talking in the past or future (I sat; I was sitting; I will sit, I may be sitting). For spelling purposes, all you really need to explain to your child is that the endings *ed* and *ing* are important.

The sounds of ed

When your child writes words about things done in the past, like *laughed, skipped,* and *hunted*, he ends those word with *ed*.

Your child writes *ed* on the end regardless of whether he hears *d (laughed),* *t (skipped),* or *ed (hunted)*.

The *ed* ending can sound a bit different when used with different words, but after you alert your child to these sounds (especially the *t* sound), she shouldn't be fooled. Table 16-6 gives you plenty of *ed* words to run through with your child. Have her read them out loud and hear the sounds for herself. You'll come back to these words in the "Placing your bets" and "Doubling the letter to keep the vowel short" activities that I include a few paragraphs farther on.

Table 16-6	Adding *ed*
ed Sounding like d or t	*ed Sounding like ed*
skipped	fainted
hopped	baited
jumped	bolted
topped	invested
feared	mended
kicked	extended
showed	depended
spilled	heated
played	cheated
called	needed

Adding ed to short-sounding words

The simple rule about adding endings onto words that have a short vowel sound is:

Double the letter to keep (or make) the vowel short.

What this rule means is that your child doesn't have to battle with words like *hoping* and *hopping* or *writing* and *written*. All she has to remember is to say the word to herself, listening for the vowel. Hearing a short vowel means that she has to double the word's last letter before attaching an ending. *Hop* becomes *hopping*, and *write* becomes *written* (the vowel sound changes so the spelling changes). Table 16-7 lists a bunch of straightforward words and it's followed by the "Placing your bets" and "Doubling the letter to keep the vowel short" activities.

The double-the-letter-to-keep-the-vowel-short rule is good for short vowel words that finish with one consonant (*hop, bed, sob*). The rule doesn't apply, however, to words that end with two consonants (*jump, sing, bond*).

Table 16-7	Adding *ed* to Short-Sounding Words	
rubbed	flipped	knitted
robbed	flopped	trotted
dropped	topped	hopped
mopped	jotted	jutted
rotted	mobbed	logged
blotted	clogged	prodded
jogged	jigged	hogged
popped	nodded	dotted
sobbed	propped	clotted
spotted	slopped	cropped

A *root word* is a word with no beginnings or endings attached to it. (The root part of *presupposed* is *suppose,* for example.)

Activity: Placing your bets

Preparation: Make a copy of Table 16-7, grab some highlighters and a watch or timer.

Follow these steps:

1. **Have your child highlight the root words.** He may want to color-code the words, using a system that he thinks up.

2. **When he's highlighted the root words, have him read all of them out loud as fast as he can.**

3. **Now recruit other family members to do the same, but before you start, have everyone guess who'll be fastest.**

4. **Time everyone and place bets with cookies or small change.**

Make sure all contestants are on even footings by devising handicaps. For example, you can make any adult who mispronounces a word start over, or chop ten seconds off the kids' times.

If you're thinking this game has nothing to do with spelling, consider this: Good spellers enjoy figuring out spellings. They see spelling as an interesting puzzle and are confident enough to try out a few different versions of a spelling. In this game, you show your child that words can be fun, and you have him look closely at spellings. The more he looks at how words are put together, the more information and tools he has at his disposal to help him crack spelling challenges later on.

Activity: Doubling the letter to keep the vowel short
Preparation: Bookmark Tables 16-6 and 16-7.

Follow these steps:

1. **Dictate root words from both tables to your child.**

2. **She has to write the word with *ed* added on, remembering whether to double the letter to keep the vowel short.**

3. **Spice up this activity by having your child draw ten dots (or smiley faces or whatever she likes).** Tell her that if she spells a word right, she can cross off a dot. If she spells it wrong, she adds a dot.

4. **When she's crossed off all ten (or more) dots, she's done.**

One more variation of this activity is to tell your child that she can win ten coins (or cookies, jelly beans, or whatever you like) from you. When she spells a word right, she gets a coin, but if she spells it wrong, you get the coin. (Drum roll . . . Who gets more coins?)

If cookies and coins leave you cold, award your child points in these games and keep a tally of them. Have him exchange his points for great things you think up (maybe special outings or toys).

Adding vowel endings (like ing and ed) to words that already end with e

When a word already ends with *e* and your child wants to add an ending that starts with *e*, she doesn't need two *e*'s. She drops (throws away, gets rid of, loses) an *e*. An easy rhyme that can help you to remember this rule about adding *ing, ed,* and all endings that start with a vowel *(er, est, ily,* and *able) is:*

Drop the *e* when you add *i-n-g.* (or any other ending that starts with a vowel).

Table 16-8 shows how it works, and the "Making a word longer" activity just ahead, goes with it.

Table 16-8		Adding Vowel Endings to Words That Already End with *e*			
ed	*ing*	*er*	*est*	*ily*	*able*
dozed	dozing	diver	cutest	dozily	notable
dived	diving	rider	ripest	nosily	tamable

ed	ing	er	est	ily	able
filed	filing	biker	whitest	stonily	likable
waved	riding	diner	palest	slimily	debatable
biked	waving	tamer	purest	lazily	changeable
noted	biking	baker	latest	crazily	movable
named	noting	maker	closest	breezily	comparable
paved	biting	faker	stalest	noisily	livable
faded	naming	shaker	largest	bouncily	drivable
tamed	taking	shaver	widest		curable
timed	paving	wider	safest		lovable
taped	posing	finer	tamest		freezable
hoped	fading	closer	nicest		erasable
waded	taming	timer	vilest		removable
nosed	timing	whiter	wisest		curable
stoned	taping	cuter	politest		traceable
dated	making	paler			manageable
liked	hoping	whiter			advisable
baked	baking	hiker			excusable
shaped	stoning	striker			noticeable
wiped	nosing	joker			serviceable
hiked	wading	smoker			adorable
joked	dating	poker			notable
smoked	shaping	wiper			persuadable

When you add *able* after soft *c* or *g,* keep the *e* so you keep that soft sound (*changeable, noticeable*).

Activity: Making a word longer

Preparation: Open this book to Tables 16-8 and have paper and pencil ready.

Follow these steps:

1. Dictate 20 root words from the words in Table 16-8 to your child.

2. Ask your child to make each (root) word longer by adding one of the endings.

3. To soup up this activity, do the dots or dimes stuff that I suggest in the "Doubling the letter to keep the vowel short" activity earlier in this chapter.

Deciding between able and ible

You may be wondering why I didn't include the *ible* ending in Table 16-8. It's because *ible* rarely follows a word that ends with e. *Ible* usually appears in words that are words in their own right, rather than root words with a suffix added on, like *legible, possible,* and *eligible* or it attaches onto words that end in a consonant, like *digestible* and *resistible.*

The simple rule for remembering whether to use *able* or *ible* is to try *able* first, because it's more common, especially if the root word makes a complete word The best thing you can do to help your child choose between *able* and *ible* is give him plenty of practice with them. Table 16-9 shows a bunch of words that go with the "Adding *able* or *ible*" activity that follows.

Table 16-9	Adding able and ible
able	**ible**
reliable	terrible
suitable	possible
reasonable	impossible
dependable	digestible
preferable	legible
commendable	visible
preventable	edible
assessable	permissible
applicable	feasible
laughable	resistible
breakable	eligible

able	ible
compactable	credible
forgettable	tangible
predictable	negligible
remarkable	susceptible
transportable	compatible
questionable	divisible
impressionable	infallible
absorbable	suggestible

Activity: Adding able or ible

Preparation: Make a copy of Table 16-9 and grab some highlighters.

Follow these steps:

1. **Remind your child about the *able/ible* rule -try *able* first, because it's more common, especially if the root word makes a complete word, and then ask him to look through Table 16-9 armed with colored highlighter.**

2. **His job is to color the *complete* words he finds inside *able* and *ible* words, like *reason* inside *reasonable*.** How many of these words-within-words are there in the *able* column? How many are there in the *ible* column? Does his answer confirm the rule?

Answers: Able column: suit, reason, depend, prefer, commend, prevent, assess, laugh, break, compact, forget, predict, remark, transport, question, impression, absorb =17 words

Ible column: digest, resist, suggest = 3 words

Yes, the rule is confirmed because *able* words contain complete root words far more often that *ible* words do.

Always give your child paper and pen and help him jot down possible spellings. The more he does this, the better he gets at sounding out syllables, choosing likely spellings, and opting for the right ones.

Adding to Words That End in y

In this section I give you two rules for adding endings onto words that end with *y*. The rules may seem tricky at first but the more your child sees and practices them for herself, the better her spelling instincts will become.

With that in mind, take a look at the two rules and then move to the "Ending for thirty points," "Finding ten ending mistakes," and Adding a quick ending" activities after Tables 16-10 and 16-11.

Rule 1: For words ending with a consonant followed by a *y* (like *marry*), change *y* to *i*, and then add the ending — except when adding *ing* — in which case, simply add the ending. The short version of this rule is

Change the *y* to *i* except with *ing* (*married, marrying*).

Rule 2: For words ending with a vowel + *y* (like *play*), simply add the ending (*playing*).

Table 16-10	Adding to Words That End with a Consonant + *y*	
Consonant + y Word	*Change y to i*	*Except for ing*
cry	cries cried	crying
dry	dries dried drier	drying
carry	carries carried carrier	carrying
marry	marries married	marrying
silly	sillier silliest	
heavy	heavier heaviest	
happy	happier happiest happily	
funny	funnies funnier funniest	
icy	icier iciest icily	
fancy	fancier fanciest fancily	
chilly	chillier chilliest	
windy	windier windiest	

Table 16-11	Adding to Words That End with a Vowel + *y*
Vowel + y Word	*Just Add On*
play	plays played player playing
pray	prays prayed prayer praying
stay	stays stayed staying
stray	strays strayed straying
delay	delays delayed delaying
enjoy	enjoys enjoyed enjoying
toy	toys toyed toying
buy	buys buyer buying

Help your child remember *say* and *pay.* They turn into *said* and *paid.*

The best way for your child to get the hang of all these words is to see them and write them often. There's quite a bit to learn, so the next three activities — "Ending for thirty points," "Finding ten ending mistakes," and Adding a quick ending" — can be used with of any of the words that you find in this chapter. Follow the instructions (and dialogue in bold) and use whichever words your child needs to practice.

Activity: Ending for thirty points

Preparation: With your book open to Tables 16-10 and 16-11, grab a large piece of paper or whiteboard.

Follow these steps:

1. **On your paper, draw a table with five columns and two rows (see the one I've provided).**

2. **Inside each square write a word from the tables.**

3. **Now write two misspelled words inside each square. Like this:**

marryied	flopping	enyoid	dryied	carrier
married	floppying	enjoyed	dried	carryer
marryed	flopping	enjoyied	dryed	carryier
happier	heaviest	staing	flies	crying
happyier	heavyest	staiing	flyes	criing
happier	heaviyest	staying	flyies	cring

4. Give the follow instructions to your child:

1. "Look at the words and choose the right spelling."

2. "If you're right, you get three points. If you're wrong, I get three points."

3. "If you beat me, you write out each correction only once and get an ice cream (and a big hug!)."

4. "If I beat you, I get a big hug!"

Keep the game fun with lighthearted consequences. You don't want your child seeing spelling as a punishment or something that makes him feel dumb.

Activity: Finding ten ending mistakes

Preparation: Write out ten sentences with spelling errors. Make the errors a mix of common words like *they* and words from the tables. Write clearly or print or type.

Follow these steps:

1. **Give your child the flawed sentences to correct. Tell him to find ten errors, one in each sentence.**

   Examples:

   • The couple got marryed.

   • The girl had neva been happier.

   • Thay went on vacation.

   • The bags were heavyer than the blankets.

   • The little girl cryed.

   • The boy was angry becuse he lost his pen.

   • I am staing in a motel.

   • She enjoyied the music.

   • It was the funnyest show.

   • It was the windyest day in years.

2. **Have him write the correct spellings.**

Tell him that if he gets all the spellings right, you'll do 20 push-ups or jumping jacks, or shoot hoops for 20 minutes, or any other creative thing that comes to you in a moment of folly, oops, I mean inspiration. Better still, tell him that your partner or other child or grandmother will do those things, but if he gets any wrong, he has to do ten push-ups.

When your child *proofreads* (looks for errors), have him read the whole sentence first. After he makes sense of the text, he then goes back to make corrections.

Activity: Adding a quick ending

Preparation: Open this book to Tables 16-10 and 16-11 and have a watch or timer.

Follow these steps:

1. **Cover the second and third columns of Table 16-10 with a blank piece of paper.**

2. **Ask your child to write on the blank paper the root words of the words in the first column with any endings.**

3. **Give her a time limit of three minutes.**

4. **Do the same with Table 16-11, but set the time limit at two minutes.**

You can think up rewards to go with these activities, but your child will like your playful attention even better. Say stupid things like "If you get all these words right, I won't have to punch you on the nose." If he makes mistakes say something like, "Well, it was only a small mistake, do you think I should step on your toe instead?" Your (razor-sharp) jokes and lightheartedness tell him that spelling can be fun and mistakes don't have to be stressful.

Mixing Suffixes and Endings

So far, you and your child have added suffixes like *ing* and *ed* to root words. Suffixes are great, but your child needs to know about other endings, too. I'm including a bunch of those other endings in the next few paragraphs. You'll spot familiar root words with suffixes added on, like *inspection,* but also words, like *lotion,* that aren't root words plus suffixes. You'll see words with sound-alike endings like *uncle* and *final.* These words are worth showing to your child, because kids often misspell them.

A suffix is an addition to a root word. It adapts the root word so it can be used in different contexts. Suffixes can turn *jump* into *jumps, jumped, jumping, jumpy, jumpier,* and *jumpiest,* and *direct* into *directs, directed, directing, director, directive,* and *direction.*

Adding *tion*, *sion*, or *cian*

The ending that often catches kids out to lunch is *tion*. Kids quite reasonably expect *tion* to be written *shun*. Table 16-12 gives you *sion*, *tion*, and *cian* words to look at with your child. Both of you need to limber up your writing hand, because the "Matching up words and endings" activity gives everyone an active role.

Table 16-12	*sion*, *tion*, and *cian*	
tion	*sion*	*cian*
station	division	magician
action	vision	musician
mention	illusion	politician
fraction	collision	electrician
inspection	confusion	beautician
reflection	decision	optician
relation	television	
direction	conclusion	
sensation	invasion	
motion	occasion	
lotion	explosion	
tradition	decision	

Activity: Matching up words and endings

Preparation: Grab some paper and pens.

Follow these steps:

1. **Write the 30 words from Table 16-12 onto a sheet of paper.**

2. **Cut out each word and then cut off all the endings.** Spread out the root words (or word parts) and the endings.

3. **Ask your child to match the words to their endings.** This activity is a good one to do together on the floor.

Looking for a challenge?

For enthusiasts and challenge seekers here are some extra *tion* words to consider:

Correction, dictation, disposition, fiction, infection, invention, refraction, relaxation, selection, suction, notion, position, and *promotion.*

When you help your child with this activity, don't take over. Say things like "Could this be right?" and "Do you think it's this one?" If your child struggles, arrange the word parts so they're close to their partners and so your child can spot the pairs better.

Adding ent or ant

When endings sound similar, your child has to get to know the looks of them. She must sharpen her visual memory. Have your child read the words in Table 16-13. With your help, have her write them out, sounding them out in chunks. Next you can dictate them to her in random order. Can she spell at least 12 of the 16 correctly? If she can, celebrate! (Drink hot chocolate together, award her points, play a game with her). If not, have her write out the ones that got away (the ones she misspelled) a few times, until they're retrieved and snugly held in her memory.

Any time a word or two escapes your child's memory, have him jot them down. If he writes them three times a day for a few days, and pins them in places where he can see them (the bathroom is good), he can get the better of them.

Table 16-13	*ent* and *ant*
ent	*ant*
enjoyment	brilliant
violent	adamant
punishment	tenant
disappointment	fragrant
judgment	relevant
compliment	confidant

(continued)

Table 16-13 *(continued)*

ent	ant
agreement	important
tournament	assistant
dependent	radiant
permanent	dominant
convenient	arrogant
intelligent	intolerant
magnificent	elegant
competent	significant
evident	irritant
argument	distant

ment endings (enjoyment) are much more common than *mant (adamant)* endings.

Words ending with *ant* end with *ance* in other uses (brilliant, brilliance).

Words ending with *ent* end with *ence* in other uses (intelligent, intelligence).

Adding *le* and *al*

Make a copy of Table 16-14 and have your child read through the words in it. He can pronounce a distinct *al* in the *al* words, if it helps him remember the right ending. Have him highlight any tricky letters. After the table, the "Remembering and spelling" activity is a quiet, but nevertheless pretty cool activity!

Table 16-14		*le* and *al*	
le Words		*al* Words	
angle	trouble	annual	usual
bangle	tangle	gradual	festival
table	tingle	manual	central
double	jungle	punctual	natural

Extras of *le* and *al*

If Table 16-13 wasn't enough, here are some more words with *le* and *al* endings:

✔ Apple, article, bicycle, bumble, bundle, candle, chuckle, circle, crackle, crinkle, cripple, dapple, dimple, double, eagle, fumble, gentle, grapple, humble, jingle, jungle, knuckle, mangle, marble, mingle, needle, nimble, pimple, purple, rifle, ripple, rumble, scramble, simple, single, sprinkle, stumble, tackle, tangle, topple, tremble, tumble, and wrangle

✔ Capital, confidential, criminal, essential, general, gradual, influential, initial, material, musical, naval, official, physical, practical, principal, psychological, racial, serial, several, social, unusual, and usual

le Words		al Words	
simple	little	equal	final
purple	uncle	rascal	hospital
handle	twinkle	special	metal

Activity: Remembering and spelling

Preparation: Make a copy of Table 16-14.

Follow these steps:

1. **Have your child look at Table 16-14 for 30 seconds.**

2. **Take the table away from him, and have him write the words that he remembers.** Tell him that spelling three words correctly is good, spelling five words correctly is great, and spelling more than five correctly is plain brilliant!

Looking at navels and principles

Navel and *principle* are two words that have practically everyone wondering about *al*'s and *le*'s, so here's the lowdown:

Your child will find his *navel* on his stomach, but his *naval* project features pictures of ships and seafaring folk. If your child has to see his *principal,* he may feel nervous. When you talk about

his *principles,* he may feel nervous, too. Maybe he needs to examine his *principles* so that he's able to stay clear of his *principal?* Can't remember all that? Don't worry, remember instead that "the princi*pal* should be your *pal*" and "in nav*al* affairs, we're *al*l on the boat together."

3. **Next give him Table 16-13, and tell him that he can cross off the words that he spelled correctly and an equal number of other words.** (If he correctly spelled five words, he crosses off those five, plus another five.)

4. **Now dictate the remaining words to him.**

Adding full and all

How easy is this? When your child adds *full* to the end of a word or *all* to the beginning, she simply drops one of the *l*'s. Table 16-15 provides some *full* and *all* words for you to check out. Have your child take a good look at the words and copy down any that look tricky to her, Then take turns writing the words with your finger on each other's back. Your child can use paper and pen, too, if she wants.

Table 16-15	Adding *full* and *all*
Adding ful	*Adding all*
careful	almost
awful	always
joyful	altogether
forceful	already
helpful	
hopeful	
beautiful	

Until has one *l*, too.

A Grand Finale of Suffixes

Want to lead your child through a different ending each week? At the end of the chapter, there are 11 add-on tables to feast on (I thought a dozen might be a bit much!). Look through them and dictate some of the words for your child to spell. If you can muster up a crowd, use these words with the group activities that I give in Chapter 20. If you're feeling dramatic, "Charades" is absolutely the game for you.

Activity: Charades

Preparation: I'm guessing that just about everybody has played charades. All you need to start is a bunch of words that can be acted out. Here are ten from the tables in this chapter: *beautiful, marriage, private, pirate, affectionate, mountain, temperature, lecture, secretary,* and *delicious.*

Follow these steps:

1. **Have one person (you or your child) silently read a word and then act it out.** This player who's acting out the word is not allowed to speak.

2. **The player who's watching must guess the word the other player is acting out.**

3. **When he shouts out the right answer, he must follow through by writing the word down** (with the correct spelling, of course). If your child spells the word incorrectly, give huge hints to help him out.

When you play charades with your child, you provide the words! You can probably get away with this activity with little kids; however, you may want to give them a peek at the words in advance to even the pitch. Older kids don't need a peek. Get an independent person to write the words down so none of the Charades players gets a sneak preview.

Table 16-16	***age***
advantage	marriage
average	message
bandage	passage
cabbage	postage
cottage	sausage
courage	village
foliage	voyage

Table 16-17	***ate***
affectionate	fortunate
alternate	intricate
chocolate	late
climate	mate

(continued)

Table 16-17 *(continued)*

deteriorate	pirate
duplicate	private
estimate	separate
fate	ultimate

Table 16-18   *ain*

bargain	curtain
captain	fountain
certain	mountain

Table 16-19   *ine*

discipline	imagine
engine	medicine
examine	vaccine

Table 16-20   *ture*

adventure	gesture
agriculture	lecture
capture	manufacture
creature	mixture
culture	moisture
departure	nature
fixture	picture
furniture	temperature
future	torture

Table 16-21	ure
exposure	measure
exterior	pleasure
failure	pressure
figure	treasure
leisure	warrior

Table 16-22	ary
boundary	primary
dictionary	salary
February	secretary
library	solitary
necessary	stationary
ordinary	voluntary

Table 16-23	ery
battery	lottery
bribery	mystery
celery	nursery
cemetery	robbery
cookery	scenery
discovery	slavery
gallery	surgery

Table 16-24	ory
factory	memory
history	territory
laboratory	victory

Table 16-25	*cial*
artificial	beneficial
facial	official
palatial	racial
social	special

Table 16-26	*cious*
delicious	fictitious
gracious	malicious
precious	precocious
spacious	suspicious

Chapter 17

Spotting What's in a Contraction

In This Chapter

▶ Spelling short and long versions of the same words

▶ Understanding the possessive apostrophe

▶ Avoiding common mistakes

The saying, "Good things come in small packages," is pertinent for things like diamonds and laptop computers, but not much use with things like scorpions. Some words are a bit like scorpions, small but potentially trouble-some. The words *don't, it's,* and *that's,* for example, rank among the top 25 most misspelled (or misused) words in written English. This chapter helps your child morph those scorpions into diamonds, at least figuratively.

Disappearing Letters

Like its name suggests, a contraction is one word that used to be more words. A *contraction* is two words that have been fused together with a letter or two taken out and replaced with an apostrophe, or a punctuation mark that looks like a high-up comma.

Understanding What's Going on with Contractions

Contractions can be confusing for some people. To make them clear for your child, remind him that the apostrophe in a contraction always replaces miss-ing letters. Your child will figure out contractions after he thinks about what he's literally writing. If, for example, he writes, "he's," it's actually short for, or a contraction of, *he is*. If he writes, "it's," it's short for *it is*. And if he writes *you're,* it's short for *you are*.

A word is a contraction only if it has an apostrophe in it and you can expand it into two words. I explain that a little more in the "It's versus its" section later in the chapter.

Getting to Know the Words That Contract

Your child will come across plenty of contractions. Table 17-1 gives you the more common ones. Look through them with your child and then cruise through the "Count and figure out," "Listen up," and "Poem search" activities that I tell you about next.

Table 17-1 Common Contractions

Contraction	Expanded words
I've	I have
we've	we have
they've	they have
you've	you have
they'd	they would
they're	they are
you're	you are
we're	we are
she's	she is
he's	he is
it's	it is
what's	what is
where's	where is
let's	let us
I'll	I will
she'll	she will
he'll	he will
who'll	who will

Contraction	Expanded words
who's	who is
we'll	we will
they'll	they will
isn't	is not
don't	do not
doesn't	does not
can't	cannot
couldn't	could not
won't	will not
wouldn't	would not
shouldn't	should not

Activity: Count and figure out

Preparation: You need your copy of *Teaching Kids to Spell For Dummies* in front of you and turned to this page. Make a copy of Table 17-1. Have pen and paper ready for your child to use.

Follow these steps (suggested dialogue is in quotation marks):

1. Have your child "Look at Table 17-1."

2. Tell your child to "Cover the right column with a piece of paper."

3. Have your child "Count to the fifth word in the left column and write what that word is short for."

4. Have your child "Count to the tenth word and write what that word is short for."

5. Do steps 1 through 4 for the 15th, 20th, and 25th words.

6. Have your child "Take away the paper to check your answers."

7. Say to your child, "Now put the paper over the left column."

8. Have your child "Look at the right column, and write the contraction for every third set of words or word."

9. Have your child "Take away the paper and check your answers."

Activity: Listen up

Preparation: Open this book to Table 17-1 and have pen and paper ready for your child to use.

Follow these steps:

1. **Dictate any five words (long form) to your child from the right column of Table 17-1.**

2. **Have your child write the short form, or contraction, for each one.**

3. **Reverse the process described in Steps 1 and 2, dictating contractions from the left column and having your child write the words in long form.**

Activity: Poem search

Preparation: Make a copy of the poem *New Boots,* which follows and have a pen ready for your child to use.

Follow these steps:

1. **Have your child read *New Boots.***

2. **Have your child find and circle the ten contractions (or maybe I miscounted!) in the poem.**

New Boots

I don't trip over

in my new boots.

They're shiny and squeaky.

They've got buckles.

My mom tried to make me get another pair

but I said they were too tight.

I didn't give in.

I knew she'd give in.

I'm stubborn.

I wouldn't, couldn't, won't ever

take off my new boots.

You'd have to give me

a million dollars

before I'd take them off.

Possessive Apostrophes

After your child is comfortable working with contractions, she needs to be on good terms with possessive apostrophes. This section shows you how to help your child wield her apostrophes wisely, without under- or overusing them.

When your child writes about people or things (nouns) and describes them as having (or possessing) something, she needs to use the possessive apostrophe. If she writes about *John's* ball, *Jane's* mom, or the *cat's* tail, or writes, "That ball is Jane's," she's writing about possession and must pop in the possessive apostrophe.

In general, the two times your child needs to use an apostrophe are

✔ In a contraction, to replace the omitted letters, like in *isn't*

✔ To show that a thing or person possesses something, like in *John's* hat or the *cat's* dish

Never use apostrophes in possessive personal pronouns (hers, his, its, ours, or yours). Of these words "its" is probably the one your child is most likely to trip up on, because it's so much like "it's." I talk about "It's versus its" later in this chapter.

For nouns that end in *s* (class, boys, boss), just add the apostrophe, as in:

✔ It's my class' turn.

✔ It was the boys' race.

✔ This is the boss' pen.

Proper nouns (names of people) are special. You can write "Tess' doll" or "Tess's doll."

Zip through the "Apostrophes in contractions and possession" and "Who has what?" activities with your child so he's sure about using apostrophes.

Activity: Apostrophes in contractions and possession

Preparation: Copy the list of 12 statements that follow and have a pen ready for your child to use.

Follow this step: Have your child put in 16 apostrophes where they're needed in the statements that follow.

✔ I went to Janes house. *(Answer: 1)*

✔ Shes Pauls sister. *(Answer: 2)*

✔ Its Matthews turn. *(Answer: 2)*

✔ Mikes cup cracked. *(Answer: 1)*

✔ The dogs ball got lost. *(Answer: 1)*

✔ Its my rooms turn to use the gym. *(Answer: 2)*

✔ Its time to go to Kellys show. *(Answer: 2)*

✔ The lamps globe was missing. *(Answer: 1)*

✔ The chairs leg broke. *(Answer: 1)*

✔ There were mice in the three boys lockers. *(Answer: 1)*

✔ It was her brothers turn. *(Answer: 1)*

✔ Jills foot hurt. *(Answer: 1)*

Activity: Who has what?

Preparation: Open this book to Table 17-2. You'll need paper and a pen.

Follow these steps:

1. **Have your child match each person or thing in the first column of Table 17-2 with an object in the second column.**

2. **Have your child write short possessive sentences like about those matches she's made.**

   She may write: *The dog's ball burst. Jane's hat fell off. My dad's sock has a hole in it.*

Table 17-2	Possessions
Person or Thing	*Object*
my dog	house
Peter	book
Sharon	bed
Jess	bone
Mom	belt
Dad	cake
Steve	dress
the class	room
Rachel	desks
my cat	basket

You can make this activity lively by thinking of real people you know and matching them with real objects. Spread out small objects on the table, and ask your child to pretend match them with friends. Make realistic or funny matches like "This lipstick is my dog's." If your child seems to be getting right into this activity, draw a poster of the matches.

Avoiding Mistakes

People always are misspelling (or to be accurate, misusing) contractions. *It's, who's,* and *you're* are particularly bothersome, so here's some information that can help your child straighten out those spellings.

A contraction is a shortened word made from two words joined together. The apostrophe takes the place of the letter or letters that are missing. Your child can decide whether he is writing a contraction by asking himself whether his word can be expanded into two words. If not, he isn't writing a contraction (and doesn't need an apostrophe).

It's versus its

It's is the contraction for *it is,* and it causes heads to ache. When your child is in the middle of writing a letter, she may not be sure whether to use *it's,* the contraction, or *its,* the possessive pronoun. Should she write *it's head* or *its head?* Because you're talking about a head that belongs to some thing, *its head* is the answer.

Your child can write *Peter's* head, *the dog's* head, and *my mom's* head, but not *it's* head. The technical reason: *It* is not a noun but rather a pronoun.

The simple reason that your child can't write *it's head* is that *its* never has an apostrophe unless you're using it to say *it is.*

Give your child the simple explanation of "*It's* versus *its*" and then dive into the "Getting it right with *its*" activity.

Activity: Getting it right with its

Preparation: Make a copy of the list of the ten sentences in this activity. You'll also need a pen or pencil.

Follow this step: Have your child put in 15 apostrophes where they're needed in the list of statements that follow. ***Note:*** I just wrote *apostrophes,* and not *apostrophe's.* If your child isn't sure whether to use an apostrophe with words ending in *s,* tell her that plurals alone *never* have apostrophes.

✔ Its a nice day today isnt it? *(Answer: 2)*

✔ It took its bone somewhere else. *(Answer: 0)*

✔ I know its late but I cant rush. *(Answer: 2)*

✔ Youd be mad to take away its blanket. *(Answer: 1)*

✔ Ill be there when its dark. *(Answer: 2)*

✔ Wed better get its bottle. *(Answer: 1)*

✔ Im sure its okay that hes gone. *(Answer: 3)*

✔ Theres a loop on its collar. *(Answer: 1)*

✔ Its been a while since youve called. *(Answer: 2)*

✔ Therell be trouble about its feed. *(Answer: 1)*

Your child must think pretty carefully about these sentences. So must I! Remember to take breaks. Shoot some hoops, grab a snack, see who can throw raisins in the air and catch them in their mouths. (Throwing raisins or mini-cookies in the air and catching them in your mouth is a time-honored art that your child will respect. Show off your forgotten skills; be wicked-awesome!)

Can't versus can,t

Can't isn't a tricky contraction, but I use it here to show you a problem that your child may have with knowing the differences between apostrophes and commas. I see some children writing *can,t,* so I'm alerting you to the dilemma of "do I put the apostrophe up or down?" If your child isn't sure where the apostrophe makes its home, remind him about the differences between apostrophes (up high) and commas (down low).

The best-selling book about English usage and grammar, *Eats, Shoots and Leaves,* by Lynne Truss, takes its name from this joke (that everyone but me heard eons ago!).

A comma shows you where to pause as you read.

An apostrophe takes the place of missing letters when you've shortened two words into a contraction.

An apostrophe also shows when a person or thing possesses something (*Sharon's* ball; the *dog's* ball; *mom's* ball), but you never use an apostrophe in *its,* like in *its* ball.

Bob's panda joke

Last week I was sitting in a café, masquerading as a cool person and typing this chapter, when a man looked over my shoulder. "What's all that about *can't* and *can,t?*" he asked. So I told him. "Ah, commas," he said. "Did you hear the one about the panda who went to the bar?" Here's the panda joke that Bob told me:

A panda orders a meal in a bar, eats it, and then shoots the unlucky fellow sitting next to him. He turns to leave the bar, but the other patrons apprehend him. "Why did you do that?" they ask. "I'm supposed to," says the panda, and hands them a (badly edited) dictionary. They flip to "panda" and read, "panda: eats, shoots, and leaves." So you see, it's like Bob says, "Those commas sure are important dudes. (He didn't really say that "dude" stuff. Sorry Bob, I got carried away with the rootin', tootin' story.)

Who's versus whose

Children sometimes write *whose* rather than *who's*. If your child makes this mistake, tell him that *who's* is short for *who is* or *who has,* and if he's saying "whose" but *not* meaning *who is* or *who has,* the spelling is *whose.* After he's thought about that distinction, help him with the "Who's or whose" activity up next.

Activity: *Who's* or *whose*

Preparation: Copy the ten sentences in this activity and make sure you have a pen or pencil ready for your child to use.

Follow this step: Have your child circle the correct word (*whose* or *who's*) in each sentence.

- ✔ "Whose/who's sweater is this?" dad asked. *(Answer: whose)*
- ✔ "That's the boy whose/who's on the chess team," Jeff said. *(Answer: who's)*
- ✔ "Whose/who's turn is it?" the teacher asked. *(Answer: whose)*
- ✔ "That's the girl whose/who's mom baked the cake," Janet told me. *(Answer: whose)*
- ✔ "Whose/who's next in line?" the waiter asked. *(Answer: who's)*
- ✔ "Whose/who's bringing oranges next week?" the coach asked. *(Answer: who's)*
- ✔ "Whose/who's taken my bag?" Brittany shouted. *(Answer: who's)*

✔ "Whose/who's got the ball?" Megan shouted. *(Answer: who's)*

✔ "She's the one whose/who's lying," Dan yelled. *(Answer: who's)*

✔ "Whose/who's in charge here?" my mom asked. *(Answer: who's)*

You're versus your

Is it *you're* or *your*? Help your child distinguish between these two words by remembering that in contractions an apostrophe takes the place of missing letters.

If you write about *your hat* or *your mom,* no letters are missing. But if you write that *you're going out,* it really means *you are* going out. Two words *(you are)* have been contracted into *you're,* with the apostrophe replacing the missing letter.

The "You're and your," "30 proverbs; 20 apostrophes," "Look who's talking," and "Ha, ha" activities give your child straightforward, change-the-mistakes practice. Go through them with your child, because basic practice, when all is said and done, is a good thing to do. Then you can move on. The last three upbeat activities are proverbs for you to ponder, conversations for you to construct, and jokes for you to split your sides over!

Activity: You're and your

Preparation: Make a copy of the 11 sentences in the list that follows, and be sure your child has either a pen or pencil.

Follow this step: Have your child make eight corrections to these sentences.

✔ Your right about your mom. *(Answer: You're right about your mom.)*

✔ Can I have your cake? *(Answer: Can I have your cake?)*

✔ I like your dog. *(Answer: I like your dog.)*

✔ Your my best friend. *(Answer: You're my best friend.)*

✔ Its your turn. *(Answer: It's your turn.)*

✔ Wheres your dad? *(Answer: Where's your dad?)*

✔ I think your right. *(Answer: I think you're right.)*

✔ Your always first. *(Answer: You're always first.)*

✔ He said your coming, too. *(Answer: He said you're coming, too.)*

✔ She took your book. *(Answer: She took your book.)*

✔ I hope your getting better. *(Answer: I hope you're getting better.)*

Activity: 30 proverbs; 20 apostrophes

For extra challenge and some good old-fashioned wisdom, I've put together these 30 proverbs with 20 missing apostrophes.

Preparation: Make a copy of the 30 statements that follow and have a pen ready for your child to use.

Follow these steps:

1. **Work together with your child to find where the missing apostrophes belong and mark them.**

2. **Read each proverb with your child, determine what they mean, and have your child give you a working example of each one.**

3. **Have your child say whether she thinks the proverbs are worthwhile or outdated.**

   1. A chain is no stronger than its weakest link. *(Answer: 0)*

   2. A mans home is his castle. *(Answer: 1)*

   3. A womans work is never done. *(Answer: 1)*

   4. Alls well that ends well. *(Answer: 1)*

   5. Beggars cant be choosers. *(Answer: 1)*

   6. Birds of a feather flock together. *(Answer: 0)*

   7. Boys will be boys. *(Answer: 0)*

   8. Dont count your chickens before they hatch. *(Answer: 1)*

   9. Dont cut off your nose to spite your face. *(Answer: 1)*

   10. Dont put all your eggs in one basket. *(Answer: 1)*

   11. Finders keepers, losers weepers. *(Answer: 0)*

   12. Give her an inch and shell take a mile. *(Answer: 1)*

   13. Good fences make good neighbors. *(Answer: 0)*

   14. Great minds think alike. *(Answer: 0)*

   15. Let sleeping dogs lie. *(Answer: 0)*

   16. Many hands make light work. *(Answer: 0)*

   17. Scratch my back and Ill scratch yours. *(Answer: 1)*

   18. There is no fool like an old fool. *(Answer: 0)*

   19. Theres no place like home. *(Answer: 1)*

   20. Theres no smoke without fire. *(Answer: 1)*

   21. Two heads are better than one. *(Answer: 0)*

   22. Two wrongs do not make a right. *(Answer: 0)*

23. What you dont know cant hurt you. *(Answer: 2)*

24. When the cat is away, the mice will play. *(Answer: 0)*

25. Where theres a will theres a way. *(Answer: 2)*

26. You cant make an omelet without breaking eggs. *(Answer: 1)*

27. You cant please everyone. *(Answer: 1)*

28. You cant judge a book by its cover. *(Answer: 1)*

29. You cant teach an old dog new tricks. *(Answer: 1)*

30. You dont get something for nothing. *(Answer: 1)*

Activity: Look who's talking

Preparation: Read the "Bear Meets Clown" story herein with your child and have pen or pencil and paper ready.

Follow these steps:

1. **Help your child write his own short story similar to the one you've just read.**

   Possible topics are: Sheep and Princess, Bull and Musician, Boy and Fish, Grandfather and Rap Band, Girl and Goblin, Spiderman and Chef, and Dog and Painter.

2. **While writing, include conversation, commas, and as many contractions as you can.**

   Try to use at least 10 contractions.

   Story: Bear Meets Clown

   "Hi clown! Don't be scared, I'm a really timid bear."

   "Oh my, you're scary! You're one big bear."

   "Sure I'm big, but you'll soon see I'm sweet tempered. Will you show me a trick? I'd love to do tricks. It's my dream."

   The clown and the bear spent the afternoon together. They had fun and said they'd meet up again some time. Do you think they really will?

Activity: Ha, ha

Preparation: Open your copy of this book to this exercise, and have pen or pencil and paper ready for your child to use.

Follow these steps:

1. **Try these silly jokes (all with apostrophes) with your child.**

2. **Have your child write out his favorites to lambaste friends and other hapless targets with.**

J: How many balls of string does it take to reach the moon?

A: Just one if it's long enough!

J: What's the best hand to write with?

A: Neither — it's best to write with a pen!

J: I'd tell you a joke about a pencil.

A: But it wouldn't have any point!

J: Why do birds fly south in the winter?

A: It's too far to walk!

J: I've got a wonder watch. It cost only 50 cents.

R: Why's it a wonder watch?

A: Every time I look at it, I wonder if it's still working!

J: Dad, there's a man at the door collecting for the new swimming pool.

A: Give him a glass of water!

J: What did the tie say to the hat?

A: You go on ahead and I'll hang around!

J: What's the best thing to take into the desert?

A: A thirst aid kit!

J: Why didn't the banana snore?

A: It was afraid of waking up the rest of the bunch!

J: What's the best day of the week to sleep?

A: Snooze-day!

J: What's the fastest thing in water?

A: A motor pike!

Part VI
The Part of Tens

The 5th Wave
By Rich Tennant

"It looks like you've been playing cards instead of practicing your spelling again."

In this part . . .

I have a friend who once tried a carrot diet. She ate plenty of carrots and drank plenty of carrot juice. Sure enough, she lost a few pounds. But her skin turned orange, and she didn't feel like she was having much fun.

In this part of the book, I give you smaller bites of information (usually ten at a time) and quick, fun strategies. You more than likely won't lose weight reading through it, but then again, neither you nor your child will turn orange (and that *has* to be good).

Chapter 18

Ten Word Families

In This Chapter

▶ Starting with *all* and *or* before tackling *ight*

▶ Toiling with *oi* and *oy* word families

▶ Sprucing up with the *ou* and *ow* families

▶ Investigating *er, ir,* and *ur*

▶ Getting the hang of *au* and *aw*

▶ Swooning over two ways to say *oo*

*E*very day my friend Emma drags me around on what could loosely be described as a walk. Emma is a beagle. She keeps her nose to the ground and does disconcerting things when she picks up a scent. I've gotten used to her sudden sprints (since the time she wrapped her lead around my ankles and yanked me to the ground before my keen reflexes kicked in), but her unearthly howling is something else. When Emma points her nose skyward and lets rip, people think unspeakable things are happening.

Emma has instincts. To be a good speller your child needs to form an instinct for breaking words into sounds. If he gets friendly with the word families in this chapter, he's well on his way.

The Easy All and Or Families

The words *all* and *or* are great for starting your child off on word families. After your child can spell these two, he's off and running and ready to spell a host of words in the same families (like the ones in Table 18-1), and he'll feel pretty darned clever in the process.

Table 18-1		all and or Words	
all Words		**or Words**	
all	mall	corn	order
ball	small	for	storm
call	stall	fork	torn
fall	tall	horse	worn
gall	wall	north	
hall		or	

The Straightforward ight Family

Not many children feel immediately comfortable with the *ight* family. Give your child time to warm to these guys in Table 18-2, and then run my next suggestion past her to see if it helps her bring the silent *gh* to mind when she needs to spell it.

Table 18-2	ight Words	
blight	bright	fight
flight	fright	height
knight	light	might
night	plight	right
sight	slight	tight

Height is a tricky word. It fits into the ight family but you have to warn your child about the *he* beginning. One tip for helping your child remember the spelling is to tell him that *height* follows the same spelling pattern as *weight* even though they sound out differently.

The oi and oy Families

Here are a couple of families that are worth your child befriending. Although I know they don't seem such a big deal here, you'd be surprised how often they hold up your child's spelling, if he isn't wary of them. See Table 18-3.

Table 18-3		*oi* and *oy* Words	
oy Words		*oi Words*	
annoy	Roy	boil	soil
boy	royal	moist	spoil
employ	toy	noise	toil
joy		oil	

The ou and ow Families

Many of the member words of the next two families have a lot of personality. Take *growl* and *slouch,* for example. They're evocative words that can add pep to your child's writing. They're good for your child to learn to spell for another reason. Because so many *ou* and *ow* words are out there, after she gets a handle on *ou* and *ow* spellings, the rest of the truck full of words in these families will be easy (see Table 18-4).

Table 18-4		*ou* and *ow* Words	
ou Words		*ow Words*	
around	loud	bow	howl
blouse	mound	brown	now
bounce	mouse	cow	owl
bound	noun	clown	scowl
cloud	out	crown	sow
clout	pound	down	town
count	proud	drown	
flour	round	fowl	
found	slouch	frown	
foul	sound	gown	
ground	spout	growl	
house	trout	how	

The er, ir, and ur Families

If your child gets into writing comic strips, she definitely needs to know how to spell *"er."* Comic characters who get biffed, bashed, or bonked almost always do so with *"er"* dangling above them in their speech or thought balloons. In the unlikely event that your child doesn't need an *er* for her comic strip, don't worry, any effort you put into Table 18-5 won't be wasted. Cast your eyes over the *er, ir,* and *ur* columns, and you'll see oft needed words like *girl* (as in "Go girl!"), purse (as in "Mom where's your purse?") and *dirt* (as in "Mo-om! Will this dirt come out of my jeans?").

Table 18-5	*er, ir,* and *ur* Words	
er Words	**ir Words**	**ur Words**
her	bird	burn
herb	birth	blur
herd	chirp	church
nerve	dirt	curb
perch	firm	curl
person	first	curse
serve	flirt	fur
stern	girl	hurl
term	shirt	hurt
	sir	nurse
	stir	purse
	squirt	spurt
	third	surf
	thirst	surge
	whirl	turn

The au and aw Families

Well, what d'ya know? I just talked about the comic strip *"er"* and here I am at *"aw,"* as in "Aw, doggone it!" Take your child carefully through the *au* and *aw* words in Table 18-6, because as nice as these words are, they're nonetheless tricky to spell.

Table 18-6	*au* and *aw* Words	
au Words	*aw Words*	
auto	brawl	pawn
author	caw	paws
cause	claw	straw
laundry	crawl	prawn
maul	dawn	raw
pause	draw	saw
sauce	hawk	straw
taught	jaw	thaw
	law	yawn
	lawn	

Soon, spoon, and moon

Two word families have *oo* in them. The biggest family uses *oo* with a long pronunciation, like in *food, and t*he smaller family uses *oo* with a short pronunciation, like in *book, took,* and *look*. Let your child get the hang of *food* and company in Table 18-7, and then show her the smaller *book, took,* and *look* family in Table 18-8.

Table 18-7	Words like *soon* and *spoon*		
boo	stool	noon	gloom
broom	too	room	groove
doom	troop	soon	loop
food	boot	spool	moon
goose	choose	swoon	noose
hoop	drool	tool	scoop

(continued)

Table 18-7 *(continued)*

loose	fool	zoom	smooth
moose	groom	bloom	spoon
pool	hoot	cool	swoop
shoot	moo	droop	tooth
snooze			

Table 18-8	**Words like *book* and *took***	
book	brook	cook
crook	foot	good
hook	look	nook
rook	shook	stood
soot	took	wood

Chapter 19

Ten Ways to Correct Your Child's Spelling

. . . .

In This Chapter

▶ Checking your child's eyes, ears, and posture

▶ Reviewing your teaching style

▶ Fine-tuning your child's handwriting

▶ Giving your child a few ways to attack tricky words

▶ Helping your child use rules and routines

. . . .

*I*f you're anything like me you feel as if much of your time goes into coercing your child to eat healthily and watch TV selectively and the rest goes into keeping track of your keys. In this chapter, I save you from wasting valuable time and energy (that you need for accusing loved ones of misplacing your keys) by giving you all the important spelling stuff you need, in a nutshell.

Seeing and Hearing; Slouching and Shifting

If you're unsettled about your child's ability to spell, you'll want to make sure that she sees and hears words clearly. Use activity books with look-and-search activities (like "Spot the difference") to roughly gauge her eyesight and play a lot of listening games together to get an idea of how well she hears.

You can have your child's hearing and vision tested too, and if you're still worried after that, get a second opinion. To be on the safe side, get a second opinion anyway. Parents whose children have vision or hearing problems that slip through the net will tell you to get a few opinions and to watch for the signs.

Indicators of possible hearing difficulties are:

✔ Your child has had a lot of ear infections.

✔ Your child shouts a lot and talks loudly.

✔ When you ask your child a question, you only sometimes get any answers.

✔ Your child often mishears things.

Hearing problems are tricky to spot, because kids are good at shouting and ignoring their parents much of the time. Get professional advice. Then you're not always uming and ahing over whether your child hears you.

Indicators of possible vision problems are that your child:

✔ Tilts his head slightly to look at things.

✔ Squints.

✔ Rubs his eyes a lot.

✔ Gets headaches.

✔ Sometimes complains of feeling dizzy.

✔ Feels tired after concentrating or focusing on things, or reading.

✔ Holds books and other reading material at an unusual angle or distance when reading or looking at them.

Lightening Up

Doing dreary things is difficult, but it's even harder for your full-of-fun child. That's why I include this subheading. I want to share with you a big lesson that I learned from teaching hundreds of kids: Be cheerful. Keep an upbeat pace. Do a variety of activities, and take breaks. When problems surface, focus on solutions and not blame. There, now you've learned in a few seconds all the good stuff that dawned on me over much more than a few years.

Homing in on Handwriting

Handwriting is a funny thing. Some people think that a neat hand is important; others don't. Some of the smartest people around have lazy, barely legible scrawls, and some of the flakiest or untidiest of folk write neat and even words. What's a parent to think? Well here's what a great elementary school teacher once told me: Kids need to develop a smooth and legible hand. They need to practice their penmanship so they get better and faster at writing. Why? Because doing so frees them to do other things. If they can read their own writing (and believe me, plenty of kids can't), they can proofread their work and are more likely to spot their errors. If they write fluidly and at a good pace, they can keep track of their thoughts — and you know how difficult that is. If they're not always stopping and starting to think of how to spell words, they have more time to think of the one or two words that are tricky to spell.

I just sold you an idea. I said that good handwriting is important. Lest you think that I'm the kind of person who doesn't look at things from a few (hundred) different angles, let me tell you about my experience with handwriting from a parent's point of view. One of my kids is a seemingly natural speller. I always thought that the effortless good speller didn't really exist, so my kid is something of a surprise to me. She spells amazingly well and hates being helped. (I'm hoping for a mellowing-down miracle some time soon.) So how does Miss Spelling Smarty Pants like handwriting drill? She hates it. So, here's where I think the middle ground is between my friend's and my daughter's points of view: Writing fluidly, with letters formed in the proper direction, is an important skill for your child to have. (I've seen kids whose writing was seriously slowed because they started letters in the wrong places and put them together any old how.) It's also important that you don't switch your child off writing by nagging him to death about his penmanship. Expect a legible hand from your child but not necessarily perfection, because some kids just write more neatly than others. If your child is a Spelling Smarty Pants, great! You may not have to tut-tut, if he scrawls and scrapes his letters. If your child is like the rest of us and needs to fix some spelling errors, you may want to invest enough time to improve his handwriting so that it's neat enough for him to actually see those mistakes.

Upping the fun side of the equation

My child is at horseback-riding camp. She's there for a week and has only completed one day so far. When I picked her up yesterday, she had mixed feelings about camp. "I picked these wild flowers and made this sword and shield," she panted. "I can't wait to be the mayor tomorrow." Then she changed her tone. "They made us clean horse poop for hours," she complained. "We're just kids, why don't *they* clean the horse poop? After all, the horses are theirs."

This morning my daughter raced back to the horse poop without complaining. She'll get through the stinky, hard-work aspects of being around horses, because she'll get to go on trail rides, gather armfuls of wildflowers and be mayor. Like all good teachers, her camp leaders are upping the fun side of the learning equation. If I were a gambling woman, I'd bet good money that my child will be eager for more of the same next summer.

Telling Your Child a Word Versus Making Your Child Figure It Out

When your child is stuck with a word, whether you give him the whole spelling or try to help him to figure it out depends first and foremost on your child's personality. Is your child the type of little person who doesn't mind you helping him or do you have to tread carefully around his fierce sense of independence? Your child probably is somewhere in between, so you can deftly skip between roles of chirpy mentor and wizened old sage without too much of the wizened and old. And what about the words with which you're dealing? Are there words that need to be swiftly and wholly given, or are there words you need to give out sparingly and with cute or cryptic clues? The answers are yes and yes. Some words, like *who* and *any,* are hard to clue your child in on. They're written differently from the way they sound and any clues you can give your child are either boring or convoluted ones like, "*Who* has a silent *w,* and then the bit you'd think was spelled *hoo* is, in fact, spelled *ho,* like in "Ho ho, boys and girls, it's Christmas." When you come across words like *who* that are hard to sound out or apply rules to, don't try to do either.

Tell your child the complete spelling of difficult words, like *who,* that don't conform to spelling rules and phonetic principles. Have him write them and hang onto a written copy. You can present the words to him later so he gets plenty of practice recalling them. Keep practicing for a few days until the spellings stick in his mind.

Oh sleep. Why doth thou elude me?

The other night my youngest daughter played host to a birthday sleepover. Four giggling, squealing little girls took their teddies and blankets into one bedroom. They told me they were going to sleep. When an hour had elapsed, I went into the bedroom with a gentle reminder, "Girls, you have a busy day tomorrow (more birthday things), so you need to be quiet." When an hour and 30 minutes had passed, I delivered a more somber message, "Girls, you need to go to sleep now, and when I leave this room, I don't want to hear any voices." When two hours had tick-tocked by, I gave my ultimatum, "Okay, I hear noise. Whoever I hear when I leave this room has to sleep in the other room."

It wasn't long before I moved my daughter into that other room. She was heartbroken. "But Mom, it's my birthday! I *promise* I'll be good, only *please* let me go back with the others." We dried her tears. She tiptoed back to her friends, and a wonderful, complete quiet enveloped our house.

When your child struggles with spelling, it's a bit like struggling to keep quiet on her birthday sleepover. It's hard. The best thing you can do is be flexible. If one strategy doesn't work, try another. When all is said and done, learning to spell in a happy, unstressed way is best for your child. (And, of course, it's best that little friends on sleepovers, even restless ones, get to lay their weary heads down together.)

Words that you can help your child with, without giving the complete spelling, are the ones that belong to word families or that sound out regularly. Misspellings like *vetrenery* and *throte* are the kinds you can nudge your child into correcting for herself. The word *veterinary* is easier if your child pronounces it phonetically. Tell her that it's spelled *ve-ter-in-ary*. Tell her that the word *throat* follows the When-two-vowels-go-walking-the first-one-does-the-talking rule.

Whenever you can, use spelling rules or word families to help your child spell entire words or parts of words. When that doesn't work, however, have your child jot down the tricky word again a few times over a few days until the look of the word sticks in his mind.

Looking for Families

I just said that you need to call on word families whenever you're in their vicinity. In case you've just opened to this chapter or you've forgotten everything that you read so far and have no idea what a word family is, here's a lightning review.

A word family is a bunch of words that share a spelling and sound pattern. Words like *small, tall,* and *ball* form the *all* family. Words like *sound, round,* and *shout* are part of the *ou* family (but know that another small *ou* bunch has a different sound, the *would, could,* and *should* family), and *merrily, happily,* and *funnily* are in the *ily* family. You can make dozens of different word families with your child. A spelling pattern is easier for her to remember when she sees it in many words, so point her in the direction of a family anytime you can. This book is full of word families.

Looking for Spelling Rules

Some rules make life hard for your child. She wants to feel the soft grass under her toes, but the sign says to keep out, or she wants to bomb into the blue water, but the lifeguard warns her against any kind of jumping. Not so with spelling rules. Spelling rules help a great deal as long as you don't overload your child with them. Three or four rules cover pretty much all the important spelling factors that your child needs to know and, hardly surprisingly, I give them to you here in this spelling oracle. You find that I talk about all the rules in depth in chapters 7, 8, and 9, but here I give you a lightning handy overview.

Rule One: Bossy e

You write Bossy *e* everywhere. That's why it's a great letter for your child to get to know. Here's the rule: Your child spells a word like *mate* by adding Bossy *e* to the end of *mat*. The *e* is bossy because it bosses the other vowel in the word to make a long sound or to shout out its name. Here are a few words that show Bossy *e* doing its thing: *plate, mate, lake, Pete, scene, ride, hide, mine, rode, bone, hope, cute, mule* and *tune*. You get the long tour through a mountain of Bossy e words in Chapter 7.

When a vowel makes a long sound, it's the same sound as its name. That's why I say that Bossy *e* makes the vowel (in the word it tags onto) have a long sound *or* shout out its name.

Rule Two: When two vowels go walking, the first one does the talking

Here's a cute rhyme to help your child remember another way of spelling long vowel sounds. When spelling words like *neat* and *boat*, your child can go over the when-two-vowels-go-walking-the-first-one-does-the-talking rhyme. Most long-*e* sounds fit the two vowels rule. Long *e* is spelled either with *ee*, like in *meet, seed,* and *weed,* or *ea*, like in *team, seat,* and *bead*. The two vowels come side by side, but the first is the one that makes its long sound. A long-*o* sound is also often spelled with two vowels. The long *o* is spelled with *oa* like in *boat, coat,* and *loan*. A long-*a* sound can be spelled with side-by-side vowels, too. In words like *pain* and *rain*, your child spells the long-*a* sound with *ai*. See how the two vowels come together? Your child needs to start them with the long vowel that he hears and then remember the partnership. The promenading pairs that he must remember are *ee, ea, oa,* and *ai* and you can find more about them in Chapter 8.

Rule Three: y behaves like a vowel

Without a doubt, vowel sounds are tricky to spell. That's why these four spelling rules are about them. Every time your child hears a long-vowel sound, he must run through the options, which explains why he always needs to use scrap paper when trying to spell them. The third option mostly has to do with long-*e* or long-*i* sounds that your child hears on the ends of words. The *y*-behaving-as-a-vowel rule applies to vowel sounds on the end of words that are spelled with a *y*. In words like *happy* and *sunny*, your child uses *y* to sound like long *e*. In little words like *by* and *shy*, he uses it to sound like long *i*.

What about words like *system, cyst,* and *gypsy?* In those words, your child spells the short-*i* sound with a *y*. The words *cyst* and *gypsy* are soft-*c* and soft-*g* spellings (as well as spellings that use *y* to make the short-*i* sound) so, you may want to flip over to Chapter 14 to read more about those softies.

You use *y* to make *e* or *i* sounds. When your child puts *y* on the ends of longer words (like *happy*), it makes a long-*e* sound, and when she puts *y* on the end of short words (like *by*), it makes a long-*i* sound. She uses *y* in the middle of some words (like *gypsy*) to make the short-*i* sound. When your child gets into the habit of jotting down her spelling options on scrap paper, she gets better and better at deciding whether to use *y*.

Although you may think that I've been a bit stingy with my explanation of when and when not to use *y* to make the *e* and *i* sounds, I have good reason. I've given you only a brief explanation rather than an elaborate one, because if you get long-winded when explaining these rules, you can send your child off into a daze. The smarter approach is to give him scrap paper and simply let him figure out some spellings with an I've-got-a-spelling-puzzle-to-solve attitude.

Rule Four: *i* before *e* except after *c* (when you hear *ee*)

When I told you that vowel sounds are challenging to spell, I wasn't kidding. Here is yet another way for your child to spell the long-*e* sound. All sorts of words have the long-*e* sound in them, and the *i*-before-*e*-except-after-*c* rule gives your child a fourth spelling option. The question becomes: Should your child write Bossy *e* like in *Pete,* or two vowels walking like in *meat* and *meet, y* as in *happy,* or *ie* as in *niece*? Whew. Where *is* that scrap paper? With *ie* spellings, be sure to help your child learn the first part of the rule — *i* before *e* except after *c* — before helping her discover the except-when-you-hear-"*ay*"-like-in-neighbor part. Practice on words like *niece, piece,* and *receive,* and after she's at ease with those, tackle the tough words like *neighbor* and *weight.* (You hear *ay,* so you don't put *i* before *e*.) In Chapter 8, I tell you more about *ie* and *ei* spellings.

Deciding to Remember the Look of a Word

Some words have crazy spellings that you can't find in any other words or many tricky sound chunks. Here are the kinds of words I'm talking about:

Who, they, because, any, come, some, could, would, should, eight, has, laugh, work, and *want*

When a word has so many twists and turns in it that you'd have to be crazy to try to sound it out completely, your child's best bet for remembering how to spell it is remembering how it looks. He can sound out the first letter or a chunk of sound in the word, and then get used to the look of the rest of it.

How, exactly, does your child get used to the look of words? Teachers have pondered this question for years and they've come up with some pretty neat answers. I respectfully lay out the four best answers before you now:

- **Look, cover, write, and check:** This little formula describes four steps that your child can go through to fix a word in his mind. He looks at the word (already spelled out), covers it over, writes his own version, and then checks his copy against the original — look, cover, write, and check.

- **Word folders:** A great way to save words so that your child can practice spelling them regularly is to use a word envelope or folder. In Chapter 10, I explain how to make and use a super-cool spelling folder. You can use the spelling folder for any words, and if you group words into families, they're that much easier for your child to remember. Look for word families and spelling chunks. Use up to ten words at a time in your folder, and spend a few days on the same words before moving on to a new set.

- **Walls and notice boards:** How many times does your child use the bathroom? You may think that I'm asking an impertinent question here, but I have good reason. Your child probably has to pause, begrudgingly, from important things like playing and eating, to answer the call of Mother Nature, at least five times a day. If you stick his words at eye level on the bathroom wall, hey presto, he gets five looks at those words. Am I making sense? Teachers adorn their walls with fancy, attractive stuff and words. Take a leaf out of their book. Capitalize on bodily functions and tape your child's words near to the porcelain bowl. If you think I've sunk to a distinct low in this section, or you're outraged by the thought of mixing spelling with — well you know — then other good places to go with your sticky tape are above the kitchen counter or facing your child's bed.

- **Word games:** Your child likes you to play board games with her. Choose kids Scrabble, Boggle, or Hangman. Keep an eye out for fun games at your school supplies store. Kits of letter tiles, especially in cute cases with word cards, hold great appeal for your child if only because she likes fitting the letters in the custom-built spaces (a bit like the way-cool socket set that I mention in Chapter 18).

Using Spelling Lists

Sometimes your evenings will be bleak. Your child brings a spelling list home from school and doesn't want to plow through it. The words on such lists usually seem chosen arbitrarily, and your child acts like he's never seen any of them before in his life. You try bribery coupled with a sunny can-do attitude, but end up cajoling and threatening. Here's another way to go:

People classify stuff. They order the information that they get so they can remember and manage it better. People mentally classify who they like, who to give a wide berth, what they'll eat and what they really shouldn't put in temptation's range. They likewise classify what they can do and what activities, for the sake of groaning knees and temperamental shoulders, are best avoided. Your child classifies things, too. His spelling list will be easier for him to remember when you help him put some order to it. At the risk of sounding repetitive, word families and spelling rules are your best friends in this situation. Have your child grab a highlighter and go looking for families, rules, and chunks of sound in his spelling list. Group like words together, and on a scrap piece of paper, have your child jot down any more like words that jog his memory and help him recall the spelling-list words.

Lists of random words are hard for your child to learn, so help her out by finding associations and patterns, breaking words into chunks, and using word families and spelling rules.

Having Sight Words Down Pat

You can help your child dramatically reduce his spelling errors by making sure that he can quickly spell the words that he needs to spell most often. I'm talking, of course, about the 220 sight words that comprise about 70 percent of all the words that people use. Your child uses words like *they* and *would* time and time again, so do him a favor by helping him make those words flow easily from his pen. Be sure to devote plenty of time to Chapter 12, because that's where I give you the whole list of 220 sight words. Over a few days, dictate the words for your child to spell and be sure to catch the ones that he's unsure of. Have him jot them down on separate slips of paper. When you have ten words on ten bits of paper, pop them into an envelope. Have your child bring his envelope to you every evening for a week for dictation. If ten words are a bit much for your child to handle, use five. Make your spelling time companionable and share a hot chocolate or follow up the ten minutes of spelling by reading to your child. Your child will have all those important sight words tucked under his belt in just a few weeks.

Libraries and bookshops stock books that consist entirely of sight words so you can easily read books together and spot sight words at the same time.

Doing Dictation

I know that I talk a lot about dictation, but dictation is good. Of course, it isn't the only good thing you can do to improve your child's spelling. You also can

- ✔ Help your child use word families.
- ✔ Show your child how to spell in chunks.
- ✔ Explain the spelling rules to your child.
- ✔ Encourage your child to proofread his writing for spelling mistakes.

But dictation is my personal favorite, primarily because it's easy for you to do and it gives your child that on-the-job-training sort of a feel. How does dictation work? Easy. Here are some tips for getting started and staying with it:

- ✔ Develop a routine where you're giving your child things to write on a regular, but not overwhelming, basis.
- ✔ Choose text that your child is comfortable with. She needs to be able to easily write most of the words and have to figure out only three or four more difficult ones.
- ✔ Choose text from books that your child's currently reading or material that she's pretty familiar with (like a paragraph from a favorite storybook).
- ✔ Always make sure your child proofreads what she's written.
- ✔ Always check your child's writing. If she made too many errors, have her write the dictation again, quicker and with no spelling mistakes.

In case these five quick guidelines left you in a blur, here's a bit more information: Put your child's spelling plan on the fast track with a ten-week blast of activity. Practice some words and do a dictation each night. When you decide to tackle spelling over so many weeks, you may still want to take an occasional break. Breaks are great for rejuvenating a spelling program, and besides, you'll probably find that your child grows weary from spelling if no holiday is on the horizon. When you get down to a spelling routine, shorter periods are best. Little kids may be able to maintain their concentration for only 10 minutes, and even bigger kids work best in 20-minute blasts.

Rummage through schoolbooks and storybooks for sentences to dictate to your child. From them, choose a couple of sentences for little kids and a paragraph or two for older kids. Choose easy text with only three or four taxing words. If your child blitzes one dictation, you can aim a little higher next time. If the text frustrates him, back off a little the next time.

Erring on the easy side is better than giving your child words and text that are too difficult. If your child thinks that dictation is too tough to handle, he'll want to protect his pride by feigning an I'm-above-this attitude or giving you a hard time in other ways.

After your child has written his sentences on paper, remind him to proofread them. Tell him to read his words and check for the right sound chunks and whether the words look right. Give him an ample supply of scrap paper so that he can jot down a few trial spellings. When he's done, check the work and explain any mistakes. Use a sympathetic tone when pointing out his mistakes and cast a thought for the way you'd like someone to correct you if the boot were on the other foot.

To finish up, have your child do a quick rerun, but time him this time. Set the challenge of aiming for an error-free piece of writing. If he doesn't like the sound of a rerun, just have him jot down the misspelled words on a clean sheet of paper. You can use the same sentences for your next dictation and ask him things like: "Do you remember the tricky words from the last time? Do you think a 100 percent correct dictation this time will be too hard?"

Before I end this section, I need to show you an easy to harder progression to take with dictations. What follows is a list of simple sentences that you may want to lead your child through. They start off very simple and gradually get harder. By the time your child is comfortable with the last sentences, he's ready to tackle paragraphs from reading books.

- ✔ A fat cat had a nap.
- ✔ Ben fed a red hen.
- ✔ A big pig sat on a lid.
- ✔ Dot got a hot pot.
- ✔ A pup had a nap in a box.
- ✔ The cat runs in the sun. It is fun.
- ✔ Pam got a pet cat. It is in the bed.
- ✔ Dan is big. He can put a mug on the top shelf.
- ✔ He had a big drink from Ben's mug.
- ✔ The men cut the tops off the plants.
- ✔ All of them ran to get a drink at the well.
- ✔ It is as black as can be in this shed.
- ✔ Can we stop to pet the animals in the hut?
- ✔ Thank you for the drink and candy.
- ✔ They went for a short ride. When they come back, we should all go to the store.

✔ What did you do to them? They left so suddenly.

✔ The chimp was swinging on a thick branch.

✔ Beth had to bring her sister to the play.

✔ The children sat on the bench to chat.

✔ It rained all week so the kids had to stay inside the house. It was very dull.

✔ The dogs are so small that we need to keep them in a blanket inside the crate. I think we should feed them milk.

✔ When she called yesterday, she said she will visit us in three weeks time. We will have to fix the house so it is clean and neat.

✔ The grapes were on top of the crate. Pete had to reach up to get them for Jean. She was so hungry she said she could eat a horse.

✔ Steve's wife liked the gift that he gave her. She said she had always wanted a coat in that shade, but she didn't often get time to shop at the large stores.

When you dictate words to your child say them clearly and over pronounce if it helps with the spelling (like pronouncing certain, as "sur-tayn"). Explain to your child that dialect and plain ole laziness creep into people's everyday speech so enunciating clearly is useful for figuring out spellings.

Baa, Baa, Who?

When my kids were toddlers, we sang great songs like "Eensy Weensy Spider" and "Old MacDonald." Call me old-fashioned (I can't hear you anyway), but "Eensy Weensy Spider" was a nicer song (by miles) than the pop stuff my kids sing these days. I was fond of good old Eensy Weensy. I was even more fond of the black sheep in the song "Baa Baa Black Sheep." At first I didn't think that those black sheep were so great, but then I happened to hear my daughter singing to herself. Not skipping a beat she was belting out, "Baa Baa Blatchley, have you any wool? Clearly, she was buying her wool from Mr. Baa Baa Blatchley, and why not? My child had heard "Baa Baa Black Sheep," the song, many times before she realized that "Baa Baa Blatchley" should've been "Baa Baa Black Sheep." When you dictate words to your child, even though she's heard them before, speak clearly. Exaggerate your pronunciation at times, if it helps her get the spelling. Later she'll be able to spell words without your creative help, and you'll miss giving it! It was a sorry day for me when I had to bid Mr. Blatchley farewell.

Chapter 20

Ten (or More) Group Activities That Rock

In This Chapter

▶ Catering to a crowd

▶ Increasing the tempo

▶ Encouraging creativity

*W*hen I was a college student, I lived in a very small house with a bunch of other students. Next door lived a man in his 80s, named Alf, whom we rarely saw. One hot summer day, my household, with sun oil, sodas, and sound system, squeezed into our tiny yard to catch some rays. Alf came out. He took in the scene and said, "Nice to be young isn't it?"

It *is* nice to be young. It's especially nice to be a kid with friends and fun things to do. After you've read through lists of words with your child and noted any weird spellings, rustle up some friends for the fun activities that I give you in this chapter. If you're a schoolteacher, you'll be pleased to find that the first few activities on my list can be used with large groups of players.

Simple Battleships

You probably remember playing "Battleships" when you were a kid. Here's a cute adaptation.

Activity: Battling with simple word ships

Preparation: Have each player draw two grids of 5 squares by 5 squares (or 25 squares in all). Under the bottom line of squares, label the columns A, B, C, D, and E. On the left of the vertical axis and starting from the bottom row, label the rows 1, 2, 3, 4, and 5.

Follow these steps:

1. **Have your players each write down the same list of any 10 words.** Have them copy the words inside one of the grids, one word per square, in any arrangement.

2. **The words are now battleships, and each player tries to sink the other player's battleships.** Here's how it works:

    1. Player 1: Using your blank grid to mark all your calls, call out a grid reference like B2 and mark it on your chart as a hit or miss (you can use the words "hit" and "miss" or symbols like a circle for a hit and a square for a miss).

    2. Player 2: Tell Player 1 whether she called a hit or a miss. If she called a hit, cross off your battleship, and wait for her next call because she gets another call for every hit.

3. **Take turns repeating the above steps.**

The last player with battleships still afloat wins.

Intense Battleships

Just like it sounds, here is a much more detailed and "intense" version of the battleships game.

Activity: Battling with intense word ships

Preparation: Have each player draw two grids of 10 squares by 10 squares (100 squares in all). Under the bottom line label the columns A, B, C, D, E, F, G, H, I, and J. On the left of the vertical axis, label the rows 1, 2, 3, 4, 5, 6, 7, 8, 9, and 10.

Follow these steps:

1. **Have your players each write the same five pairs of words, plotted on the grid next to each other like a continuous word and 10 single words.**

    Pairs of words are submarines and must share a common characteristic, such as coming from the same word family or starting with the same letter. A sub counts as one unit, so if one square gets hit, the whole sub is hit. You can add more kinds of words and call them names like helicopters and jets, if you want to get really whiz-bang about it.

2. **Have players plot their subs and ships and continue just as you would in the "Battling with simple word ships" activity.**

Word Bingo

I probably wouldn't tell anyone but you this but I adore a good game of Bingo. Rustle up some friends and simple prizes (like markers, notepads, or chocolates) and have fun with this easy adaptation.

Activity: Whole-word bingo

Preparation: Make a list of 20 words. Have players make their own bingo cards, by drawing grids of 5 squares by 4 squares (20 squares in all).

Follow these steps:

1. **Ask players to fill their bingo cards with 1 word in each square, from a list of 20 words that you give them.**

2. **From your own copy of the words, call out words for players to cross off their cards.** BINGO can be either a full card crossed out or a line crossed out (vertically, horizontally, or diagonally).

Bits-of-Words Bingo

I warned you that I'm a closet bingo fan so you're probably expecting yet another variation of Bingo. This cute version gets players thinking about a stack of spelling chunks; in fact, any that you want your child to get more practice with.

Activity: Word-part bingo

Preparation: Have your copy of this book open to this list of 20 word parts: *ing, ed, le, al, able, ent, ant, tion, cian, sion, tch, all, re, ly, th, wh, ch, sh, ee,* and *oa.* Have players make their own bingo cards, by drawing grids of 5 squares by 4 squares (20 squares in all). You'll, of course, need paper and pens or pencils.

Follow these step:

1. **Read the list of word parts to the players.**

2. **Ask the players to make words from each part and then fill out their bingo cards with the words.**

3. **Call out the word parts and check spellings at the end of the game (or trade cards and have playing partners check each others' spellings).**

Putting Your Hands on the Table

Here's a really fun activity for a group. You may want to match spelling words to each player's ability. Beginners get easier words, like *brick,* while experts get words like *superstitious.*

Activity: Hands on the table

Preparation: Gather a bunch of players, minimum of four so you have two teams each of two players, and prepare a list of words to read out loud to the teams. You have access to plenty of them in your copy of Teaching Kids to Spell For Dummies, so preparation shouldn't be too difficult. Have paper and pens and pencils ready for the players or teams.

Follow these steps:

1. **Divide players into two or more teams.**

2. **Ask one player from the first team to write down a word that you read aloud.**

3. **If the player gets it right, ask a player from the next team to write a word.**

4. **Give each player on the teams a chance to write and spell a word.**

5. **Whenever a player gives an incorrect spelling, he puts his hands on the table, and his question moves to the next player on the opposing team in the usual order.**

The team whose players all have their hands on the table first loses.

To add spice to the "Hands on the table" activity, try any or all these frills:

- Give each player a set amount of time to answer and ring a bell when the time's up.

- Award goodbye gifts when a child puts his hands on the table (jelly beans, raisins, cookies, and so on).

- Play this game in rounds and play a blast of music at the end of each round.

- Present a winner's token: A mug (returnable) filled with marshmallows to eat in class, a cute or funny soft toy to keep for the day, stickers, erasers, or pencils.

- Include surprise questions like, "What color of sweater is Mr. Hill wearing today?"

Finding Your Family

The "Finding your word family" activity is a fun game when players use indoor voices and don't pull cards off players' backs. Tell your kids this and compliment players who mingle politely. You'll soon see why I mention this.

Activity: Finding your word family

Preparation: You need at least 12 players for this activity and space for them to mill around. Have four or five word families in mind before play begins, with at least three words in each family (like *ball, call, small,* and *tall; string, thing, sing,* and *fling; moon, broom, spook,* and *food;* and *meet, seed, wheel,* and *free*). You need some adhesive tape and each player needs an index card and pen.

Follow these steps:

1. **Divide the group into teams of three or four.**

2. **Give each player an index card with tape so that it can be stuck to someone else's back.**

3. **Name each team with a word family (*all, ing, oo,* and *ee*).**

4. **Have players on each team write a different word (from their respective families) on their index cards (players do this together, cooperatively).**

5. **Next, all players cover their words and find a player from a different team on whose back they can stick their words so that each one shows on another person's back.**

6. **After everyone's back is tagged with a word, players are told to mill around the entire group trying to find out what words are on their backs.**

   Each player can find out what his word is by asking what the word is or asking one player to tell him the first letter, another to tell him the second, and so on until he has the whole word or asking other players questions that they can only respond to with yes or no (like is there an a in my word, is the a the first letter, and suchlike).

7. **Players finish the game by joining together with the other members of their new word-family teams.**

Time the entire group to see how quickly they complete this activity.

Run and Write

The "Racing and writing" activity up next is best for groups of six or more players. You may want to limber up and don your sneakers for this one.

Activity: Racing and writing

Preparation: Divide players up into teams of at least two players. Place 10 or 20 words into a bucket or other container for each team, duplicating the words so each team gets the same words. Each team also needs either a whiteboard and marker or poster paper and a marker to play.

Follow these steps:

1. **Put the bucket or container of words at one end of a room and the paper or board at the other end.** (You can even span a few rooms if you want, but if you do, you'll probably need to designate a referee to keep watch.)

2. **Team members take turns racing to pick a word from their buckets, taking it in hand to the board, and writing it.** All teams start at the same time.

The team that finishes first wins. If the winning team makes any spelling errors, have a short rematch with five new words.

You may want to set strict rules before you start. For instance, unsporting behavior from a player earns his entire team 20 push-ups apiece.

For extra hype, play loud, fast music when teams are racing.

To emphasize the look, cover, write method, place a bucket just in front of the board. Players must drop the word into the bucket before writing it on the board.

Run and Finger-Write

Your kids need physical movement, and this activity is a good way to get it. To help them remain quiet during the finger-writing, have them do a small workout before starting the game. Try ten push-ups, ten high kicks (like the Can-Can dance), and ten jumping jacks.

The "Racing and finger-writing" activity up next is best for groups of six or more players.

Activity: Racing and finger-writing

Preparation: Like in "Racing and writing," divide players in to teams of at least two players, and have a bucket of the same words for each team. Provide a whiteboard and marker, or poster paper and marker for each team.

Follow these steps:

1. **Play this game just like "Racing and writing," but in this game the runner has to finger-write (no ink, just finger pressure) the word onto the next player's back.**

2. **The player on whose back the word was written then writes the word onto the whiteboard (no talking allowed) and then takes his turn running for a new word.**

3. **The last player runs three extra laps (a lap is to the bucket and back), because he doesn't get to do any finger-writing.**

If the winning team makes spelling errors, have a short rematch of five new words.

Run, Figure Out, and Write

Here's a game that pretty much has it all — movement, mental challenge, and getting spellings onto paper.

Activity: Racing and defining

Preparation: The preparation for this game is the same as for "Racing and writing," but instead of placing words into the buckets, use clues about words. The clues that I give you here are for the words in Table 20-1, but you can adapt this activity to virtually any of the tables in this book. Don't let your kids in on the answers the way I have for you in parentheses (as my kids would say now, "Well, duh!"), but give each team a copy of Table 20-1 so they can find the answers for themselves.

Follow these steps:

1. **Put the buckets of clues at one end of a room and the papers or boards at the other end.**

2. **Players have to go in turn to pick a clue from their bucket, race to their board, and when they've cracked the clue, write the right word.**

3. **All teams start together. The fastest team wins two points; a correct answer wins one point.** If the winning team makes errors (wrong words and/or wrong spellings), have a short rematch with five new words.

   List of clues:

   • Not possible *(Answer: impossible)*

   • Someone who's in your family *(Answer: relation)*

   • I can count on you; you're this *(Answer: reliable)*

   • Extremely good or bright *(Answer: brilliant)*

- A competition *(Answer: tournament)*

- I saw you right away, you're . . . *(Answer: noticeable)*

- Where you catch a train *(Answer: station)*

- You change your mind a lot; you're this *(Answer: changeable)*

- Easily seen *(Answer: visible)*

- You can eat it; it's . . . *(Answer: edible)*

- What you see in a mirror or pond *(Answer: reflection)*

- When someone says something nice about you it's a *(Answer: compliment)*

- When you agree about something you may sign a written *(Answer: agreement)*

- A helper *(Answer: assistant)*

- Faraway *(Answer: distant)*

When handing out Table 20-1 to each team, you may want to remind players about these two rules for adding suffixes:

✔ Drop the *e* before you add *i-n-g* (or any other suffix that starts with a vowel) with words like *make*. So why, you're asking, do you keep the *e* in *notice* when you tack on *able* to write *noticeable?* Because the *e* retains the soft-*c* sound. Do the same with soft-*g* words like *changeable*.

✔ Change the *y* to *i* and then add *ed* (or any other suffix that starts with a vowel — except *ing*) with words like *rely*. You can't have two *i*'s together, so to speak, so hang onto the *y* to turn *rely* into *relying*.

Table 20-1		Mixed Suffixes		
relation	reliable	impossible	compliment	distant
station	noticeable	visible	agreement	assistant
reflection	changeable	edible	tournament	brilliant

Boxes

The "Drawing boxes with words" activity up next is good for three or more players.

Activity: Drawing boxes with words

Preparation: Draw a grid of 4 dots by 4 dots (16 dots altogether) on a whiteboard or poster.

Follow these steps:

1. **If possible, divide the players into two teams.**

2. **Players must take turns spelling the words that you give them.**

3. **For each correct answer, players get to draw a line between two dots on the grid — vertically or horizontally.**

4. **Teams try to complete boxes, because the player who completes a box marks it with team's insignia (or letter) and gets to draw one extra line and the team that gets most boxes wins.**

The challenging part of Boxes is to win boxes without enabling the opposition to get boxes. Remember, any time your team fills in the third line of a box, the opposition gets to fill in the fourth line and claim that box.

You can play "Boxes" with only two players, but more than two is much more fun, because everyone likes to advise other players where to draw their lines. If you end up playing with two players, and you're one of them, give your child five spellings to start off the game. For each correct spelling, he gets to draw a line and you wait. This gives him a potential lead over you of five lines. After his five spellings, take turns drawing a line with no spellings required.

Pictures

Okay, so you caught me; I've now reached my quota of ten games. But hey, everyone loves a good game! So here are three more, and while I'm at it, I'll show you a game for a happy duo.

Games for Grandma

I always give a copy of my latest book to my mom and dad (I'm hopelessly generous!). I don't really expect them to read my books, but I know they like to have them on display. Last week my mom phoned me. "Your book's great," she gushed. I thought she was just being kind, but then she explained how the book had actually come in handy: One of my nieces visits my parents regularly and, of course, likes to play. She doesn't have any siblings, though, so my parents often end up scratching their heads for inspiration about what to do. During the most recent visit, my mom was showing off my book, "Teaching Kids to Read For Dummies," to my sister-in-law. The pages fell open at the games, and voilà! Apparently everyone played nicely for the entire afternoon and now my mom's reading the book from cover to cover. Go Grandma!

The "Drawing pictures with words" activity is an adaptation of the game Pictionary.

Activity: Drawing pictures with words

Preparation: You'll need large paper and marker, or even better, a whiteboard and marker or blackboard chalk. Fill a bowl with words that lend themselves to drawings (*fright, flight, knit, and squash,* for example).

Follow these steps:

1. **Divide players into two teams, each with a "scribe" whose job is to draw and write. Teams with more than two players can rotate this role.**

2. **The scribe from one team takes a word from the bowl and must write one letter on her board and provide lines as spaces for the other letters of the word.**

3. **Next she draws a picture of the word (no letters or numbers allowed in the picture).**

4. **While she's drawing, players call out what they think the word is (no need to take turns or be civilized, just let rip!)**

5. **The player who guesses the word must spell the word without any help from teammates for the scribe to write (now teammates must be quiet).**

6. **Set a time limit of two minutes per word and disallow words whenever players talk during spelling time.**

7. **The next turn goes to the other team.** Every third and fourth turn is *open play,* in which the scribe from each team draws the picture for her team, and both teams race to be the first to guess the word.

The first team to get ten words (or points) wins.

Modify and tweak "Drawing pictures with words" to suit the players: Set a three-minute time limit for younger kids. If players are rowdy, award bonus points for quiet play. Allow younger kids to be given two letters.

Oh No!

The "Oh, no!" activity is an adaptation of the card game Old Maid.

Activity: Oh, no!

Preparation: For all intents and purposes, this game is actually Old Maid (if you know that game), except that you call the Old Maid card the *Oh No* card. Choose eight words and write each one on four separate cards. Make an "*Oh No*" card, giving you a total of 33 cards.

Follow these steps:

1. **Shuffle all cards. Deal them all out.**

2. **Players have to make sets of four identical words.** Starting with the player to the left of the dealer, players take a card from the players to their right, and add the card to their packs.(Each time it's their turn, players try to make a set of cards, and then fan out their pack for the player on the left to select another card.

3. **When a player has a set (or four identical cards), he must lay it face down and spell the word out loud.** If he spells the word correctly, he keeps the set; if he doesn't it goes into a lost pile that no one can have.

The player with the most sets wins. The player who ends up with the *Oh No* card has to pack away the cards.

To make this game more challenging you can make family sets (like ball, call, fall, and wall) rather than identical word sets (like wall, wall, wall, and wall).

You can make the *Oh No* card anything you want (Sore Loser, Ha Ha, So Yesterday, and so on), but remember that the backs of the cards all have to look the same. You can be fairly sure that one of your kids will try bending a corner of the *Oh No* card when no one's looking, so give your "I have eyes in the back of my head" speech early on!

Wake Up!

The "Wake up and spell the word!" activity is a game that's good for young kids. If you're used to playing games with older kids, and they're not easily embarrassed, they may also like this activity .

Activity: Wake up and spell the word!

Preparation: Jot down six words you want each player to spell. Have all players lie down on their backs.

Follow this step: Ask each player in turn to spell a word. A correct answer enables the player to make one move toward standing up, in this order:

1. Roll onto your side.

2. Prop yourself up on one arm.

3. Kneel on all fours.

4. Squat back on your heels.

5. Put one knee up.

6. Stand up.

If a player can't spell the word, you can do different things, depending on the age of your players. You can:

- ✔ Provide clues until the child gets the answer right
- ✔ Let another player answer on behalf of the player who got the word wrong
- ✔ Move to the next player

When all players are standing, have them do an on-the-spot drill comprised of simulated wake-up activities: jogging to loosen those limbs, stretching and yawning, racing to the bathroom, cleaning your teeth, brushing your hair, running to the school bus, or climbing the steps. Whew you made it!

For fun give players a sleeping prop (pillow, blanket, candy pacifier) and play sleepy music. And you can have someone blow a horn or whistle after each correct word. Make sure that you praise kids who stay quietest and stillest.

Big kids want players to stay down when they make spelling mistakes, so make light of that. Award a sour candy as a bitter spelling pill or entrust a teddy bear to the sleepy player for a set amount of time. Make it so that no one minds staying down in this game; in fact, it's sort of fun.

If you want to modify this game next time around, have players start in a different position. Have them lie down with their legs in the air, arms twisted (like the eagle pose in yoga), and eyes shut. They unravel a bit each time they get a correct answer (one leg down, two legs down, arms untwisted, eyes open, kneel on two knees, kneel on one knee, stand, and so on).

One More! Just for Two

I guess that two people don't really count as a group, but I include the good old "Chutes and ladders" activity for two players, because it's simple and great for kids who like to create. Making the board can be an artistic bonanza and you can laminate the finished product so that it sees you through plenty of play.

Activity: Chutes and ladders (with spell-to-throw)

Preparations: Have your kids draw a big chutes and ladders board, 10 squares by 10 squares, numbering the squares along the bottom row from 1 to 10 left to right, and then from 11 to 20 left to right in the next row up and so on all the way to 100. Have them draw chutes and ladders on the board at varying inclines. Because you need a pack of spelling words, you can either write them yourself or have another child do it. You also need a cup and a dice for players to share, and playing pieces for each player — you can use buttons or pieces from other games you have or, as a creative extra, ask players if they want to provide their own special piece (preferably one that fits inside a single square, like a button and not something like a toy giant panda).

Follow these steps:

1. **The player who isn't taking his turn takes a spelling card and reads the word to the other player.**

2. **That player then spells the word.**

3. **If he spells correctly, he shakes and throws the dice and moves his marker according to the number on the dice.** He can use paper and pen to try out different spellings before he gives you his answer but forfeits his turn when he gives an incorrect answer.

4. **A score of six on the dice gets that player an extra throw of the dice.**

The first player to reach square 100 wins.

Poetry magnets are fun too and come in huge assortments. Many come in word parts: the "ly" magnet, for example, comes separately from the love magnet.

Enjoying toyshop favorites

You can find several word-based games in toyshops. The two that have been around for years are Scrabble and Boggle. Both games are available in junior and hand-held electronic versions. You can also watch for letter tiles and magnetic letters to put on your refrigerator. Bear in mind, however, that magnetic tiles aren't usually a big hit with kids until you join in the fun. Get together with your child in front of your refrigerator and make words together. Make a *word of the day* every day for a week. Put the letters away and bring them out again in a few weeks so they seem new and interesting all over again!

Chapter 21

Ten Spelling Games for Car Trips

In This Chapter

▶ Going beyond "I Spy"

▶ Working out word patterns

*N*obody in their right mind wants to be holed up in a car with fractious kids. But it happens. When I'm trapped in my car with my kids and they're chock-full of junk food and have broken all the free toys in hand-to-hand combat, we play the games I describe to you in this chapter.

Cards in the Car

Your child can be a better speller simply by doing regular spelling in a fun way. One fun way to fix spellings in your child's mind is to take a pack of them with you in the car or in your bag (spellings, not kids). Your child can spell them out to you in one continuous stream (taking a breath now and then), or you can test him on words when you're waiting in line or at lights. Here are some card-using tips:

✔ If you write your own words, make sure that you have an envelope to keep them in.

✔ Have your child write the date and number of words correctly spelled on the envelope or stick stickers on it to keep track. Color-code the stickers to show how many words he spelled right each time.

✔ Keep adding new words.

✔ Keep a notepad and pencil, a blackboard and chalk, or whiteboard and dry markers in the car (pencil, chalk, and dry markers won't mar your upholstery).

If you want to buy boxes of preprinted words, check out these:

✔ *Easy Vowels* boxed set by Frank Schaffer. Includes three-letter, short-vowel words you can start with and long-vowel words to use later.

✔ *Easy Blends and Digraphs* boxed set by Frank Schaffer. Use these after three-letter words. Do the blends first and then work on the long vowels.

✔ *Sight Words* boxed sets by Frank Schaffer. These cards come in boxes of 100 words (first 100, second 100, and so on). You get the word on one side of the card and the word in a sentence on the other side.

✔ *Beginning to Read Phonics: Fishing for Silent "e" Words* by Judy/Instructo.

✔ *Beginning to Read Phonics: Word Family Fun, Long Vowels* by Judy/Instructo.

You can get Frank Schaffer products, published by Frank Schaffer Publications in school supplies stores or online at http://www.teacherspecialty.com. You can get Judy/Instructo products, published by Judy/Instructo Company, in school supplies stores.

Hangman

In case you're not familiar with Hangman (which sounds terribly gruesome but is only real creepy!), here's how it works. Your child thinks of a word. She writes down a bunch of underscores equal to the number of letters in her word. She tells you how many letters are in her word and you have to guess what letters are used. When you guess a correct letter, your child writes that letter on its appropriate underscore. If you incorrectly guess a letter, she jots down the letter (so you both know that that letter's already been used) and begins to draw a person in the process of being hanged (that's the creepy factor!). The basic hangman picture is a gallows (ugh) that looks like a basketball hoop, only the net is a rope, with a stick-figure person attached. Your child draws the figure bit-by-bit adding one bit each time you guess an incorrect letter. (She starts by drawing a head for the first wrong letter. With the next wrong letter she adds a line for the body. With each additional wrong letter she adds a body part such as an arm or leg, followed by hands and feet. Depending on how long she wants you to guess she can add each of the ten fingers and toes!)

Describing and Drawing the Letters

I invented this game on a particularly long and arduous car journey and was amazed by how long it amused my kids. I started out desperately attempting to divert my kids from yet another fight. "Look at that *A!*" I cried enthusiastically. "Doesn't it look just like a tepee with a bed in it." After a brief puzzled silence, my kids got right into this visualization. They came up with ideas for every letter, capitals and lowercase, and took turns (almost unheard of!) drawing their images on a blackboard that before then lay untouched for months in the car.

I Spy with My Little Eye

I Spy With My Little Eye is a timeless favorite on car journeys. If you were never recruited by an I Spyer as a kid, here's how the game goes. Look out for an object inside or outside of your car and have your child guess what the object is. Give him a clue by saying, "I spy with my little eye something beginning with *B* (or whatever letter starts the name of your object). Adapt your clue for little kids, by saying, "I spy with my little eye something beginning with *buh* (the sound of the letter)."

Going to Aunt Maud's

This game is all about cracking a word rule. To start the game, say the following sentence, but fill in the blank space with any word you like:

"I'm going to Aunt Maud's and I'm taking a _____ with me."

Maybe you decide that only words with a double letter can be used in the game, so you take your *boots.* Your child's job is to figure out that your secret rule is "words with double letters." Read this dialogue and you'll see how the game progresses (your hints are in bold):

I'm going to Aunt Maud's and I'm taking my boots with me.

I'm going to Aunt Maud's too, can I bring a bag?

Sorry, no, you can't bring a bag.

I'm going to Aunt Maud's and I'm taking some cheese with me.

I'm going to Aunt Maud's too, can I bring a blanket?

Sorry, no, you can't bring a blanket.

Your child can take things like *mittens, eggs, apples, cheese, glasses, books,* and *balloons,* but she can't take things like *milk, socks, shoes,* and *chocolate.*

Names

The names game is easy. The spelling skills required are at the little-kid level, but your big kids will jump right in on this activity, too. All you have to do is go through each letter of the alphabet thinking of a person's name for each letter. Start with girls' names (there are more of them!) and see how you fare when you get to the letter *U.* One of my kids once came up with "Umbrella" when she was stuck on *U,* and we had a cute diversion into the kind of problems Umbrella might face and what would be the worse name to have.

Shopping at Macy's

Another work-your-way-through-the-alphabet game, Shopping at Macy's, asks players to think of an item they'd buy at Macy's and then each successive player has to repeat all the items that have already been mentioned before adding her own. The dialogue looks like this.

> **First player: I went to Macy's and bought an amber ring.**
>
> **Second player: I went to Macy's and bought an amber ring and a red bag.**
>
> **Third player: I went to Macy's and bought an amber ring, a red bag, and a purple coat.**

Songs

Most of us enjoy breaking out in song even when those around us aren't all that appreciative. Songs are good. They draw your child's attention to rhyme and wordplay, which help her auditory discrimination and her phonemic awareness. So you have every reason to teach your child the songs you grew up with. Some of my stalwarts are:

- ✔ *Ten Green Bottles*
- ✔ *She'll Be Coming Round The Mountain When She Comes*
- ✔ *One Man Went To Mow*
- ✔ *At The Quartermaster's Store*
- ✔ *There Were Ten In The Bed (And The Little One Said)*

Word Find

A good game for keeping your child amused in the store, in Word Find, you give your child a notepad and pencil, jot down five letters and ask him to find words that begin with those letters. Other write-them-down topics can be favorite foods, or animals, or long words that he can see around him. You can use this game in the car as well as in the store.

Fortunetellers (or Origami Cruets)

Although not a great hit with boys, this activity keeps girls amused for ages. The kids call it Fortunes, but my husband tells me (and he swears that he knows such things) that it originates from pre-saltshaker days. Apparently when salt was less refined and was pinched (in lumps) onto your food, it was put into a cruet along with pepper and other condiments. You pinched up what you needed out of the four little dishes of the cruet. Whenever you traveled, you made a cruet from paper. When you turn this fortuneteller upside down, you'll see that it's a cruet. (Or else my husband made it up!)

Activity: Fortuneteller

Preparation: Get a piece of writing paper (computer paper works well). Tear off a strip to make the paper a square.

Follow these steps:

1. **Fold the four corners into the center of the square so that you've made a smaller square with four triangle flaps facing you.**

2. **Turn the paper over and do the same thing again. You may want to rotate your square first to get a good grip on the corners.**

3. **Keeping your paper this way up, pick it up and fold it in half so that you see four pockets on the outside.**

4. **Put the finger and thumb of one hand into two of these pockets and pinch them together. Do the same on the other side.**

5. **You'll be able to move the fortune-teller open and shut in two directions with your fingers and thumbs in four compartments that move.**

6. **Flatten your fortuneteller like it was before. On the side with four square flaps, have your child write the name of one color on each flap.**

7. **Have your child turn the fortuneteller over and number (1 through 8) the eight small triangles facing you.**

8. **Next you open these eight triangles and write a fortune on the back of each one.** The eight fortunes can be things like:

   • You will marry before you're 20.

   • You'll have six kids.

   • You'll be rich.

   • You'll live to 100.

   • Your true love will find you.

   • You love animals.

   • You'll be very lucky.

   • A boy likes you.

Now you're all set. Your child pesters you forevermore. Her routine is this:

Her: **"What color?"** (Showing you your choices of four different colors.)

You: **"Red."** (Choosing a nice short word!)

Her: *"R-E-D."* (She moves her fortuneteller three times (corresponding with the three letters in "RED"), revealing a set of numbers.) **"What number?"**

You: (You read her numbers and choose . . .) **"One."** (Of course, because it's going to take less time!)

Her: **"One."** (. . . she says as she moves her fortuneteller one move.) **What number?**

You: **"Two."**

Her: (She unfolds No. 2 and reads your fortune.)

You're hoping for "I will go away and give you several hours of peace."

You can find this and other fun activities at `www.enchantedlearning.com/crafts/origami/fortuneteller`.

Index

• *Numerics* •

3 by 3 by 3 (activity), 240
30 proverbs; 20 apostrophes (activity), 305–306

• *A* •

a (letter)
  lazy, 179
  long sound, 88–89, 123–124, 133, 322
  schwa, 177, 178–180
  short sound, 88
  uh sound, 88
  y as long-*a* sound, 152
able (suffix), 280–282
ack (word family), 172–173
acronyms, 212
activities. *See specific activities; specific games*
Activity icon, 5
Adding a quick ending (activity), 285–286
Adding able or ible (activity), 281–282
Adding s's quick and easy (activity), 268–269
age (suffix), 292
ai pair, 134–135
ain (suffix), 292
air (word family), 147–148, 202–203
ake words, 73–74
al (suffix), 289–290
alk (word family), 183–184
all (suffix), 290–291
all (word family), 183–184, 208, 311–312
alternated reading, 34–35
Always *ct* (never *kt*) (activity), 104–105
an (word family), 172
anagrams, 55
ank (word family), 172–173
ant (suffix), 288–289
antonym, 57
ap (word family), 172

apostrophes
  commas compared, 302
  in contractions, 295–296, 301–302, 304–307
  possessive, 299–301
Apostrophes in contractions and possessions (activity), 299–300
ar sound, 189
ar (word family), 185–187
are (word family), 148, 202–203
ary (suffix), 293
ash (word family), 172–173
at (word family), 172
ate (suffix), 292
au (word family), 200–201, 314–315
aught (word family), 191–193
aw (word family), 200–201, 314–315
awt sound, 192
ay sound, 88–89, 144, 152, 192, 323

• *B* •

b (silent), 228–229
Back to front and front to back (activity), 125–126
Back-to-front syllables (activity), 75
ball and jacks (game), 169
Bang! (game), 146
Battleship (activity), 329–330
beanbag toss (game), 146
Beginning to Read Phonics: Fishing for Silent "e" Words (Judy/Instructo), 19, 344
Beginning to Read Phonics: Word Family Fun, Long Vowels (Judy/Instructo), 19, 344
Bingo (activity), 331
bl (blend), 94
blend
  Always *ct* (never *kt*) (activity), 104–105
  cc words, 99–101
  ct, 104–105
  description, 93–94
  digraphs compared, 94, 110
  at the end, 103–108

blend *(continued)*
Extending yourself with *ex* words
(activity), 102–103
at the front, 103–108
lk, 106
Looking at *ex* words (activity), 101–102
Making great use of a pizza box (activity),
96–97
ng, 107–108
nk, 106, 107–108
practicing, 51
Seven super shapes (activity), 97
sk, 97–99, 106
skr, 99
Sorting your double-*c*'s (activity), 100–101
Boggle (game), 324, 341
books, choosing, 34
Bossy-*e* spelling rule
Back to front and front to back (activity),
125–126
benefits of knowing, 61
description, 121–122, 322
Finding 18 errors (activity), 126–127
Forming Bossy *e* pictures (activity), 131
Joking around with Bossy *e* (activity), 130
long-vowel sound, 121–122
sight words and, 214–215
spelling Bossy-*e* words, 126–130
spotting Bossy-*e* words, 122–126
Thinking in threes (activity), 129–130
Three Bossy *e* quizzes (activity), 127–129
boys, spelling and, 20
breaks, 47
Building word families (activity), 210–211
busy teachers cafe (Web site), 60

• C •

c (letter)
cuh sound, 69
hard sound, 100
soft-*c* sound, 63–64, 69, 98, 234–237
ss sound, 69, 99
ca words, 71
Cadaco (Spell Time kit), 18
car trips, games for, 343–348
card games, 343–344
The Cat in the Hat (Dr. Seuss), 173

cc words, 74, 99–101
ch (digraph)
in long-vowel words, 112–113
Mastering *ch* with Lay-3 card game
(activity), 111–112
in short-vowel words, 110–111
Sorting long-vowel words with *ch* endings
(activity), 113
Changing a first letter (activity), 81–82
Changing a last letter (activity), 82
Changing a vowel (activity), 82–83
Changing between short and long vowels
(activity), 137
Changing the last letter (activity), 203
Charades (activity), 291
charts, reward system and, 16, 17
chat rooms, 40
Chinese jump-rope (game), 169
Choosing your spelling list (activity), 254
choral reading, 34
chunks of sound
blends, 51
digraphs, 52
long vowels, 51
long words from short-vowel chunks,
85–86
rhymes, 52
single letters, 51
spelling in chunks, 84–85
syllables as, 245
Chutes and ladders (activity), 340–341
Chutes and ladders with chances
(activity), 241–242
cial (suffix), 294
cian (suffix), 286–287
cious (suffix), 294
ck words, 72–73, 105–106
Clapping out syllables (activity), 246
Cleaver cards (activity), 223–224
close activity, 40
co words, 71
Coffee for the jockey and me (activity), 158
Color-coding sight words (activity), 207
Colors and chunks (activity), 194
commas, 302, 303
compound words, 248–250
computers, 20
confidence, in spelling, 55

consonants
  blends at the end, 103–108
  blends at the front, 94–103
  breaking words between, 253–255
  different spellings for same sound, 76
  double, 250–253
contractions
  activities, 297–298, 301–307
  can't versus can,t, 302–303
  common, table of, 296–297
  definition, 295
  it's versus its, 301–302
  understanding, 295–296
  who's versus whose, 303–304
  you're versus your, 198
corrections
  judicious, 55–56
  look-say-cover-write-check formula, 42–43
  with pencil instead of red pen, 56
  pronunciation, 178
  proofreading, 44–45
  reading mistakes, 35–37
  tips for, 46
Count and figure out (activity), 297
Cracking the *ph* cryptic code (activity), 117
Creating *th* word crosses (activity), 116
cs sound, 100
ct (blend), 69, 104–105
cu words, 71
cuh sound, 69
Cutting extra letters (activity), 76

• D •

Demon dozen (activity), 263
Department of Health and Human Services
  (DHHS), 45
Dictated spellings (activity), 236
dictation, 43–44, 59–60, 326–328
dictionary, 19–20
digraph
  blend compared, 94, 110
  ch, 110–113
  definition, 109, 247
  ph, 116–117
  practicing, 52
  sh, 113–115
  th, 115–116

vowel, 110
  wh, 118, 168
diphthong, 110
double consonants, 250–253
double letters, 76–79
Doubling the letter to keep the vowel short
  (activity), 278
Dr. Seuss
  The Cat in the Hat, 173
  Hop on Pop-Up, 173
Drawing boxes with words (activity),
  336–337
Drawing pictures with words (activity),
  337–338

• E •

e (letter). *See also* Bossy-*e* spelling rule
  ey sound, 89
  long sound, 89, 123, 133, 322–323
  schwa, 177
  short sound, 146
  silent, 89
  soft-*s* and *j*, 89
  y as long-*e* sound, 122, 152–159, 216,
    322–323
ea words, 134–135, 139–141, 146–147
ear (word family), 148–149, 189, 202–203
Easy Action Picture Words (Frank Schaffer
  Publications), 19
Easy Blends and Digraphs (Frank Schaffer
  Publications), 19, 344
Easy, medium, and hard (activity), 256
Easy Sight Words (Frank Schaffer
  Publications), 19
Easy Vowels (Frank Schaffer Publications),
  19, 343
Eats, Shoots and Leaves (Lynne Truss), 302
ed (suffix), 105, 275–280
Educational Learning Games (Web site), 18
ee pair, 134–135, 139–141
ee sound, 152–159
ei words, 145
Eight itchy gnomes have ticks
  (activity), 191
eight (word family), 191–193
Eight-square bingo (activity), 225–226
ell (word family), 174

emergent writing, 56

enchantedlearning.com (Web site), 180

Ending for thirty points (activity), 284

endings. *See* suffixes

ent (suffix), 288–289

ent (word family), 174

er sound, 185, 187, 189

er (word family), 185–187, 314

ery (suffix), 293–294

es (plural), 269–273

est (word family), 174

ewe sound, 90

ex words, 100–103

Extending yourself with *ex* words (activity), 102–103

Extravagant excuses (activity), 200

ey sound, 89

eye sound, 89

• F •

f words, 273–275

ff words, 77

Filling in missing letters (activity), 75

Finding an *ear* match (activity), 189–190

Finding an *our*, *oar*, or *oor* match (activity), 189

Finding 18 errors (activity), 126–127

Finding, running, and writing (activity), 275

Finding ten ending mistakes (activity), 284–285

Finding the gap (activity), 86

Finding the word (activity), 274

Finding three little words (activity), 54–55

Finding your spelling strategies (activity), 212–213

Finding your word family (activity), 333

fine-motor skills, 23

finger olympics, 23

Finishing words (activity), 161

Five up (activity), 138

Fixing a muddle (activity), 241

flashcards, 18–19

Forming Bossy *e* pictures (activity), 131

fortuneteller (game), 346–348

Four pairs of vowels (activity), 136–137

fr (blend), 94

Frank Schaffer Publications

Easy Action Picture Words, 19

Easy Blends and Digraphs, 19, 344

Easy Sight Words, 19

Easy Vowels, 19, 343

Sight Words, 19, 344

full (suffix), 290–291

• G •

g (letter)

silent, 227–228

soft-*g* words, 63–64, 238–241

games. *See specific games*

Games Kids Play (Web site), 169

Getting it right with its (activity), 301–302

gh (silent), 222–223

Going to Aunt Maud's (game), 345

group activities

Battleship, 329–330

Bingo, 331

Chutes and ladders, 340–341

Drawing boxes with words, 336–337

Drawing pictures with words, 337–338

Finding your word family, 333

Hands on the table, 332

Oh No!, 338–339

Racing and defining, 335–336

Racing and finger-writing, 334–335

Racing and writing, 333–334

Wake up and spell the word, 339–340

gu words, 226

gue words, 226–227

• H •

h (silent), 230–231

Ha, ha (activity), 306–307

Half and half (activity), 154

Hands on the table (activity), 332

handwriting, 26, 41, 318–319

Hangman (game), 62, 324, 344

hard sound, 68, 98

hearing, assessing, 26, 317–318

High five (activity), 252

homograph, 57, 58, 147, 199

homonym, 57

Homonyms Match (Judy/Instructo), 19
homophone, 57, 59
Hop on Pop-Up (Dr. Seuss), 173
Hula-Hoop (game), 169

• *I* •

i (letter)
  eye sound, 89
  long sound, 89, 123–124, 144
  schwa, 177
  short sound, 89, 322–323
  y as long-*i* sound, 122, 159–162, 216,
    322–323
  y as short-*i* sound, 162–163
I Spy (game), 345
i-before-*e*-except-after-*c* spelling rule,
  144, 323
ible (suffix), 280–282
ic words, 69–70, 105, 106
ick (word family), 175
icons, used in book, 5
identical sounds
  j or soft-*g*, 233, 240–241
  s or soft-*c*, 233, 237
ie words, 142–144
igh (word family), 190
ight (word family), 190, 312
ike words, 73–74
ill (word family), 175
Imagining sentences (activity), 240
in (word family), 174
ine (suffix), 292
ing (word family), 175
ink (word family), 175
Internet message boards and chat
  rooms, 40
interrupted reading, 34, 35
invented spellings, 55
ip (word family), 174
ir (word family), 185–186, 314
it (word family), 174

• *J* •

jargon, 26–30
Joking around with Bossy *e* (activity), 130
journal, shared, 39

Judy/Instructo
  *Beginning to Read Phonics: Fishing for
    Silent "e" Words*, 19, 344
  *Beginning to Read Phonics: Word Family
    Fun, Long Vowels*, 19, 344
  Homonyms Match, 19

• *K* •

k (letter)
  after long vowel, 106
  after short-vowel sound + a consonant, 73
  digraphs in front of, 73
  ending words, 105
  ke and *ki* words, 70, 98
  silent, 221–222
ke words, 70, 98
ki words, 70, 98
kits, 18
kn words, 221–222
ks sound, 74–75
kuh sound, 69–76

• *L* •

l (silent), 229–230
le (suffix), 289–290
left-handers, making accommodations
  for, 25
letters. *See also* consonants; vowels;
  specific letters
  double, 76–79
  order of study, 68
  practicing single, 51
  sounds from single letters, 68
License plates (activity), 160
Listen up (activity), 298
listening
  phonemic awareness, 49–51
  to your child read, 35
Listening up for long vowels (activity), 136
lk (blend), 106
ll words, 77, 157, 174
long vowels
  a, 88–89, 123–124, 133, 322
  Bossy-*e* and, 121–122
  ch endings, 112–113
  description, 105, 122

long vowels *(continued)*
 e, 89, 123, 133, 322–323
 i, 89, 123–124, 144
 o, 90, 123–124, 133, 322
 in open syllables, 90–91, 255–256
 practicing, 51
 spelling, 138–139
 two vowels combined, 122
 u, 90, 123
 y as long *a*, 152
 y as long *e*, 122, 152–159, 216, 322–323
 y as long *i*, 122, 159–162, 216, 322–323
long words, from short-vowel chunks,
 85–86
long-term memory, 48
look of words, remembering, 323–324
Look who's talking (activity), 306
Looking at *ex* words (activity), 101–102
looking at letters
 importance of, 53
 words within words, 54–55
Looking, marking, and writing
 (activity), 185
look-say-cover-write-check formula, 42–43
ly words, 155–157

• *M* •

magnetic letters, 341
Making a word longer (activity), 279–280
Making great use of a pizza box (activity),
 96–97
Making sense (activity), 250
Mancala Spellorama! (activity), 264–265
Marathon spelling contest (activity), 60
marbles (game), 169
Marking up words (activity), 162
Mastering *ch* with the Lay-3 card game
 (activity), 111–112
Matching up words and endings
 (activity), 287
memory joggers, 45
message boards, Internet, 40
mistakes, learning from, 55–56
mn words, 232
mnemonic, 45, 192, 193
modeling reading, 33
mood lifters, 15

More challenging *sh* rhymes (activity),
 114–115
motivation, 15–16

• *N* •

names game, 345
National Institutes of Health
 (NIH, Web site), 45
ng (blend), 107–108
nk (blend), 106, 107–108
notes, from child to parent, 41
Nuts about Nuts (Michael Rosen), 33

• *O* •

o (letter)
 long sound, 90, 123–124, 133, 322
 oh sound, 90
 schwa, 177
 short sound, 90
o (word family), 193–194, 208–209
oa pair, 134–135
oar words, 189
ock (word family), 175–176
og (word family), 175–176
Oh No! (activity), 338–339
oh sound, 90, 199
oi (word family), 196–198, 312–313
oke words, 73–74
one-syllable words, 247
Only ungrateful girls hate toys
 (activity), 192
oo (word family), 195–196, 315–316
oor words, 189
op (word family), 175–176
open syllables, 90–91
open vowel words, 90–91, 255–256
or sound, 187, 188–189
or (word family), 185–187, 311–312
origami cruets (game), 346–348
ory (suffix), 294
ou (word family), 193–194, 198–199, 208,
 209, 313
ought (word family), 191–193
ould (word family), 208
our words, 189
overpronunciation, 52–53

ow (word family), 198–199, 313
oxymorons, 55
oy (word family), 196–197, 312–313
oy-oi quiz (activity), 197

• P •

p (silent), 231–232
Pairs of vowels (activity), 139–141
palindromes, 56, 181
parrot reading, 45
pencil grip, 22–24
ph (digraph), 116–117
phonemic awareness, 49–51
phonetic pronunciation, 52, 321
phonics, 49, 50
phonograms, 168
Pictures and mnemonics (activity),
    230–231
Placing your bets (activity), 277
plcmc.org (Web site), 180
plurals
    es, 269–273
    f words, 273–275
    s, 268–269
poem, mistake-filled, 21
Poem search (activity), 298
Pointing and spelling (activity), 271–272
points, reward system and, 16, 17
possessive apostrophes, 299–301
posters, writing, 38–39
posture, 22–24
Prefix run (activity), 258
prefixes
    definition, 256
    description, 63
    syllables and, 256–261
profanity, 17
pronunciation
    correcting, 178
    exaggerating, 53, 328
    phonetic, 52, 321
proofreading, 44–45

• Q •

q (letter), silent *u* with, 94
qu words, 224–225

• R •

r (letter)
    after two vowels, 188–190
    vowel+*r* words, 81, 184–190
Racing and defining (activity), 335–336
Racing and finger-writing (activity),
    334–335
Racing and writing (activity), 333–334
readiness, for spelling well, 20–26
reading
    alternated, 34–35
    choosing books, 34
    choral, 34
    correcting mistakes, 35–37
    interrupted, 34, 35
    listening to your child read, 35
    modeling, 33
    parrot, 45
    remembering to read, 61
    to your child, 32
    with your child, 32–37
Remember icon, 5
Remembering and spelling (activity), 290
remembering unusual words, 213–214
rhymes
    as memory joggers, 45
    practicing, 52
Rhyming riddles (activity), 78–79
Rhyming time with *sh* (activity), 114
Riddles of things you shouldn't do
    (activity), 78
Right or wrong? (activity), 252–253
root word, 196
Rosen, Michael (*Nuts about Nuts*), 33
rote, learning by, 43
routines
    benefits, 42
    dictation, 43–44, 59–60
    look-say-cover-write-check formula, 42–43
    proofreading, 44–45

• S •

s (plural), 268–269
sc (blend), 97–99
schwa
    at the beginning of words, 178–179
    description, 177

schwa *(continued)*
  at the end of words, 179
  in the middle of words, 180–181
  Spelling continents (activity), 180
scr words, 72
Scrabble (game), 62, 324, 341
See it, say it, spell it (activity), 157
Seven super shapes (activity), 97
sh (digraph)
  More challenging *sh* rhymes (activity),
    114–115
  Rhyming time with *sh* (activity), 114
  words beginning with, 113
  words ending with, 113–114
Sharing a journal (activity), 39
Shopping at Macy's (game), 346
short vowels
  ch in short-vowel words, 110–111
  Changing a first letter (activity), 81–82
  Changing a last letter (activity), 82
  Changing a vowel (activity), 82–83
  description, 68–69, 122
  importance, 67
  inside sight words, 86–88
  kuh sound, 69–76
  long words from short-vowel chunks,
    85–86
  Spelling circle (activity), 84
  spelling in chunks, 84–85
  table of short-vowel words, 80–81
  Ten words in a chain (activity), 83–84
short-sounding words, adding *ed* to,
    276–278
short-term memory, 47–48
sight word activities
  boxes, 219
  games, 219–220
  hiding and seeking, 217–218
  mediums, varying, 218–219
  oral spellings, 219
  oral spellings with a theme, 219
  picture words, 220
  racing the clock, 218
  seeing and writing, 217
  tracking progress, 218
  words on your back, 219

sight words
  Bossy-*e* spelling rule, 214–215
  eccentric individuals, 211–214
  families, 207–211
  games, 219–220
  learning in bite-sized pieces, 220
  long-*e* and long-*i* sounds, 216
  made from short-vowel spelling
    chunks, 87
  remembering unusual words, 213–214
  spelling quickly, 216
  spelling rules, 214–216
  table of most common, 206–207
  working on, 62, 325
  writing short vowels inside, 86–88
Sight Words (Frank Schaffer Publications),
    344
silent letters
  b, 228–229
  description, 63
  g, 227–228
  gh, 222–223
  h, 230–231
  k, 221–222
  l, 229–230
  p, 231–232
  t, 231
  u, 94, 224–226
  w, 224
Silly sentences (activity), 236–237
similes, 55
sion (suffix), 286–287
sk (blend), 97–99, 106
ske words, 71–72
ski words, 71–72
skr (blend), 99
soft-*c* words
  ci letter combination, 98
  recognizing soft-*c* words, 234–235
  rule, 234
  working on, 63–64
  writing soft-*c* words, 236–237
soft-*g* words
  j, distinguishing from, 240–241
  recognizing soft-*g* words, 238–239
  rule, 238

working on, 63–64

writing soft-*g* words, 240

songs (car trip game), 346

Sorting long-vowel words with *ch* endings (activity), 113

Sorting prefixes (activity), 257–258

Sorting sounds into groups (activity), 154–155

Sorting your double-*c*'s (activity), 100–101

Sorting your tomatoes and heroes (activity), 273

Sounds right; looks wrong (activity), 139

Spell Time kit (Cadaco), 18

spell-checker, computer, 20

Spelling back to front (activity), 181

Spelling buddies (activity), 143–144

Spelling by flashlight (activity), 87–88

spelling chunks. *See also* chunks of sound

defined, 117

short-vowel chunks, 84–85

word family, 167–168

Spelling circle (activity), 84

Spelling compound words (activity), 249

Spelling continents (activity), 180

Spelling folder (activity), 170–171

spelling lists, 324–325

spelling patterns, key, 263–265

spelling rules

Bossy-*e*, 61, 121–122, 214–215, 322

i-before-*e*-except-after-*c*, 137, 144

looking for, 321–323

sight words, 214–216

when-two-vowels-go-walking-the-first-one-does-the-talking rule, 61, 110, 133–134, 215, 322

y-acting-like-a-vowel rule, 79, 322–323

spelling, with your child, 41–42

Spotting soft-*c* spellings (activity), 235

Spotting soft-*g* spellings (activity), 239

squ (blend), 94

ss sound, 73, 99

ss words, 77

stories, writing, 40

stress, decreasing, 46–47

suffixes

age, 292

ain, 292

ary, 293

ate, 292

cial, 294

cious, 294

description, 63

ent or *ant*, 288–289

ery, 293–294

full and *all*, 290–291

ine, 292

le and *al*, 289–290

mixed, 336

ory, 294

plurals, 268–275

syllables and, 261

tenses, 275–282

tion, *sion*, or *cian*, 286–287

ture, 293

ure, 293

y, 282–286

syllables

compound words, 248–250

double consonants, 250–253

friendly letters, 246–247

hearing in words, 245–246

one-syllable words, 247

open vowel words, 90–91, 255–256

prefixes, 256–261

suffixes, 261

three-syllable words and larger, 261–263

two consonants, 253–255

two-syllable words, 248–261

VCCV rule, 253, 262

VCV rule, 255, 262

vowels in, 245, 246

synonym, 57

• T •

t (silent), 231

Tackling a tampered-with story (activity), 237

Taking the word away! (activity), 270

teaching techniques

backing off, 11

charts, 16, 17

lightening up, 14–15

mood lifters, 15

teaching techniques *(continued)*
motivation, 15–16
points and rewards, 16, 17
reasons to spell well, 12
say and then spell words, 12–14
sharing, 10–11
short and sweet, keeping things, 14
showing and practicing, 10
solving problems, 11–12
teaching tools, 17–19
team games, 62
Technical Stuff icon, 5
Ten neat word families (activity), 210
Ten words in a chain (activity), 83–84
tenses, 275–282
terminology, 27–30
th (digraph), 115–116
Thinking in threes (activity), 129–130
30 proverbs; 20 apostrophes (activity), 305–306
Three Bossy *e* quizzes (activity), 127–129
3 by 3 by 3 (activity), 240
three-syllable words, 261–263
tiddlywinks, words associated with, 169
Tidmarsh, David (National Spelling Bee champion), 107
tion (suffix), 286–287
Tip icon, 5
To *b* or not to *b* (activity), 228–229
tools
flashcards, 18–19
kits, 18
Toothpicks (activity), 157–158
Truss, Lynne (*Eats, Shoots and Leaves*), 302
try words, 155–156
ture (suffix), 293
Twins (activity), 250–251
two vowels (word family), 208
two-syllable words
compound words, 248–250
double consonants, 250–253
open vowel words, 255–256
prefixes, 256–261
suffixes, 261
two consonants, 253–255
Two-vowel word quiz (activity), 141

• *U* •

u (letter)
ewe sound, 90
long sound, 90, 123
schwa, 177
short sound, 90
silent, 94, 224–226
u sound, 193–194
uck (word family), 176–177
ug (word family), 176–177
uh sound, 88, 94, 177–181
ump (word family), 176–177
unk (word family), 176–177
ur (word family), 185–186, 314
ure (suffix), 293

• *V* •

VCCV rule, 253, 262
VCV rule, 255, 262
vision, assessing, 24–26, 317–318
vowel digraphs, 110
vowel+*r* words
description, 81, 184–185
Looking, marking, and writing (activity), 185
r after two vowels, 188–190
tables of words, 186–187
vowels. *See also* long vowels; short vowels; *specific vowels*
Changing between short and long vowels (activity), 137
copy-cat, 142–149
ei words, 145
Five up (activity), 138
Four pairs of vowels (activity), 136–137
ie words, 142–144
Listening up for long vowels (activity), 136
open vowel words, 90–91, 255–256
Pairs of vowels (activity), 139–141
schwas, 177–181
Sounds right; looks wrong (activity), 139
Spelling buddies (activity), 143–144
in syllables, 245, 246
Two-vowel word quiz (activity), 141
y-acting-like-a-vowel rule, 79, 322–323

• W •

w (silent), 224
wa (word family), 208
The Wacky World of Words (Web site), 55
Wake up and spell the word (activity), 339–340
war (word family), 208–209
Warning! icon, 5
Web site
  busy teachers cafe, 60
  Educational Learning Games, 18
  enchantedlearning.com, 180
  Games Kids Play, 169
  handwriting worksheets, 26
  National Institutes of Health (NIH), 45
  plcmc.org, 180
  tiddlywinks.org, 169
  The Wacky World of Words, 55
wh (digraph), 118
wh (word family), 208
What's in a word? (activity), 13–14
when-two-vowels-go-walking-the-first-one-
    does-the-talking spelling rule, 61, 110,
    133–134, 215, 322
Which word? (activity), 202–203
Which word does this describe? (activity),
    229–230
Who has what? (activity), 300–301
Who's or whose (activity), 303–304
wor (word family), 208–209
word cross, 116
word family
  at, 172
  in, 174
  ack, 172–173
  air, 147–148, 202–203
  alk, 183–184
  all, 183–184, 208, 311–312
  an, 172
  ank, 172–173
  ap, 172
  ar, 185–187
  are, 148, 202–203
  ash, 172–173

au, 200–201, 314–315
aught, 191–193
aw, 200–201, 314–315
description, 36, 168, 321
Dr. Seuss and, 173
ear, 148–149, 189, 202–203
eight, 191–193
ell, 174
ent, 174
er, 185–186, 314
est, 174
ick, 175
igh, 190
ight, 190, 312
ill, 175
ing, 175
ink, 175
ip, 174
ir, 185–186, 314
it, 174
o, 193–194, 208–209
ock, 175–176
og, 175–176
oi, 196–198, 312–313
one-syllable, 171–177
oo, 195–196, 315–316
op, 175–176
or, 185–187, 311–312
ou, 193–194, 198–199, 208, 209, 313
ought, 191–193
ould, 208
ow, 198–199, 313
oy, 196–197, 312–313
oy-oi quiz (activity), 197
rhymes, 51
sight words, 207–211
spelling chunks, 167–168
two vowels, 208
two vowels+*r*, 188–190
uck, 176–177
ug, 176–177
ump, 176–177
unk, 176–177
ur, 185–186, 314
vowel+*r* words, 184–190
wa, 208

word family *(continued)*
  war, 208–209
  wh, 208
  wor, 208–209
word family activities
  Building word families, 210–211
  Changing a first letter, 81–82
  Changing the last letter, 203
  Colors and chunks, 194
  Eight itchy gnomes have ticks, 191
  Extravagant excuses, 200
  Finding an *ear* match, 189–190
  Finding an *our*, *oar*, or *oor* match, 189
  Finding your word family, 333
  Looking, marking, and writing, 185
  Only ungrateful girls hate toys, 192
  Spelling folder, 170–171
  Ten neat word families, 210
  Which word?, 202–203
word find (game), 346
word searches, downloading, 62
words within words, 54–55
writing
  close activity, 40
  emergent, 56
  handwriting, 41
  Internet message boards and chat
    rooms, 40
  journal, shared, 39
  notes from child to parent, 41

  posters, 38–39
  stories, 40
  to your child, 37–38
  with your child, 38–42
Writing a loony letter (activity), 228

• X •

x sounds, 100

• Y •

y (letter)
  draping *e* and adding *y*, 164
  long-*a* sound, 152
  long-*e* sound, 122, 152–159, 216, 322–323
  long-*i* sound, 122, 159–162, 216, 322–323
  in middle of words, 162
  short-*i* sound, 162–163
  spelling words with, 151–152
  suffix, 282–286
y quiz (activity), 163
y-acting-like-a-vowel rule, 79, 322–323
y-at-the-end quiz (activity), 153
You're and your (activity), 304

• Z •

zz words, 77

BUSINESS, CAREERS & PERSONAL FINANCE

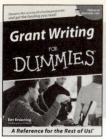

Grant Writing For Dummies
0-7645-5307-0

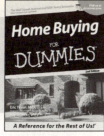

Home Buying For Dummies
0-7645-5331-3 *†

Also available:
- Accounting For Dummies †
  0-7645-5314-3
- Business Plans Kit For Dummies †
  0-7645-5365-8
- Cover Letters For Dummies
  0-7645-5224-4
- Frugal Living For Dummies
  0-7645-5403-4
- Leadership For Dummies
  0-7645-5176-0
- Managing For Dummies
  0-7645-1771-6

- Marketing For Dummies
  0-7645-5600-2
- Personal Finance For Dummies *
  0-7645-2590-5
- Project Management For Dummies
  0-7645-5283-X
- Resumes For Dummies †
  0-7645-5471-9
- Selling For Dummies
  0-7645-5363-1
- Small Business Kit For Dummies *†
  0-7645-5093-4

HOME & BUSINESS COMPUTER BASICS

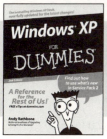

Windows XP For Dummies
0-7645-4074-2

Excel 2003 All-in-One Desk Reference For Dummies
0-7645-3758-X

Also available:
- ACT! 6 For Dummies
  0-7645-2645-6
- iLife '04 All-in-One Desk Reference For Dummies
  0-7645-7347-0
- iPAQ For Dummies
  0-7645-6769-1
- Mac OS X Panther Timesaving Techniques For Dummies
  0-7645-5812-9
- Macs For Dummies
  0-7645-5656-8

- Microsoft Money 2004 For Dummies
  0-7645-4195-1
- Office 2003 All-in-One Desk Reference For Dummies
  0-7645-3883-7
- Outlook 2003 For Dummies
  0-7645-3759-8
- PCs For Dummies
  0-7645-4074-2
- TiVo For Dummies
  0-7645-6923-6
- Upgrading and Fixing PCs For Dummies
  0-7645-1665-5
- Windows XP Timesaving Techniques For Dummies
  0-7645-3748-2

FOOD, HOME, GARDEN, HOBBIES, MUSIC & PETS

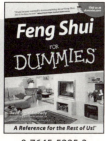

Feng Shui For Dummies
0-7645-5295-3

Poker For Dummies
0-7645-5232-5

Also available:
- Bass Guitar For Dummies
  0-7645-2487-9
- Diabetes Cookbook For Dummies
  0-7645-5230-9
- Gardening For Dummies *
  0-7645-5130-2
- Guitar For Dummies
  0-7645-5106-X
- Holiday Decorating For Dummies
  0-7645-2570-0
- Home Improvement All-in-One For Dummies
  0-7645-5680-0

- Knitting For Dummies
  0-7645-5395-X
- Piano For Dummies
  0-7645-5105-1
- Puppies For Dummies
  0-7645-5255-4
- Scrapbooking For Dummies
  0-7645-7208-3
- Senior Dogs For Dummies
  0-7645-5818-8
- Singing For Dummies
  0-7645-2475-5
- 30-Minute Meals For Dummies
  0-7645-2589-1

INTERNET & DIGITAL MEDIA

Digital Photography For Dummies
0-7645-1664-7

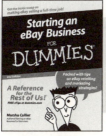

Starting an eBay Business For Dummies
0-7645-6924-4

Also available:
- 2005 Online Shopping Directory For Dummies
  0-7645-7495-7
- CD & DVD Recording For Dummies
  0-7645-5956-7
- eBay For Dummies
  0-7645-5654-1
- Fighting Spam For Dummies
  0-7645-5965-6
- Genealogy Online For Dummies
  0-7645-5964-8
- Google For Dummies
  0-7645-4420-9

- Home Recording For Musicians For Dummies
  0-7645-1634-5
- The Internet For Dummies
  0-7645-4173-0
- iPod & iTunes For Dummies
  0-7645-7772-7
- Preventing Identity Theft For Dummies
  0-7645-7336-5
- Pro Tools All-in-One Desk Reference For Dummies
  0-7645-5714-9
- Roxio Easy Media Creator For Dummies
  0-7645-7131-1

* Separate Canadian edition also available
† Separate U.K. edition also available

Available wherever books are sold. For more information or to order direct: U.S. customers visit www.dummies.com or call 1-877-762-2974.
U.K. customers visit www.wileyeurope.com or call 0800 243407. Canadian customers visit www.wiley.ca or call 1-800-567-4797.

 WILEY

SPORTS, FITNESS, PARENTING, RELIGION & SPIRITUALITY

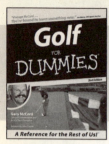

0-7645-5146-9

0-7645-5418-2

Also available:
- Adoption For Dummies
  0-7645-5488-3
- Basketball For Dummies
  0-7645-5248-1
- The Bible For Dummies
  0-7645-5296-1
- Buddhism For Dummies
  0-7645-5359-3
- Catholicism For Dummies
  0-7645-5391-7
- Hockey For Dummies
  0-7645-5228-7

- Judaism For Dummies
  0-7645-5299-6
- Martial Arts For Dummies
  0-7645-5358-5
- Pilates For Dummies
  0-7645-5397-6
- Religion For Dummies
  0-7645-5264-3
- Teaching Kids to Read For Dummies
  0-7645-4043-2
- Weight Training For Dummies
  0-7645-5168-X
- Yoga For Dummies
  0-7645-5117-5

TRAVEL

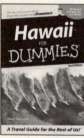

0-7645-5438-7

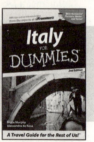

0-7645-5453-0

Also available:
- Alaska For Dummies
  0-7645-1761-9
- Arizona For Dummies
  0-7645-6938-4
- Cancún and the Yucatán For Dummies
  0-7645-2437-2
- Cruise Vacations For Dummies
  0-7645-6941-4
- Europe For Dummies
  0-7645-5456-5
- Ireland For Dummies
  0-7645-5455-7

- Las Vegas For Dummies
  0-7645-5448-4
- London For Dummies
  0-7645-4277-X
- New York City For Dummies
  0-7645-6945-7
- Paris For Dummies
  0-7645-5494-8
- RV Vacations For Dummies
  0-7645-5443-3
- Walt Disney World & Orlando For Dummies
  0-7645-6943-0

GRAPHICS, DESIGN & WEB DEVELOPMENT

0-7645-4345-8

0-7645-5589-8

Also available:
- Adobe Acrobat 6 PDF For Dummies
  0-7645-3760-1
- Building a Web Site For Dummies
  0-7645-7144-3
- Dreamweaver MX 2004 For Dummies
  0-7645-4342-3
- FrontPage 2003 For Dummies
  0-7645-3882-9
- HTML 4 For Dummies
  0-7645-1995-6
- Illustrator CS For Dummies
  0-7645-4084-X

- Macromedia Flash MX 2004 For Dummies
  0-7645-4358-X
- Photoshop 7 All-in-One Desk
  Reference For Dummies
  0-7645-1667-1
- Photoshop CS Timesaving Techniques
  For Dummies
  0-7645-6782-9
- PHP 5 For Dummies
  0-7645-4166-8
- PowerPoint 2003 For Dummies
  0-7645-3908-6
- QuarkXPress 6 For Dummies
  0-7645-2593-X

NETWORKING, SECURITY, PROGRAMMING & DATABASES

0-7645-6852-3

0-7645-5784-X

Also available:
- A+ Certification For Dummies
  0-7645-4187-0
- Access 2003 All-in-One Desk
  Reference For Dummies
  0-7645-3988-4
- Beginning Programming For Dummies
  0-7645-4997-9
- C For Dummies
  0-7645-7068-4
- Firewalls For Dummies
  0-7645-4048-3
- Home Networking For Dummies
  0-7645-42796

- Network Security For Dummies
  0-7645-1679-5
- Networking For Dummies
  0-7645-1677-9
- TCP/IP For Dummies
  0-7645-1760-0
- VBA For Dummies
  0-7645-3989-2
- Wireless All In-One Desk Reference
  For Dummies
  0-7645-7496-5
- Wireless Home Networking For Dummies
  0-7645-3910-8